Leasing Retail Space

Leasing Retail Space

 Institute of Real Estate Management
of the **NATIONAL ASSOCIATION OF REALTORS®**
430 NORTH MICHIGAN AVENUE • CHICAGO, ILLINOIS 60611

Library of Congress Cataloging-in-Publication Data

Leasing Retail Space
    p.   cm.
Includes bibliographical references.
ISBN 0-944298-41-9 :
    1. Stores, Retail.   2. Commercial leases.   I. Institute of Real
Estate Management.
HD1393.26.S67L43   1990
658.8'7—dc20   89–83354
                                                                CIP

Printed in the United States of America

1 2 3 4 5 6 7 8 9 10 Printing / Year 99 98 97 96 95 94 93 92 91 90

Contents

Foreword

The Institute of Real Estate Management (IREM), since its founding in 1933, has been at the forefront of all of the phases of real estate management. Initially more active in multifamily residential properties and office buildings, the retail area was not a major concentration until Course 303, Leasing and Management of Shopping Centers and Retail Space, was inaugurated. Since the initial offering of Course 303, IREM has attracted a broader constituency of professionals who have had experience in the field of retail management and leasing.

The eleventh and twelfth editions of Downs' *Principles of Real Estate Management,* published by IREM, had good chapters on the shopping center. Then in 1983, IREM published *Managing the Shopping Center,* which included the efforts of a number of stalwart CPM® members with shopping center and retail experience. *Managing the Shopping Center* has been a continuing seller for IREM and is highly regarded by other professional organizations involved with retail properties.

Now comes *Leasing Retail Space,* which has been developed with guidance, assistance, and review by a dedicated group of leasing and property management professionals who have made sure the book is a practical hands-on guide to leasing retail space.

The Institute's continuing commitment to this field is also reflected in a decision in 1989 to launch an experience exchange and publish an income and expense analysis of shopping centers beginning in the 1990s.

Shopping centers in this country probably have been the most dynamic of the real estate types because the American public has never been static in its demand for retail goods and services. So shopping "areas" have evolved from the corner grocery store and retail tenants along dedicated streets in towns to shopping center prototypes such as the architecturally unified blocks of stores in Roland Park, Kansas, in 1907 and the unified shopping district of Country Club Plaza in Kansas City in the 1920s.

The first free-standing community shopping center with no dedicated streets running through it was Highland Park Village in Dallas, Texas, in 1931. The first suburban regional mall, Northgate, opened in Seattle in 1950. It was first an open mall, then later expanded and enclosed. The first enclosed mall built as such was Southdale in Edina, Minnesota, in 1956. Then came the refinements and permutations:

- Centers in mixed-use developments such as the Galleria in Houston in 1969
- Multilevel downtown centers like Chicago's Water Tower Place in 1976
- The "festival" center—e.g., Faneuil Hall Marketplace in Boston in 1976
- Specialty or theme centers such as Pier 39 in San Francisco in 1978
- The super-duper regional center, with eight anchors and numerous recreational attractions—West Edmonton Mall in Alberta, Canada, in 1981.

A further innovation was the introduction of off-price malls like Potomac Mills in the Washington, D.C., area in 1985 and the evolution of a variety of other types, including anchorless strips, preservation sites, and infill centers.

The traditional neighborhood shopping center with a supermarket as the anchor tenant has gone through some subtle and important changes. In the 1930s, the grocery store anchor tenant was considered large at 15,000 square feet. These stores grew to 25,000 square feet, then to 40,000 square feet, and a number are now as large as 50,000 and 60,000 square feet. This has caused a revolution in the secondary stores surrounding the major anchor tenant, in that many of the types of merchandise and services offered previously by smaller tenants have been absorbed into the anchor stores.

Not to be forgotten is the European import, the hypermarket, some of which have 220,000 square feet of store area and are shopping centers in themselves. In addition to groceries, they include soft goods and warehouse sections and a number of supplemental service shops—all under one roof.

Power centers with a number of large 30,000–50,000-square-foot destination-oriented tenants have become popular, either as peripherals to regional malls or as attractions on their own, often with few or no smaller tenants between the powerhouse attractions.

Looking to the end of the twentieth century and the beginning of the twenty-first century, we will see fads in shopping and trends in retailing that are the result of changing demographic patterns. Consumers are getting older on average, and a growing number of women are working. Also, traditional retail space in city neighborhoods is reviving as viable outlying sites become harder to find.

Acquisitions, consolidations, and sell-offs of established department store chains that are experiencing hard times will continue to change the traditional makeup of shopping centers. Many mall shops suffer from the same problems as the department stores, and this reduces the quality of service, the maintenance of stores, advertising, and the amount and quality of merchandise. All of these changes create new areas of endeavor for retail leasing specialists.

Some present trends in retailing and retail development are:

- Open and enclosed malls representing themselves as true manufacturers' outlets
- Development of specialized car care centers and centers specializing in materials and equipment for home repairs
- An increased interest in high-rise centers as part of mixed-use developments on major shopping streets in large metropolitan areas
- The updating and renovation of centers that were built twenty to thirty years ago.

In the development of new shopping centers or renovations or retenanting of existing shopping centers, the rules for success continue to be:

1. Appropriate demographic profile
2. Location at the intersection of major thoroughfares
3. Good visibility
4. Easy access
5. Dynamic and harmonious tenant mix

The job, then, of the retail leasing agent along with the owner and manager of the shopping center is to provide the best platform to do all these things successfully. The leasing agent has the opportunity and the challenge to put together the dynamic and compatible tenant mix. Working together with the manager and the owner, the leasing agent can see that all parts of the puzzle fit into their proper places, supply the consumer or customer with what is needed and wanted, and provide a sound financial investment for the developer and owner. *Leasing Retail Space* is a comprehensive guide for anyone involved in this diverse and exciting field.

A. Alexander Bül, CPM®

Publisher's Preface

Leasing Retail Space was first proposed to the Institute of Real Estate Management by A. Alexander Bül, CPM®. Mr. Bül has served as the primary editorial consultant, providing encouragement and guidance throughout the project. He generously shared his knowledge and experience and recommended other experts in retail leasing management as additional resources. As a result, this unique book truly reflects the variety of retail properties to be leased and the challenge they present to the leasing agent. The Institute is deeply grateful to Mr. Bül and all the others whose generous contributions of time and expertise have made this publication possible.

Editorial Consultants

A. Alexander Bül, CPM®, CSM, CRE, CIPS, is Vice Chairman of the Board of Henry S. Miller Management Corporation, a Grubb & Ellis Company, in Dallas, Texas. The firm is an ACCREDITED MANAGEMENT ORGANIZATION® with an extensive portfolio of properties under management, a large portion of them being neighborhood and community shopping centers. Mr. Bül has more than twenty-five years experience in real estate management, with prior experience in city management and urban renewal. He is also a well-known teacher, having been Director of the Ryan-Reilly Center for Urban Land Utilization and Associate Professor of Real Estate and Finance at the University of Texas at Arlington. As a member of the Institute of Real Estate Management, he is a member of the National Faculty and has been involved in designation course development. He also served as Chapter President and Regional Vice President. Mr. Bül is a member of ULI—the Urban Land Institute, where he serves as Lead Instructor for shopping center development seminars. He is also a member of the International Council of Shopping Centers, for which he has taught designation preparatory courses. Mr. Bül is active in numerous other professional organizations, including FIABCI-USA (the American Chapter of the International Real Estate Federation, an affiliate of the NATIONAL ASSOCIATION OF REALTORS®). He is coauthor or contributing author of several books, including *Managing the Shopping Center,* and *Principles of Real Estate Management,* both published by the Institute of Real Estate Management.

Alan A. Alexander, CPM®, CSM, CRE, is President of Alexander Consultants in San Bruno, California. The firm specializes in management, leasing, development, and consultation for income-producing residential and commercial properties, including shopping centers. Mr. Alexander has more than twenty-five years experience in real estate management, which includes responsibility for a wide variety of shopping center types and sizes. Mr. Alexander is a member of the Institute of Real Estate Management, where he is on the National Faculty and has served as a Chapter President. He is also a member of the International Council of Shopping Centers, for which he is a frequent speaker, and he has moderated numerous seminars offered by the Northwest Center for Professional Education. He is the author of several articles on commercial leasing and management published in IREM's *Journal of Property Management* and other real estate publications. Mr. Alexander is coauthor of *Managing and Leasing Commercial Properties,* published by John Wiley & Sons, and a contributing author of *Managing the Shopping Center,* published by the Institute of Real Estate Management. He was inducted into the IREM "Academy of Authors" in 1984.

Jim Bane, CPM®, is Director of Property Management for L. C. Fulenwider, Inc., an ACCREDITED MANAGEMENT ORGANIZATION® in Denver, Colorado. Previously Mr. Bane was President of The Retail Property Management Company in Denver (also an AMO®), with a portfolio including 1.3 million square feet of commercial property. He has fifteen years experience in property management, focused primarily on commercial and retail properties. He is an active member of several professional real estate organizations, including the Institute of Real Estate Management and the International Council of Shopping Centers. He is a frequent lecturer in the Denver area.

Harold J. Carlson, CPM®, CSM, is President of Harold J. Carlson Associates, Inc., a subsidiary of Draper & Kramer, Inc., an ACCREDITED MANAGEMENT ORGANIZATION® in Rosemont, Illinois. The firm provides shopping center management and consultation exclusively. Mr. Carlson has more than thirty-five years experience in real estate management, focused almost entirely on shopping center management. He is an active faculty member of the International Council of Shopping Centers and recipient of their Distinguished Service Award. His professional association memberships include the Institute of Real Estate Management, the International Council of Shopping Centers, and the American Institute of Real Estate Appraisers. Mr. Carlson is publisher of *CarlsonReport,* a monthly newsletter for shopping center managers, and a contributing author of *Managing the Shopping Center,* published by the Institute of Real Estate Management.

Stephen J. Coates, CPM®, CSM, is President of Coates & Sowards, Inc., in San Jose, California. The firm is an ACCREDITED MANAGEMENT ORGANIZATION® that specializes in the management, leasing, and sales of shopping centers, office buildings, and industrial buildings. Mr. Coates is a member of the Institute of Real Estate Management, where he is on the National Faculty and is a Past President of the San Jose South Bay Chapter. He is also a member of the International Council of Shopping Centers, where he is a National Instructor, and he teaches for the Building Owners and Managers Association International (BOMA) and in the California Community College system. Mr. Coates has managed and leased more than three million square feet of retail space in neighborhood and community shopping centers during his seventeen-year career.

Joseph W. Karp, CPM®, CSM, is Vice President of Weingarten Realty Management Company in Houston, Texas. The firm is the exclusive developer and manager for Weingarten Realty Investors, a NYSE-listed Real Estate Investment Trust with a portfolio including shopping centers and other commercial properties in a six-state area. Mr. Karp has a long career in management and leasing of income-producing real estate. He is an active member of the Institute of Real Estate Management, where he is on the National Faculty of courses required for the CPM® designation and has served as a Chapter President. Currently he is National Course Board Director for IREM Course 303 Leasing and Management of Shopping Centers and Retail Space. Mr. Karp is also active in the International Council of Shopping Centers for which he is a regular speaker and a published author.

Robert J. Lofton, CPM®, is Senior Vice President of Boyle Investment Company in Memphis, Tennessee. The firm is a major developer and manager of income-producing properties throughout the South, including shopping centers and other commercial properties. Mr. Lofton has more than twenty-five years experience in real estate management and is currently in charge of all of Boyle's leasing, sales and management activities. As a member of the Institute of Real Estate Management, he is on the National Faculty and has served as Course Board Director and as Chapter President. Mr. Lofton is also a member of the International Council of Shopping Centers and on the faculty of Memphis State University where he teaches courses on shopping center development, leasing, and management in the Division of Continuing Education. He is a contributing author of *Managing the Shopping Center,* published by the Institute of Real Estate Management.

Richard F. Muhlebach, CPM®, CSM, CRE, RPA, is President of TRF Management Corporation in Bellevue, Washington, a commercial property management company and ACCREDITED MANAGEMENT ORGANIZATION®, and Vice President of Leasing of TRF Pacific, a developer of shopping centers and malls in the Northwest and Alaska. Mr. Muhlebach has more than twenty years experience in leasing and management of shopping centers, including strip, neighborhood, and community centers, regional malls, multilevel downtown malls, and mixed-use developments. He is author of numerous articles on retail property management published in IREM's *Journal of Property Management* and other real estate publications, coauthor of *Managing and Leasing Commercial Properties,* published by John Wiley and Sons in New York, and was an editorial consultant for *Managing the Shopping Center,* published by the Institute of Real Estate Management. Mr. Muhlebach is a member of the Institute of Real Estate Management, where he is a Senior Instructor on the National Faculty. He is also a member of the International Council of Shopping Centers and on their faculty. He has also taught for the Northwest Center for Professional Education and at the college level.

John W. Phelps, CPM®, CSM, is Vice President of the Retail Property Division of the Tishman West Companies, an ACCREDITED MANAGEMENT ORGANIZATION® in Orange, California. Mr. Phelps has more than twenty-seven years experience in the leasing, management, and development of retail properties, and he has written numerous articles on these subjects for publication in real estate periodicals. He is a consultant and lecturer in real estate leasing and management with a strong emphasis on retail properties. Mr. Phelps is an active member of the Orange County Chapter of the Institute of Real Estate Management, where he has held numerous positions including the office of Chapter President, and regularly serves on several IREM National committees. He was the organizer and continues to serve as coordinator of quarterly meetings of the Southern California regional shopping center managers and is a participant in the metro-politan Los Angeles leasing agent organization. Mr. Phelps is listed in *Who's Who in the Shopping Center Industry,* published by the *National Mall Monitor.*

Raymond Poche, is affiliated with Weingarten Realty Management in Houston, Texas, with responsibility for corporate acquisitions, development of new shopping centers, and anchor tenant relationships. Mr. Poche's 17-year career in real estate development and management includes more than seven years selecting store sites for A & P Food Stores and Target Department Stores and more than seven years as Executive Vice President of the Development Group of Henry S. Miller Company, with responsibility for all aspects of shopping center leasing, management, and development. As a Faculty member of ULI—the Urban Land Institute, he teaches seminars on shopping center development. Mr. Poche also teaches classes for the International Council of Shopping Centers.

For sharing their knowledge and expertise, the Institute also wishes to thank: **Thomas Dobyns,** attorney-at-law, Tuston, California, who reviewed chapter 7 on The Lease, and **Candice A. Tillack,** CPM®, Senior Property Manager at Weingarten Realty Management Company, Houston, Texas, who reviewed the information on retailing in chapter 1.

Russell Schneck Design of Glenview, Illinois, developed cover and dustjacket art and designed the interior typography for *Leasing Retail Space.*

Who Should Read This Book?

For the reader who is beginning a career as a leasing professional, *Leasing Retail Space* offers a sound basis for developing the skills you will need day to day. For the experienced leasing agent, this book provides a ready reference to reaffirm and expand upon what has already been learned. Every leasing situation varies with the property and the agent involved and with a host of other factors. Not all of the topics covered in this book will apply in every leasing situation, and unique properties or leasing assignments may pose challenges that have not been addressed here.

There is no substitute for actually working as a leasing agent, but *Leasing Retail Space* can help the agent gain a broader understanding of this exciting profession. The general information presented here can be applied to a wide variety of leasing situations. Not every leasing agent will perform every leasing-related task or use every skill described in the text. It is hoped that this book will guide readers who wish to pursue their own interests and learn more about those specific aspects of retail space leasing that apply to the properties and prospective tenants with whom they will be dealing.

Whether you are reading *Leasing Retail Space* as an introduction to this specialized career area or to refresh your memory on particular details of contemporary retail space leasing, this book is a source for practical ideas to maximize your successes from the many opportunities you encounter as well as a useful shelf reference.

What the Book Has to Say

Chapter 1 presents an introductory discussion of retailing and describes contemporary forms of retail space and the development of retail space leasing as a profession. The discussion of retailing is limited because the agent's need for and use of this type of information is limited. However, it is useful for the agent to know how retailers set prices and compute profits because the resultant sales dollars are the source of the income from which the retail tenant pays rent.

In chapter 2, the concept of market research as it applies to retail properties is developed. This includes evaluation of the property's location and sales potential. Chapter 3 covers development of the leasing plan used in establishing rents, including different types of rents and different types of leases. For purposes of this book, all rents are quoted as dollars per square foot per year for uniformity. Rents may be quoted on different bases in different regions, and actual lease documents usually state both the annual rate and the total rent for the duration of the lease. There may be other variants as well. Chapter 4 is a discussion of how type of store, type of merchandise, and operational size are evaluated in setting up the best mix of retail tenants for a particular type of shopping center.

In chapter 5, the basics of prospecting for and qualifying prospective tenants are described. Ideally, one seeks to place the best possible retail business in a given space—one that can and will succeed in that location. On the other hand, it may not be possible to fully qualify a particular prospect whose main attraction is that their line of merchandise is a sought-after element of the proposed tenant mix. Both tenant and center owner may "take a chance" on the retailer's success. Occasionally market conditions—vacancies, in particular—will dictate a need to lease to a less-than-ideal prospect. Owners will sometimes make such a compromise in order to fill a space or to meet financial commitments—or in order *not* to lose customer traffic to the center as a whole because of an apparent lack of stores in operation.

The impact of center design on the placement of tenants in shopping centers is covered in chapter 6. Chapter 7 describes the basic lease document and discusses in general terms the variety of clauses and considerations that can or should be included in a properly drafted retail lease. Consultation with legal advisors in the course of developing specific lease forms will certainly uncover additional items that could not be included in a book of this size and scope. Many elements of retail space leases are negotiable, and specifics related to the negotiation process are detailed in chapter 8, including the leasing agent's role in successful negotiations. Chapter 9 deals with the leasing of downtown retail space, how these types of properties differ from suburban shopping malls, and the challenges posed to the leasing agent by downtown leasing. Some data represented in tables and figures in chapter 9 were included in order to provide meaningful comparisons within the context of the discussion of a downtown demographic profile, despite changes over time.

Because rental income and operating expenses vary considerably among the different types of centers, such data generally have been excluded from the comparisons presented in *Leasing Retail Space*. Information on shopping center rents and operating expenses can be found in a variety of published sources. However, the reader is cautioned to be aware of publication dates and compilation periods when using such sources because the passage of time can render these data less accurate. Also, some reports may include figures for anchor tenants and factor in rental rates established in older, long-term leases, resulting in artificially *lower* figures for a center as a whole or for the center's market area. Published data cannot substitute for personal knowledge gained in the marketplace where the agent is actually leasing space.

Throughout this book, the term "retailer" is used to refer to the owner or operator of a retail business, whatever its size; "owner" refers to the individual who owns the shopping center. In a lease document, these two parties would be referred to, respectively, as "tenant" and "landlord."

A number of forms are included as examples to clarify points made in the text. The reader is encouraged to develop his or her own unique forms for the job at hand. Examples included in a book of this nature cannot begin to address all of the considerations that may be required by various legal jurisdictions or that may be important for an individual shopping center. Documentation of any contractual arrangements—for example, commission agreements—should be developed in consultation with appropriate legal counsel.

The Special Nature of Retail Space Leasing

Before shopping centers became a dominant force in real estate markets, retail space was found primarily on the ground floors of commercial or residential buildings in urban, downtown business areas. Leasing was performed by local real estate brokerage firms or by the property manager or the owner. As retail businesses have relocated to the suburbs and larger and more complex shopping centers have been built, retail leasing has become the domain of a specialist. For large new developments, advance leasing commitments from major or anchor tenants are a requirement to secure financing before construction can begin. Targeting the property to the right segment of the retail market is an art in itself. In response to the increasing complexity of the leasing process, retail leasing has developed into a distinctly separate full-time career.

A leasing agent's job may encompass some or all of the following tasks:

- Helping to conduct market research
- Advising on site plan to ensure leasability
- Setting or advising ownership regarding rental rates
- Developing and executing a leasing plan
- Executing a marketing plan to attract potential tenants
- Selecting or advising ownership regarding tenant mix
- Evaluating prospects and in-place tenants
- Negotiating leases
- Helping the property manager arrange tenant move-ins

Other duties may include a role in lease renewals and tenant buyouts, evaluation of a potential tenant's financial statement and business plan, preparation of marketing materials, budgeting, and looking for opportunities to increase the leasable area of the property.

Because of the use to which retail space is put, it differs markedly from other types of leased space, and the process by which it is leased is similarly unique. The retail tenant usually sells a product or service directly to the general public. Therefore visibility and accessibility are major considerations in the choice of a location. However, one of the keys to successful retailing is finding a *profitable* location.

When leasing retail space, the agent must sell the prospective tenant on a particular space and the potential profitability of its location. The benefits to the retailer relate to the size of the space, its position in relation to other retailers—especially those viewed as competition, and the desirability of or need for the retailer's products or services in the particular marketplace. The leasing agent must also know how to judge the potential profitability of the retailer's merchandise and how a particular location enhances that profitability. Knowledge of retailers' businesses and how they evaluate profits are further requirements of agents who lease retail space. A well-thought-out leasing program will generate an optimum tenant mix such that each retailer contributes to and benefits from the range of customers attracted to the center by all the retailers.

Leasing agents generally are employed by a property owner or manager to lease retail space at a particular center or location. Some leasing agents are employed by commercial real estate brokerage firms to represent sites; others, called site selectors, work directly for large retailers that are constantly seeking new space and new markets. The information in this book most directly concerns leasing agents who represent available space.

In most leasing situations, the agent works either directly or indirectly *for the owner,* yet it is important for the agent to remember that the tenant that benefits from a choice location will benefit the owner as well. If a retailer occupies a storefront or a position in a mall that is ill-suited for marketing its goods, that business could eventually become a liability to the owner because of low sales volume, poor "fit" into the tenant mix, or inability to meet its rent obligations. Only in retail leasing is the landlord concerned about the success and business practices of its tenants beyond their ability to pay their bills. Thus one of the agent's most important responsibilities is careful selection and placement of tenants to maximize each one's sales potential.

Being able to evaluate the prospect's chances for success is more important in leasing retail space than in any other type of leasing. Retail leasing is also the only type of leasing activity in which the tenant's customers are a consideration. Many of the benefits of the property that the agent will "sell" to the prospective retail tenant require examination from the customer's perspective as well. This includes appropriateness of center design, compatibility of the mix of retailers, and competition.

In order to properly evaluate the prospective tenant's chances for success, the leasing agent must acquire sufficient knowledge of retailing to be able to speak the prospect's language. This chapter discusses those areas of retailing that the leasing agent should understand and describes contemporary forms of retail space. It concludes with an overview of retail leasing as a profession.

THE RETAILING FIELD

Retailing has evolved into a much more sophisticated and systematic process than the simple transaction of selling goods and services to consumers that it once was. Today's retailers are not only independent merchants operating family businesses in small shops but also major corporations that operate large stores complete with separate departments to handle each facet of merchandising and operations. To be successful, a retailer has to have a working knowledge of manufacturing, marketing, accounting, theories of retail buying and selling, human resource management, and consumer psychology. Mathematical formulas and theories are used to help the retailer choose the ideal location. Because the leasing agent will often approach prospects who are retail specialists—rather than simply merchants in the narrow sense of the word—he or she should be well-informed about the retailing field.

The retail leasing agent is concerned with four aspects of a prospective tenant's business.

- Method of operation
- Expense structure
- Target market
- Sales performance potential

Leasing Retail Space cannot cover the business of retailing to a very great extent, so it is to the agent's advantage to research the topic independently as well.

Retailers have to make a number of decisions in order to operate a store profitably. Principal among them are (1) what merchandise to carry in stock, (2) how many of each item to buy and carry in stock, (3) how much selling space to allow each item, (4) what price to charge, and (5) how to display, advertise, and promote the item. The leasing agent should share an interest in these aspects of retailing because they are related to the prospect's sales performance, which in turn is related to the prospect's ability to pay rent. In judging the financial capabilities of a prospective tenant, the most important concept for the agent to understand is profit margin. In this regard, there are three particular elements of retailing that the leasing agent should be familiar with: gross profits, stock turnover, and pricing.

Gross Profits

In retail merchandising, *gross profit* is the difference between the cost of the merchandise and the price for which it is sold. It is the amount of income generated *before* any costs of doing business are taken into account. Rent, salaries, and other business expenses—known as *overhead*—are deducted from the gross profit to determine the actual or *net profit*.

Gross profit can be calculated in two ways. The simplest way is to take the selling price of an item and subtract its cost.

Selling Price − Cost = Gross profit

However, accountants and many retailers prefer to calculate gross profit by subtracting the total cost of merchandise sold from *net* sales. Because many stores permit customers to return merchandise, some of which then has to be sold at less than full price, net sales are total sales (as rung up on the cash register) less any returns.

Total Sales − Returns = Net Sales
Net Sales − Cost of Goods = Gross Profit

Stock Turnover

Another important element in retailing is *stock turnover,* which refers to the number of times the average inventory of an item has been sold or turned over. Goods that are not sold occupy valuable shelf and display space and represent considerable financial investment.

Stock turnover is computed by dividing annual net sales by the average inventory at the retail value of the items in stock.

$$\frac{\text{Net Sales}}{\text{Average Inventory at Retail}} = \text{Stock Turnover}$$

Stock turnover can be determined on a per item basis as well. *Average inventory* at retail is the sum of the starting and closing inventory values divided by two. As an example, a store might have an inventory valued at retail of $100,000 at the beginning of the year. At year's end, the inventory is $120,000, and during the year there were net sales of $500,000. Stock turnover would be computed as follows:

$$\frac{\text{Beginning Inventory} + \text{Ending Inventory}}{2} = \frac{\text{Average Inventory}}{\text{at Retail}}$$

$$\frac{\$100,000 + \$120,000}{2} = \$110,000$$

$$\frac{\$500,000 \text{ (Net Sales)}}{\$110,000 \text{ (Average Inventory)}} = 4.5 \text{ (Stock Turnover)}$$

A stock turnover of 4.5 means the store in this example turned over its inventory 4.5 times during the course of the year. Retailers view turnover as a measure of their productivity, and a higher turnover rate—even coupled with a low margin—will usually generate more sales dollars.

Stock turnover is usually computed on an annual basis. However, inventories are usually at their lowest at the beginning and end of the year. To minimize distortion of the results, most retailers average their monthly inventories (beginning and ending inventories and eleven monthly amounts in between) and divide by thirteen. Stock turnover provides a useful way to measure a retailer's sales performance. Stores that carry high-priced merchandise (jewelry stores for example) generally have low turnover rates; grocery stores usually have high turnover rates. Retailers compare turnover rates from year to year to detect changes that may require analysis of sales and inventory operations. Comparison with turnover rates of other retailers in similar businesses can also be made.

Because sales performance information is important to the tenant qualification process, the leasing agent should become familiar with typical stock turnover rates for major retail types. It also helps the agent to evaluate the retailer's business practices because too low a turnover rate can indicate that too much inventory is being carried, which is a signal that too many dollars are tied up in inventory, which can possibly point to difficulty in paying rent.

Pricing

Retailers price goods with two goals in mind. They want to achieve a profit and they also want to be competitive in the marketplace. Pricing has a great impact on sales volume. In a competitive environment, pricing must be monitored constantly.

Three different types of retail prices can be recognized: (1) the original retail price placed on goods when first purchased and put in stock, (2) the current retail price of goods in stock—which may be more or less than the original retail price, and (3) the sales retail price—the price at which the goods are actually sold after markdowns, if any, have been taken.

Margins.   Retailers price an item in order to make a profit. An amount is added to the cost of the item to recover the expense of selling it—plus a little more. The difference between the cost and the selling price, when compared to the selling price, yields a percentage that is the retailer's *margin* of profit. The margin is always calculated on the selling price of the item rather than its cost. For example, a coat that is purchased wholesale for $120 and sold for $160 yields a profit of $40, which is 25 percent of the selling price—the profit margin.

$160 (Retail Price) − $120 (Wholesale Cost) = $40 (Profit)

$$\frac{\$40\ (Profit)}{\$160\ (Retail\ Price)} = .25\ or\ 25\%\ (Margin)$$

Markups.   The difference between the cost of merchandise and its selling price is also known as *markup*. Both margin and markup are identical in dollars; however, the percentages are different because of the way they relate to the selling price.

Although markup may be computed as a percentage of either cost or selling price, it is easier to use cost. Markup is the percent of the cost that must be added to it to create a selling price that will yield the desired margin of profit.

In the preceding example of the coat that cost $120 wholesale and sold for $160 retail, the retailer had to mark up the cost by $40. The relation of the $40 profit to the $120 cost of the coat—33.3 percent—is the markup. Clearly the amount of the markup represents a greater percentage of the cost than the desired margin percentage.

$$\frac{\$40\ (Profit)}{\$120\ (Cost)} = 0.333 = 33.3\%\ (Markup)$$

If retailers calculated profit by applying the desired margin directly to the cost, they would lose money—in this instance $10 per item sold—and would not achieve the necessary amount of profit. Table 1.1 shows the relationship between margin and markup using as an example an item that costs the retailer $17.50 wholesale. The first column is used to find the desired margin or gross profit percentage. The second column is then used to find the required markup, which is multiplied by the cost of the article (in this case, $17.50). The third column shows the dollar amount to be added to the cost and the fourth column shows the resultant selling

T A B L E   1.1

Markups and Margins Compared

Margin (% of Price to Customer)	Markup (% of Cost to Retailer)	For item that costs a retailer $17.50	
		Markup Amount ($)	Selling Price to Customer ($)
9	10	1.75	19.25
10	11.1	1.94	19.44
13	15	2.63	20.13
15	17.7	3.10	20.60
16.7	20	3.50	21.00
20	25	4.38	21.88
23.1	30	5.25	22.75
25	33.3	5.83	23.33

price. Note that in order to achieve a gross margin of 25 percent (one-fourth) requires addition of 33.3 percent (one-third) to the cost, whereas a markup of 25 percent (one-fourth) yields a profit margin of only 20 percent (one-fifth).

There are other terms related to markup that the leasing agent should know. Many apparel stores seek a *keystone markup* which is equivalent to the cost of the item. Thus the retail price is double the cost. This goal may be difficult to maintain in a competitive retail environment. For a particular item, the average of all markups over a period of time—the *maintained markup*—is usually less than the original markup.

Markdowns.   The opposite of a markup is a *markdown*. This is a retail price reduction usually instituted because of poor sales at the original retail price or changes in the season. Markdown prices reflect a depreciation in the value of the goods. The markdown policy followed by a retailer will affect its ability to turnover merchandise and produce the cash to acquire new merchandise.

If one retailer's prices on some items are somewhat lower than those of its competitors, that store can probably attract more customers and sell more merchandise. For other items, especially merchandise that is unique to a given store, it may be possible or even necessary to set a higher selling price because it may not be possible (or necessary) to sell a larger number of those items and thus achieve an acceptable margin of profit overall. Most retailers experiment with different prices to establish their pricing policy.

Sales.   Along with markdowns, specially identified sales form an important component of the retailer's pricing mechanism. Most stores have established three basic types of sales: start-of-season, holiday, and clearance.

- *Start-of-season sales* are run to introduce the shopper to new merchandise. They also help the store gain a competitive edge.
- *Holiday sales* are always effective due to the large number of people shopping for gifts.
- *Clearance sales* are held to drastically reduce inventory. Marking down the least-desirable merchandise along with end-of-season merchandise will not only help slow-moving items disappear but also provide cash to replenish inventory with new, seasonal, and more-profitable merchandise.

Even selling merchandise at cost usually entails no loss because the retailer is then able to replace the old goods with better-moving merchandise. Sales attract more people into the store, and often these customers will shop for regular-priced goods as well.

The foregoing discussion of retailing has addressed only some of the terms the agent will encounter in his or her efforts to get to know different retailers and their businesses. In general, understanding the terminology of retailing equips the leasing agent to communicate more effectively with prospective tenants, facilitate negotiations, and enhance a property's profitability.

TYPES OF CONTEMPORARY RETAIL SPACE

The dominant form of retail space in the United States is the suburban shopping center. Five major types of shopping centers exist: the regional center, the community center, the neighborhood center, the specialty center, and the convenience center. (Downtown malls and other forms of urban retail space—including freestanding stores—are discussed in chapter 9.) In addition, several variations on these forms have been developed as the shopping center industry has matured. Shopping centers are typically defined by their dominant or anchor tenants and their gross leasable area or GLA (table 1.2) and, to some extent, by the population or trade area that they serve.

T A B L E   1.2

Characteristics of Shopping Centers

	GLA Range	Anchor Tenant(s)	Ancillary Tenants
Super Regional	1,000,000 or more	Three or more full-line department stores	Men's and women's apparel, shoes (including athletic footwear), electronic equipment, toy stores
Regional	400,000– 1,000,000	One or more full-line department stores	Men's and women's apparel, health food stores, optical shops, electronic equipment, jewelry, banks
Community	150,000– 400,000	Junior department store; hardware; supermarket	Men's and women's apparel, family shoe stores, banks, medical and dental offices
Neighborhood*	50,000– 150,000	Supermarket or drugstore or a combination of the two	Dry cleaners, beauty shops, donut shops, liquor stores, video tape rentals, travel agents, cards and gifts
Specialty	Less than 50,000 to 375,000	Anchorless or off-price or discount store	Gifts and novelties, gourmet food stores and food service
Convenience	Less than 50,000	Small grocery; service station	Barber shops, self-service laundries, dry cleaners, liquor stores

*Supermarkets have grown from 25,000 square feet of GLA in the 1950s to 35,000 square feet in the 1970s and 40,000 square feet in the 1980s, with projected further growth to 50,000–70,000 square feet of GLA in the early 1990s. Neighborhood and community centers anchored by supermarkets can be expected to grow along with them.

Note: There is a great deal of overlap of store types between regional and super regional shopping centers, with the latter having more examples and greater variety of ancillaries. Specialty centers may focus on apparel; those drawing predominantly on tourist trade will feature gifts and food items.

Regional Shopping Centers

Regional shopping centers are the most visible form of retail space, yet they represent only about 5 percent of the more than 32,500 shopping centers in the United States (1988 estimate). Regional shopping centers are designed to provide the range and quality of goods comparable to what is available in the downtown area of a small city. They are characterized by the presence of one or more full-line department stores that offer a broad selection of general merchandise and apparel. Most regional centers have two or three large department stores and some of the very largest feature as many as five or six.

Ancillary tenants most frequently found in U.S. regional shopping centers are ladies' ready-to-wear apparel stores, jewelry stores, fast food restaurants, shoe stores, men's apparel stores, and bookstores.

In addition to merchandise, many regional shopping centers offer services, entertainment, and recreational facilities. The comprehensive nature of the regional shopping center means there is virtually no limit to the kinds of goods and services that can be purchased there. As a modern, compact version of the traditional downtown retail district, the regional shopping center can offer nearly every type of product or service for which there is a demand in its *trade area*—the geographic area from which it will draw most of its customers. However, the traditional focus of the regional center is toward fashion. Many retail businesses that cannot generate sufficient sales volume or mark up their goods or services enough to be profitable are not able to afford regional shopping center rents.

Super regional centers are simply bigger regional centers, with at least a million square feet of GLA and a minimum of three full-line department stores. The number of retailers in each category of merchandise is comparable to what would be found in the central business district of a large city; otherwise, super regional centers offer the same type and quality of goods as regional centers.

Community Shopping Centers

While the focal points of regional centers are large department stores, community shopping centers are often anchored by junior department stores that feature primarily soft goods and apparel. Other anchors for community centers include discount or off-price stores, hardware and home improvement stores, electronic super stores, supermarkets, and garden centers—any of which might be combined with variety or drug stores. The median total GLA in community centers ranges from 150,000 to 400,000 square feet. These centers account for approximately 25–30 percent of the shopping center facilities in the United States.

Common ancillary tenants are food service operations and family apparel stores. Service stores are also viable in these locations. Top-ranking ancillary tenants for community shopping centers are women's ready-to-wear stores, restaurants that serve liquor, beauty salons, card shops, family shoe stores, and fast food operations.

Neighborhood Shopping Centers

Designed to provide day-to-day necessities to people living within a five- to ten-minute drive of the site, the neighborhood center commonly has a supermarket as its anchor tenant, usually accompanied by a drugstore. Such centers often include several service stores—barber shops, beauty parlors, shoe repair stores, dry cleaners—as well as fast food stores and restaurants in a gross leasable area of 50,000–175,000 square feet. Although neighborhood centers are comparatively small, people visit them because of their convenience and proximity. The tenant mix of neighborhood centers in particular is tailored to the specific needs of the surrounding trade area. Nearly two-thirds of the shopping centers in the United States can be characterized as neighborhood centers, making them the most prevalent form of shopping center.

Growth of the supermarket has expanded the size of these centers. From predominantly food items, supermarkets have extended their merchandise beyond a few drug sundries, and they commonly include specialty food offerings—fresh bakery goods, fresh fish, deli meats—along with video rentals and some housewares. As a result, supermarkets can offer one-stop shopping, and the customer need not seek out a separate drug or hardware store.

On the other hand, neighborhood centers themselves are becoming increasingly specialized, and in some cases supermarket anchors have been replaced by a group of individual stores that offer the same range of goods as the typical supermarket. New centers are being designed to be architecturally compatible with residential developments constructed nearby.

Specialty Shopping Centers

The characteristic that distinguishes a specialty center from other types of shopping centers is the use of a dominant theme or image that results in concentration on a particular type of merchandise. There is seldom a conventional anchor tenant, and restaurants commonly serve as the main attraction.

Some specialty centers are entirely focused toward tourists, with typical tenants including gourmet food shops, restaurants, gift stores, jewelry, and so-called luxury merchandise. These centers are usually developed in locations that enjoy a high volume of tourist traffic—Ghirardelli Square in San Francisco, Trolley Square in Salt Lake City, Faneuil Hall Marketplace in Boston, The Pavilion at The Old Post Office in Washington, D.C., Harborplace in Baltimore. They tend to occupy relatively small sites and rarely contain more than 300,000 square feet of GLA. However, the trade area of this type of specialty center is quite extensive, often equivalent to that of a regional center, because the success of such specialty retailers frequently depends on the trade area being large enough to include groups of consumers with the income and demand for nonessential and high-quality goods. The trade area for a tourist-oriented specialty center must also be large enough to compensate for the fact that specialty retailers cannot depend on repeat purchases as other retailers can.

There are specialty centers that concentrate on high-fashion apparel and cater to an upper-income trade area where the population has the means to purchase luxury or high-quality merchandise. There are also so-called "industrial shopping centers" designed around a group of specialty retailers that offer such items as plumbing fixtures, automotive services, or hardware. An auto care center, for example, would include tenants that offer a wide variety of automotive products and services, from car stereo equipment to regular tune-ups.

Outlet and off-price centers are two other variations of the specialty shopping center concept. *Outlet centers* are comprised of at least 50 percent factory outlet stores that offer name-brand goods at lower prices by eliminating the price increases required by the intermediary wholesale distributor. The individual manufacturers represented in the center usually operate the stores selling their merchandise. Clothing, shoes, linens, luggage, kitchenware, and home decorating accessories are among the products typically available at outlet centers. Because the manufacturers do not want to compete directly with the retailers that distribute their products, these centers are usually located greater distances from a metropolitan trade area than are more traditional regional shopping centers. Frequently they serve an "extra regional" market, with 25 to 50 percent of their sales being to customers who travel more than 50 miles to shop. Factory Outlet Centre in Kenosha, Wisconsin, and Lighthouse Place in Michigan City, Indiana, both attract customers from the Chicago metropolitan area even though they are somewhat out of the way.

An *off-price center* is comprised of retailers that offer name-brand merchandise at 20 to 60 percent below normal retail prices. In addition to factory overruns, seconds and dated merchandise, and overstock items from conventional department stores, they buy many different kinds of merchandise on consignment from manufacturers. Off-price centers generally feature more fashion and apparel stores than do factory outlet centers.

Both outlet and off-price centers have available anywhere from 60,000 to 400,000 square feet of GLA. Larger centers do exist, however; Potomac Mills in Maryland is one example of an extremely large off-price shopping center equivalent in size to a regional center.

Outlet and off-price centers are fairly new entries in discount merchandising. Discount stores selling brand-name *hard goods* at less-than-retail prices have been on the American scene for many years. It is the sale of brand-name *apparel* at discount prices that has established the off-price and outlet centers in their market niches. However, the differences between these two types of value-oriented shopping centers have become less pronounced over time. The merchandise available and the presentation of lower-priced goods are now very similar. Many of these centers have been upgraded so that shoppers often save on merchandise in an atmosphere similar to a department store, a presentation format that reinforces the customers' perception of value.

In keeping with the emphasis on low cost, tenants in off-price centers generally try to rent the least amount of store space possible so they can keep rents low and pass the savings on to their customers. Some large tenants, however, may occupy as much as 40,000 square feet of GLA, and they can negotiate favorable lease terms as a result. The success of both outlet and off-price centers is based on low occupancy costs and high sales volume. Center owners are able to charge low rents because they keep design frills and other amenities to a minimum. The fact that consumers will accept modest surroundings in order to be able to purchase name-brand goods at low prices is borne out by the success of both outlet and off-price centers. Leasing agents should not assume that only low-income areas will be feasible for these centers; many affluent suburban residents also frequently shop at outlet and off-price centers.

Convenience Centers

By definition, a *convenience center* is anchored by a convenience food store that provides quick-stop necessities and grocery items. The anchor may be a regional or national chain such as White Hen Pantry or 7-Eleven. Convenience centers commonly provide space for several other retail tenants, and service-oriented businesses—dry cleaners, liquor stores, self-service laundries, barber shops, and fast food restaurants—are typical ancillary tenants. The entire site for a convenience center may measure only 10,000–15,000 square feet and have parking space for only ten to twenty cars. The actual structure of the center may occupy only 4,000–5,000 square feet of space.

Also known as mini-centers, convenience centers cater to busy shoppers who are unwilling to travel long distances for daily necessities. There may be a population of 100,000 consumers within a two-mile radius of these sites, and daily traffic counts on adjoining streets may total 40,000 to 50,000 cars. However, a convenience center can be supported where the population is less than 5,000 if the site is strategically located and there are no competing centers nearby. Shoppers repeatedly demonstrate a willingness to pay the higher prices charged at such centers in order to avoid the trouble and expense of lengthy trips to more distant centers.

New Forms of Shopping Centers

A newer development of interest to the leasing agent is the *megamall,* which is at least three or four times larger than an ordinary regional center. An example is the gigantic West Edmonton Mall outside the city of Edmonton in Alberta, Canada. This five-million-square-foot, totally enclosed mall includes among its many attractions an Olympic-sized swimming pool and an amusement park—complete with a submarine ride. In addition, the mall contains numerous restaurants and shops, a hotel, and several department stores. The mall has become so famous internationally that special "shopping flights" to Edmonton are available, with shuttle bus service connecting the airport and the center. In the United States, the Mall of America scheduled to open in Bloomington, Minnesota, in 1992 will have 2.6 million square feet of retail GLA and include eight major stores plus some 600–800 specialty shops, eighteen theaters, a health club, and several restaurants and nightclubs. The complex will include three hotels and a theme park when it is completed.

Supermarkets and discount stores, too, have undergone changes in both size and design. The success of membership warehouse clubs, where customers pay annual membership fees in order to receive discounts at out-of-the-way stores, has inspired several retailers to expand upon the concept. The stores offer some 3,500 food and general merchandise items on average and operate at a gross margin of 10 percent or less. Sam's Wholesale Club and The Price Club are two examples of successful warehouse operations in the United States.

A new concept for U.S. retailing is the *hypermarket*. Originated in France, the hypermarket combines elements of both the supermarket and the discount warehouse store into one gigantic structure. Hypermarkets are usually owned by retailers; many times they are freestanding or have limited service concessions such as fast food stands leased inside the store. Hypermart USA, developed by Tom Thumb Grocers and Wal-Mart, is one such store. Although hypermarkets cannot be considered "shopping centers" by definition, their size alone allows them to serve a larger trade area than that of the traditional neighborhood shopping center anchored by a supermarket. While the average size is approximately 150,000 square feet, it is not unusual for hypermarkets to be much larger—Hypermart USA in Dallas has 250,000 square feet of GLA. Typical merchandise offered includes groceries, electronic equipment, appliances, clothing, toys, household goods, office supplies, furniture, automotive supplies, and even jewelry. High-volume buying and a no-frills approach to merchandising mean pricing can be substantially lower than that of the competition.

Whether hypermarkets will prove as successful in the United States as in France is yet to be seen. Generally, the American shopper is not accustomed to buying food and general merchandise items at the same shopping location. In addition, hypermarket shoppers must travel long distances—a disadvantage in all but very rural areas. In spite of the lower prices that a hypermarket offers, most consumers would probably choose the convenience of a nearby traditional supermarket over a hypermarket located 10 or 12 miles from their homes. The size of such stores could also prove to be a deterrent. Walking to hard-to-find items can be exhausting for the average shopper. Hypermart USA has attempted to overcome this problem by placing benches and information phone booths at varied locations throughout their stores and by outfitting some employees with rollerskates so that they can reach shoppers more quickly. Reasoning that customers would prefer not to walk through the entire store to find a particular item, Hypermart USA is also divided into separate sections—food, apparel, general merchandise, and specialty departments. In general, hypermarkets present exciting new retailing potential, but they also pose new challenges in marketing.

Yet another innovation in shopping center design is the *power center.* Power centers show a much higher ratio of anchor space to small stores than is usually seen in community shopping centers. There may be three to five or more anchors in each center—discount foodstores, super drugstores, large toy stores, sporting goods stores, electronics superstores, or house and garden stores. They have the customer draw of a regional center while appealing to shoppers who are looking for discount and convenience items. The "power" behind power centers comes from their size and their concentration of anchor tenants; they range in size from 250,000 to 700,000 square feet of GLA—nearly twice the size of a standard community center. By combining the scope of a regional mall with the convenience of a community center, they are able to attract more business than a standard community center. One disadvantage of power centers, however, is that most of their tenants offer merchandise that shoppers seek out specifically (toys, sporting goods) rather than items purchased on impulse, and therefore the centers themselves have little of the ambiance of a community or regional center where there is a mix of tenants that benefit from each other's presence.

Megamalls, hypermarkets, and power centers are developments to be watched in the future. The questions the leasing agent may well ask are when and how will these types of retail properties become leasing opportunities. The answers to these questions will become known as more of these and other new types of centers are built—and succeed.

THE RETAIL LEASING PROFESSION

Retail space leasing can encompass a variety of tasks. In its simplest form, it may involve finding an appropriate tenant for a single, freestanding retail store and negotiating a lease that will be acceptable to both the tenant and the property owner. Leasing agents also locate tenants to fill large new developments or to re-lease or revitalize an existing center.

Although retail leasing has evolved into a specialized profession in its own right, it is often a function within a property management company or full-service real estate firm. There is an advantage to the owner or developer who hires a management firm that distinguishes its operations functions from its leasing functions. Because the management company will receive the fees for both property management and leasing, it should have adequate funds to justify proper staffing and is therefore more likely to be able to give the property the attention it deserves.

In general, the property manager is the one who will collect rents, pay bills, provide maintenance and security, manage promotional campaigns, respond to tenant complaints, and attempt to resolve disputes between the tenants and the owner. The property manager may also supervise or undertake the leasing activity in centers that are already fully leased. In addition, the manager will submit regular reports to the owner on income and expenditures. The owner's goal is to enhance the value of the property and to receive sufficient returns on investment; the property manager helps fulfill these financial objectives by maintaining high occupancy levels and making sure the property is capable of maximizing its potential rents. This is where the leasing agent comes in. At most centers, leasing is an ongoing process, and the leasing agent's knowledge of the market can be a valuable resource to the property manager who is renewing leases or renovating a property. The leasing agent will be able to provide the property manager with information on demographic and economic changes in the trade area and fluctuations in market rents, as well as suggest ways to implement new strategies for marketing and leasing.

A good leasing agent will also learn from the property manager's close connection to the property and its day-to-day operations. Although the leasing agent's primary focus will be on what types of tenants are making deals and how much rent they are paying, the agent should also be more than simply a "leasing machine." The owner's financial goals and the physical layout of the center or store itself are also important considerations in the development of a leasing campaign.

The Agency Broker

Basically, there are two types of retail leasing agents—those who work for a salary on the in-house staff of a developer and those who work on commission for a real estate brokerage firm. In addition, there are agents who represent retailers as prospective tenants; they often work directly for large local, regional, or national real estate agencies. The tenant representative may also represent a specific retailer or chain that is seeking an entry into a part of the country where it has no previously established outlets.

In-house leasing is project-oriented: Agents are better able to control leasing plans and to develop standardized leasing policies that will help them achieve long-term goals. They can also deal more effectively with saturation of the target market because they concentrate primarily on the surrounding trade area. In a sluggish market, working in-house has its advantages, mainly a regular salary. The agent employed by an aggressive developer will make excellent contacts. Because developers are constantly expanding their portfolios of properties, the in-house agent has less of a problem with dwindling opportunities; efforts are concentrated on finding tenants, not building an inventory of available space. The developer also may be more likely to share information on the business with an in-house agent because such sharing will be seen as a worthwhile investment in the developer's own staff.

Most of the tenants in regional centers are part of national organizations that have multiple tenancies in other similar centers. Because mall developers and managers already know who these major players are, they tend to refuse to cooperate with outside brokers. (That way they avoid payment of commissions as well as potential conflicts of interest.) In fact, leasing to anchor tenants is a specialty in itself. It is rare for an outside broker to work on leasing a regional or super regional center. Most of that type of leasing is done by the developer's in-house staff, giving the developer greater control over tenant mix and tenant placement.

The majority of agents are agency brokers who lease retail space in community or neighborhood centers. Agency brokers are deal-oriented, committed to getting a lease signed and bringing the transaction between a potential tenant and the owner to a satisfactory close. Thus the deal, rather than the parties involved, is the most important aspect of the agency broker's job.

These agents can represent either the property or the tenant. Generally, an *overbuilt market,* where space is abundant, favors the tenant; an *underbuilt market,* where there is not enough space to go around, favors the property. It is to the agent's advantage to represent the scarcer commodity in any given market. The intent is to secure the owner's or the tenant's agreement not to work with another agent on a particular deal—in other words, an exclusive listing. Tenant brokerage is far less common than owner representation, however; and for this reason, *Leasing Retail Space* focuses primarily on the work of the agency broker who is representing owners.

Every leasing agent's job is different, depending on the circumstances of the deal and the characteristics of the owner and the property involved. It is not possible to give a precise description of a leasing agent's daily tasks because the very nature of the job demands flexibility and a willingness to adapt to different circumstances. The agent's main objective is to gauge the environment of the deal—to determine the main concerns of both prospective tenant and owner and, given these stipulations, to formulate his or her leasing techniques accordingly.

However, most leasing agents will have at least some activities in common, even though they may not devote equal time to each of them or will put more emphasis on one task than on another. Briefly, these activities are as follows:

- *Cold calling and canvassing for prospects.* Most leasing agents are required to make a specific number of contacts per day and will spend much of their time making telephone calls. Cold calling serves a dual purpose: It helps leasing agents find the right tenant for the space, and it allows them to make an inventory of the market that will be useful for future deals. It also provides them with leads for other centers they are leasing. (Cold calling will be explained in more detail in chapter 5.)

- *Developing a database of tenants and properties.* Site plans, tenancies, vacancies, rental rates, and other specifics related to competing centers are vital to successful leasing. This database is the direct result of cold calling. The longer an agent is in the business, the more people he or she will know, and the less time it will take to make contacts with potential tenants.
- *Evaluating demographic data and preparing sales materials.* The agent uses demographic data primarily to aid prospective tenants in forecasting sales, in order to determine whether the prospect will be able to succeed in the new location. Demographic data are also used to focus information about the property for the prospective tenant.
- *Qualifying tenants.* Every leasing agent should be able to evaluate a retailer's financial stability, space and operational requirements, merchandising policies, and business history. It is the agent's responsibility to find the best possible tenant for any given space. (Qualifying will be covered in detail in chapter 5.)
- *Cooperating with other brokers.* Cooperation speeds up the process of finding suitable tenants; deals will be made much more quickly. In the retail leasing community, cooperation is a fact of life.
- *Networking.* The agent should not overlook the public relations aspect of the job. Being involved in community activities and attending trade shows, seminars, and conferences related to shopping center development and retailing will help the agent make valuable contacts useful for present as well as future deals.

Leasing agents are always working to increase their contacts in the retail community. Even retail space owners and developers who are not currently looking for tenants might eventually need the leasing agent's services. By keeping track of vacant stores or space in competing shopping centers, the leasing agent will be able to approach the owner in the future, when the time is right. The more leasing decisionmakers the agent gets to know, the greater the possibility of getting future listings.

One of the most difficult aspects of the leasing agent's job, and the hardest one for inexperienced agents to become accustomed to, is the almost perpetual rejection encountered when making cold calls. In order to close a few deals, the leasing agent may contact hundreds of prospects, most of whom will turn the agent down at the first contact. For every fifty phone calls an agent makes to potential tenants, perhaps only ten will express interest in the site. Of those ten, seven will likely decide the site is not what they wanted, or they will not be qualified for the space; of the three remaining prospects, only one will actually sign a lease. The leasing agent will repeat this process for every listing. A typical large brokerage firm that employs 120 agents will normally generate 2,000 leases in a year—an average of approximately 16.6 deals per agent. Considering the many hours of prospecting effort each deal represents, that is not a large number. Of course, the time needed to acquire a particular tenant depends on the size of the space, market conditions, and the reputation of the center or store site, as well as the extent of the agent's contacts and knowledge of the business.

Exclusive versus Nonexclusive Listings

An agent who approaches the owner or developer of a particular retail site will usually try to obtain an *exclusive listing* with that owner. Briefly, this means that the agent is assured in writing that the owner will not deal with any other leasing agent without paying a fee to the original agent—the original agent is guaranteed a commission if the deal is closed, no matter who brought the tenant to the owner.

An open or *nonexclusive listing* gives the owner the right to deal with other agents. If the original agent actually closes the deal, he or she gets paid a commission. Otherwise, the owner is not required to pay the original agent any fee. Some owners believe that the nonexclusive arrangement gives them more freedom of choice because it does not lock them into one agent's efforts—instead of accepting offers from only one agent, they may see offers from several agents.

From the leasing agent's point of view, an exclusive listing is much more desirable. Most brokers with some experience in the business refuse to work on a nonexclusive basis. An agent's ability to obtain an exclusive listing depends on a number of factors, including market conditions and the law of supply and demand. In general, an owner is *more likely* to grant an exclusive if there are fewer tenants available to fill a large number of vacancies; if there are more tenants looking for space than there are sites available, the owner is *less likely* to grant an exclusive. An exclusive listing provides more assurance to the owner that the agent will work hard at leasing the space and also gives the agent confidence to be able to spend more time on securing that lease.

The arrangement between the agent and the owner should be spelled out in a specific agreement. An *exclusive authorization to lease* form states that the agent will receive a commission for any tenant prospect the agent has introduced who signs a lease within a certain period, including a period of time following the expiration date of the agreement. The agent will receive the commission regardless of who actually concludes the lease negotiation. (Leases negotiated up to 180 days after expiration of the authorization agreement are commonly covered; however, this may vary from firm to firm or by locality. The term may be only thirty to sixty days.) Sometimes a second agent will bring the deal to a close, in which case the commission will be split between the two agents. An exclusive authorization ensures that a second agent will not receive the entire commission for a lease to a prospect for whom the original agent did the groundwork. In other words, each participating agent receives credit for the work he or she has done. To assure proper credit for leases ultimately brought to a close, the agent should register all prospects with the owner on a regular basis, submitting their names, their business, and their retail space needs in writing. If not done when the space is shown, registration of prospects should certainly be done within thirty days of the expiration date of the authorization agreement in order to document the agent's right to a possible future commission.

Attention to detail is important when completing the exclusive authorization to lease form. The listing period should include a specific expiration date; without one, the entire form may be void. Other key considerations include acceptable terms of a lease such as the rent per square foot, the duration of the lease, and escalation clauses. All of the leasing terms should be as specific as possible. Then if the agent produces a prospective tenant who agrees to sign a lease under the given conditions—but the owner rejects that prospect—the agent will still be entitled to a commission.

Under the terms of a *nonexclusive authorization to lease,* the agent receives a commission only if a lease is actually executed with a prospect. However, the same 180-day extension beyond the expiration date of the authorization agreement usually applies as long as the agent has registered prospective tenants with the owner, and the owner has accepted the registrations. Many of the same completion guidelines apply to both the nonexclusive and exclusive authorizations: the dates covering the duration of the agent's contract should be stated and the lease terms should be as specific as possible. (Examples of these two forms are shown in appendixes A.1 and A.2.)

In general, all prospects are registered by the leasing agent in writing, in order to protect his or her interest in the property and to assure that a commission will be received. The listing agreement can be in the form of a contract, or it can be a letter the agent drafts stating specific details. The listing agreement is also crucial in dealings with other, secondary agents because it will help prevent misunderstandings about who approached the owner first and will ensure that commissions are divided on a fair basis.

Because the owner's motivation to accept the agent's participation will be greatest at the beginning of the deal, when the agent's introductory role is crucial, it is preferable to record transactions early, before lease negotiations begin. Market conditions may not always favor the agent.

When demand for space is high, owners may refuse to pay commissions, reasoning that acceptable prospects will eventually approach them directly, bypassing an agent. Knowing the owners they are dealing with is the best assurance that leasing agents will be paid the commissions they've earned. This is also why broker cooperation and a wide knowledge of the market and the leasing community become so important to the individual leasing agent.

Commission Agreements

The leasing commission is usually paid by the property owner, although prospective tenants concerned with protecting their interests will sometimes pay agents to work for them. The amount of the commission and the time at which it is paid are both fully negotiable; they depend in large part on the nature of the market as well as the nature of the deal. The leasing commission almost always represents *a percentage of the rent for the entire term of the tenant's lease*—in other words, the gross rent. In some instances, the commission may be based on a set fee per square foot of GLA, regardless of rental rate or lease term. Each owner-agent relationship will require a different structure for commission payment. Basically, there are two types of commission structures, cash-out and deferred.

Cash-out.   In some cases, commissions are paid to the agent up front, usually at a rate of 3–5 percent of the gross rents. Depending on market conditions or the owner's financial situation, full payment may not always be possible, especially when there is a long-term lease and the commission is substantial. The owner's cash flow may be low before a tenant takes possession of the property, and a large commission may be too much to pay the agent up front. As an alternative, the agent may be paid 50 percent of the commission when the lease is signed and 50 percent after the tenant has moved in (or after six months or another agreed-upon period). Sometimes the agent is paid one third at the signing, one third at the actual move-in, and one third six months after commencement of the lease term. In many cases, commissions are paid when rents are collected. Each situation is different.

Deferred.   Sometimes a deferred payment structure is arranged. Deferred payments are also used if the tenant is less creditworthy. In a deferred-payment schedule, the owner may pay the agent in installments over the course of the entire lease term, decreasing the commission percentage in succeeding years. An example of how this might work is shown below.

Suppose a retailer has signed a three-year lease. Rent is $1,200 per month or $14,400 per year. The commission has been negotiated at 7 percent the first year, 6 percent the second year, and 5 percent the third year. Here is how the commission would be calculated:

    1st year—$14,400 at 7% = $1,008
    2nd year—$14,400 at 6% = $ 864
    3rd year—$14,400 at 5% = $ 720
            Total Commission = $2,592

Commission rates payable on deferred schedules are slightly higher than cash-out payments—5–10 percent of the total rent amount. This is done to account for the impact of inflation on the value of the dollar over time. Because the commission paid cash-out is calculated as a straight percentage, the resulting amount is usually a little larger than a deferred commission paid at the same rate would be. Offering a larger percentage in a deferred payment program makes up the difference. In addition, agents who are paid commissions on a deferred schedule may also be entitled to receive commissions on percentage rents and on renewals or extensions of leases or expansions of leased space; agents paid cash-out commissions usually do not receive such additional payments. Agents sometimes prefer deferred payment because it permits them to budget their incomes.

Split Commissions.   Commissions are often divided among two or more agents; this is the norm in retail leasing, where broker cooperation is a necessity. Often the deal is negotiated between two agents—one representing the owner and the other representing the prospective tenant. Split commissions are especially common when deals are complex or involve large amounts of space and rent. Often an outside agent will generate interest from a prospect the original agent would not otherwise approach, or the agent working one property may develop a prospect whose business would better suit a property or location represented by another broker. Sharing of commissions may be documented in advance with a *broker cooperation agreement.* (An example of such an agreement is presented in appendix A.3.)

The inexperienced agent may be reluctant to share a commission with another broker, especially if he or she has an exclusive listing with a particular owner. While it may be tempting to hold out for the next prospect rather than accept a suitable prospect brought in by an outside agent, such behavior is unethical and not in the best interest of the agent's client (the owner of the property). Also, the agent who does not cooperate with outside brokers will gain a poor reputation in the leasing community.

The agent with an exclusive listing has a binding legal fiduciary relationship or is therefore committed to the owner, and the owner's desire is to lease the space as quickly as possible. The agent may not lose money if the space is not leased to the first suitable prospect, but the owner might.

Usually the owner has debts to service and wants to generate cash flow immediately. It is the agent's responsibility to help the owner accomplish this. On the other hand, both the agent and the owner should be certain that the prospect is the best candidate for the particular space and a good match for the center's tenant mix.

Forms. Commission payments are established on a mutually agreed-upon plan; this agreement between the owner and the agent is legally binding. Therefore, the agent must fully understand all the conditions of a transaction before signing any forms. A *schedule of commissions* should be attached to the *commission agreement,* stating the percentage of the commission and when the commission will be paid. (The exact amount of the commission will not be known until the rental rates and lease terms are established, and payment may be made on agreement, at final lease closing, on tenant move-in, or on some other schedule.) Any specifics regarding deferred payments or additional commissions should be spelled out in detail.

When presented to the owner, these two documents—commission agreement and schedule of commissions—are usually treated as two parts of a single document because one without the other will not guarantee that an agent is paid. A schedule of commissions tells the owner *how* and *what* the agent is to be paid; the commission agreement is legal proof that a commission *will* be paid. An exclusive authorization to lease includes a statement about commission agreements (no separate or additional commission agreement is necessary), but a schedule of commissions should be attached to it to complete the legal documentation. (Examples of a commission agreement and a schedule of commissions are given in appendixes A.4 and A.5, respectively.)

SUMMARY

In response to the continuing growth and diversification of shopping centers, the leasing of retail space has become a highly specialized profession. In order to succeed as a retail leasing specialist, one has to be familiar with the business of retailing, the different types of contemporary retail space, and the nature of the retail leasing profession.

The leasing agent has to be well-informed about the aspects of the tenant's business that affect sales performance and merchandising, both of which influence rental income. It is important to know that merchandise is priced to (1) reflect the cost of the goods, (2) create an adequate profit margin, and (3) be competitive in the marketplace. The leasing agent learns about a potential tenant's operation by noting when an item is under- or overstocked (at the beginning or end of a season, or at holidays), when price markdowns are made, and when the retailer has special sales. Gross profits—the difference between the cost of goods sold and the net sales income (total sales minus returns)—are the measure the retailer uses to estimate how well the business has done during the year. A retailer's skill at handling these different aspects of retailing is an important indicator of the business's potential success and contribution to a retail location.

Contemporary retail space is dominated by the suburban shopping center, although urban retail space is experiencing a rebirth. The different types of shopping centers—super regional, regional, community, neighborhood, specialty, and convenience centers—are defined by their gross leasable area (GLA), their tenant mix (especially type of anchor tenant), and their typical location. Regional and super regional centers most often are enclosed malls located in the suburbs and anchored by one or more department stores. Community and neighborhood centers are generally found in busy urban or suburban areas and are anchored by discount stores and supermarkets. Specialty centers tend to occupy smaller sites and are often built around a particular "theme," with a tenant mix that thrives on tourist trade. Convenience centers that offer necessities such as groceries and gasoline (and may include service businesses like dry cleaners) are located primarily in residential areas or on a corner of a busy intersection. New forms of shopping centers that offer more diversity or greater concentrations of specific types of merchandise (megamalls, hypermarkets, power centers) are also entering the picture, and these may provide opportunities for the leasing agent in the future.

Even though retail leasing has evolved into a separate profession, the leasing function may still be part of the overall property management. Leasing agents do not oversee the day-to-day operations of the shopping center, but the agent who is prospecting for retail tenants must be aware of the owner's goals as well as the plans for the future of the center. Agents work either in-house—as part of a salaried staff for a large developer or management company—or on commission for a brokerage firm. In the latter case, they may represent the center owner or the prospective tenant. The agent's duties include prospecting for tenants, market research and preparation of demographic studies and sales materials, and qualifying prospective tenants. Leasing agents also show the property for lease and must know the inventory of available space as well as the lease terms that apply to each unit. The leasing agent is an expert who matches retail businesses to profitable locations. Cooperation with other brokers and networking with people in the retailing industry prepare the agent to do the best job possible.

Independent agents prefer to obtain an exclusive listing from a shopping center owner. This assures that the agent will receive a commission regardless of who recruits the accepted tenant. In a market where there are more potential tenants and less available space, however, a non-exclusive listing may be the agent's only option. Before any campaigning begins, a commission agreement stating the agent's fee, how and when it is to be paid, and the conditions under which it is earned should be signed. Commissions are traditionally paid by the owner of the space, and they can be split among two or more brokers who have collaborated on the deal.

To formulate an effective leasing plan, the agent needs a concrete knowledge of the property's market. Tenant selection and rental rates are the result of an evaluation of the area's retail needs and demographic characteristics. Such market assessment is described in detail in the next chapter.

2

Assessing the Market

The developer is interested in turning relatively low-priced land into a profitable investment by leasing space in the new building to the strongest retailers for the highest rents the market can command. The individual retailer is interested in finding a location that will yield the highest possible sales for its goods or services. To a great extent, the developer's (or owner's) success depends on the retail tenant's success, and for that reason, both developer and retailer will want the same kinds of information about the trade area in which a retail property is located. Some of the questions they both ask are listed below.

- Is there a market for specific retail goods or services?
- What share of the market can a retailer capture?
- How much sales area (square footage) for specific goods or services will the market support?
- What volume of sales per square foot must be generated to yield a profit?
- What rental rates are currently charged in the market?
- What rental rates can the center's location support?
- How much rent can individual retailers pay?
- Is the market changing in any significant way?

The answers to these questions are found by conducting *market research.*

Retail sites, particularly new ones, draw on several sources of traffic:

general population growth which increases the number of customers that are not absorbed by competing centers, customers that can be lured away from existing centers, and customers seeking goods that are not currently available in the area. For the retailer, market research answers questions about the overall sales potential of a location in terms of customers, market share, and profitability.

For the owner, market research helps in establishing rental rates for the property. An owner wants to achieve the highest cash flow and occupancy levels possible. Because the amount of rent in large part determines not only cash flow and occupancy but also the ultimate value of the property, the owner has to know what rental rates the property will support. Base and percentage rents are based on a combination of many factors, including the current per-square-foot rates in the general market. (Rental schedules are described in detail in chapter 3.) Market research is undertaken both by large retailers considering a particular location and by developers selecting a site for a new store or shopping center. It may be conducted by an in-house marketing staff, by independent firms that specialize in market research, or by consultants. The leasing agent may not actually conduct the market research, but familiarity with the results of such studies is important to successful leasing.

A major component of market research is the *market survey* which contains both quantitative and qualitative data about the site. The market survey can provide background material for the leasing effort and serve as a promotional tool during prospecting. The principal aspects of retail space that prospective tenants usually take into consideration are location, competition, and sales potential. The survey should cover all of these in detail. When forecasting sales, each retailer will focus on a different aspect of the market based on the nature of its business. A jeweler might be more interested in demographic data that indicate specific income and that the area has a high per capita expenditure for nonconvenience items; a grocer will want to know the proximity and strength of the competition, and a service station operator will be interested in attributes of the site location such as traffic counts and ease of access. Because of these differences in retailers' operations, the agent will have to tailor the leasing campaign to each prospective tenant's individual needs.

EVALUATING THE LOCATION

A good location study will help sell a retailer on the location. It will include economic and demographic information about the overall region in which the retail property is situated as well as the narrower "trade area" where the retailer will be doing business. Many retail sites are rejected because they are not suitable for a particular business. A retailer evaluates a center's location on the basis of such factors as the regional economic climate, trade area characteristics, specific site attributes (accessibility, visibility, traffic counts, terrain, etc.), and an assessment of the competition. The data should include a *demographic profile*—population counts (both present and projected), community growth patterns, income and expenditures in the various trade areas, and a profile of local shoppers.

The Regional Economy

A *regional analysis* will provide a broad perspective of the retail site. The term "region" refers to the large general area around a property that influences its profitability. Although a region can refer to a state, a section of the country (such as the Midwest or the Sunbelt), a county, or only a large metropolitan area such as New York City, the size of a retail property's region is directly related to the property's size and type. A regional shopping center with two or more department stores and sixty to one hundred smaller shops offering a wide variety of merchandise draws customers from a larger area than a community shopping center does.

The objective of a regional analysis is to determine the economic strength of the area as well as its economic health. It will focus primarily on the economic trends that affect each retail store or center. Reports on regional business activity and data on employment can be obtained from the U.S. Department of Commerce and state employment departments. Information about the available labor force, types of jobs or occupations, and names of major employers in the area are usually available. Population forecasts and per capita income are other important factors, and these data are available from the U.S. Bureau of the Census as well as other sources. Utility companies, local traffic zone studies, and retail sales tax records are other useful resources. Numerous commercial data vendors compile and sell specifically focused market information. (A variety of information sources and a number of specific publications that are helpful in market research are included in the bibliography of resources.)

Both retailers and developers will also be interested in whether there are a variety of retail businesses because variety provides a better draw to the area. The local chamber of commerce is a source for this type of information. It is also important to know the extent to which smaller businesses are linked to major employers in the area. Some cities are dominated by a certain business—the rubber industry in Akron, Ohio, for example, and the auto industry in Detroit, Michigan.

In some areas, rehabbing and renovation may be more desirable than new development. This will depend on the nature of the trade area and whether it has been overbuilt. In many parts of the Midwest, especially in Chicago, such "infill" projects are prevalent and encouraged. Los Angeles, however, has had a large number of retail sites developed on former service station corners, and the limited parking and high density of these "centers" necessitated legislation declaring a moratorium on such development. Thus, local zoning laws and governmental real estate controls are considerations, although these are of more interest to developers than to retailers. In some regions, regulations forbid certain types of construction or certain types of retail tenants, and local ordinances may affect rental rates. Scarcity of space zoned for retail use can promote competition among developers; in the northeastern United States, for example, space limitations have driven rental rates up. On the other hand, taxes distributed over a growing population base—as in a healthy, developing region—are less likely to be increased than taxes in slow-growth areas that must meet community needs. Where services are well-established, taxes may be less of a consideration than they must be where new services require new or additional assessments.

Other factors influencing retail activity are climate and natural resources. An area where agriculture dominates will not support many high-end specialty retailers if the region does not include a large metropolitan area. The population of farming regions is more likely to be distributed among small cities and rural communities, with retail activity dominated by farming equipment and family-oriented goods and services—clothing, home furnishings, and restaurants—rather than luxury goods.

Retailers are aware that the economic structure of a region and the geographic features that influence its business activity will have an impact on how retailing grows in that area. When business districts in inner-city communities are depressed or nonexistent, residents often have to travel great distances to shop, and there are fewer community-based jobs. Downtown development can be risky and difficult, as exemplified by The Underground in Atlanta, which at one time had to be closed for several years because of the high crime rate. However, certain areas that were once thought to be unfeasible as locations for new stores are proving to be a success. Developers are beginning to design community shopping centers especially for the inner city. The Watts district in Los Angeles and the North Lawndale neighborhood in Chicago are two such areas. The inner city can be a viable market for retailers, a fact that agents should emphasize when leasing in this type of environment.

On the other hand, many regions are saturated with retail businesses or with certain types of merchandise. A careful study of the region can show whether there are too many women's clothing stores to support one more. Population forecasts that predict a minor baby boom might make a children's store feasible. Active housing construction and an expanding job market could indicate the need for a larger shopping center than the one being planned.

T A B L E   2.1

**Minimum Population* Required to Support
Different Types of Shopping Centers**

Type of Center	Population Minimum
Convenience	1,000 to 2,500
Neighborhood	5,000 to 40,000
Community	100,000 to 150,000
Regional	150,000 to 300,000
Super Regional	300,000 and up
Discount/Outlet	150,000 and up
Specialty (Upscale/Theme)	150,000 and up
"Power"	150,000 and up

*Figures are guidelines only.

As the geographic area under study narrows, the degree of detail of the market analysis increases. The next step in the market assessment is an analysis of the immediate trade area around the site.

Trade Area Analysis

Regional analysis projects the degree of success in a given area for retail development generally; subsequent *trade area analysis* will indicate the potential for a specific site to be successful. The trade area is the portion of the larger region from which the retail site actually draws its customers. The trade area population needed to support a particular retail site is related to the size or type of retail center. Minimum population requirements for different types of shopping centers are shown in table 2.1.

The trade area analysis usually generates in-depth information about the geographic zones where consumers are likely to be found, including maps showing population density and the location of competing retail stores, a demographic profile of the area, and a survey of local consumers and shopping habits.

Trade Area Zones. Typically, the trade area is divided into three zones—primary, secondary, and tertiary—based on the area from which a store will derive sales. Because these zones vary in size for every type of retailer and every type of center, it is not possible to offer a definition that can be used for every market research survey. Some general observations

T A B L E   2.2

Trade Area Zone Definitions*

Zone	Customer Draw	Radius (miles)	Driving Time (minutes)
Primary	60–75%	Less than 3	Up to 10
Secondary	10–20%	3–7	15–20
Tertiary	5–15%	15–50	25–30

*Figures given are general guidelines. Zone sizes and driving times will vary with the specific type of shopping center and its location.

about consumer habits can be made, however. Studies show that the average shopper will travel 1½ miles for food, 3–5 miles for apparel and household items, and 8–10 miles to comparison shop. Thus, the sizes of trade area zones for a particular center or store can have a significant relationship to its success. However, travel time is often more important than physical distance, especially in areas surrounded by rougher terrain. Travel times can be estimated by driving through the trade area in typical weather conditions and traffic situations. Table 2.2 summarizes comparative information about the different trade area zones.

Retailers consider the *primary trade area* as the area they can dominate. It represents their most significant penetration of the market. Therefore, it is the primary trade area which is the most important when considering a retail property's position in the market and its merchandising policies. In general, the primary trade area is the immediate area around the site. This is the area from which the retailer or the center draws 60–75 percent of its sales and is usually not more than a ten-minute drive away for most customers. However, distance in miles is also related to the size or the nature of the retailer's business. While the primary trade area of a small convenience grocery store such as 7-Eleven may extend only 1–3 miles, that for a typical 40,000-square-foot supermarket might be 1–4 miles, and the primary trade area for a *hypermarket* might be more than 10 miles. Also, consumers within easy reach of a particular store or shopping center cannot be considered in the "primary" trade area if a major retail property located nearby—a comparable center or competitor—would be passed by the shopper on the way to the subject site. On the other hand, a nearby center that "complements" the subject center can increase the general attraction of the area and draw customers from farther away, thereby extending its and the subject center's trade areas.

The *secondary trade area* accounts for about 10–20 percent of total sales at a retail site. It usually extends some 3–7 miles from the site (for a regional center) and represents a drive time of no more than fifteen or twenty minutes. This area is generally less defensible from competition. The range of the secondary area can be determined in several different ways depending on the location of competitive stores and population clusters. In areas where there are few retail facilities, the secondary trade area may extend a long distance from the property.

The *tertiary trade area* is the most difficult to pinpoint. It accounts for about 5–15 percent of a retailer's sales and can extend 15 miles from the site in major metropolitan areas to as much as 50 miles from the site in less-populated markets; driving time can be twenty-five to thirty minutes or more, depending on the situation. However, the radius of the tertiary trade area cannot always be measured in miles. Retailers often have no idea where these customers are coming from. They may be attracted to the store because it has better parking, because they are visiting from out of town and happen to be in that neighborhood, because they are tourists and have heard about the center, or because of special sales or availability of specialty items. So-called tertiary trade also exists in areas where distance is not an issue—downtown centers, for example, where lunchtime customers in a restaurant or visitors staying at a hotel are considered part of the tertiary trade (see chapter 9).

Mapping.   Representations of the trade area on maps provide an excellent basis for examining the problems and opportunities facing a retailer. For the leasing agent, maps can be an invaluable resource when prospecting for tenants.

Several methods can be used to determine trade area boundaries. The analog approach involves extrapolation from estimates of the trade areas of comparable centers. Data for such estimates can be obtained by conducting surveys at the comparable centers, asking customers to indicate the intersection nearest to their residences as well as answer questions about their buying habits. Plotting the locations of customers' homes on a map of the area will reveal "population clusters" that show where people live in relation to the store or center.

The next step is to estimate the boundaries of the so-called primary, secondary, and tertiary zones, adjusting for such differences as natural and man-made barriers to access, distribution of public thoroughfares, and location of competing properties. Because a variety of factors influences the boundaries of the trade area, the outer edge of each zone will not form a perfect circle around the retail site.

If a proposed new center is to be located geographically close to a comparable center, the projected trade area boundaries for the comparable center should apply to the new center by extrapolation. However, centers used to develop comparison data may yield good results—in other words, clearly defined trade areas, but they may not be located where geographic overlap with a proposed center can be assumed. In that case, extrapolation may mean plotting available data for the area of the proposed center on a map and using the trade area radiuses estimated for the comparable center to extrapolate primary, secondary, and tertiary trade areas for the proposed center. For example, market survey data for three successful regional centers—comparable in size, number of retailers, and types of merchandise but serving different markets—might reveal average estimated primary, secondary, and tertiary trade area radiuses of 5, 10, and 20 miles, respectively. Establishing the same zone radiuses on the map for the proposed center will permit at least an approximation of its potential market size and customer base.

The locations of rivers, parks, railroads, and other features in relation to a site can be important considerations. (Topographical maps showing physical features of the local terrain can be obtained from the U.S. Geological Survey.) Major access routes can be highlighted, and planned (future) highways or roads should be indicated, showing direction of traffic flow if necessary, as on a one-way street. Future residential developments can be shown as well. The completed map should indicate the dimensions of the trade area and suggest the degree to which the center can penetrate its market.

Location of the competition is probably one of the most crucial aspects of market analysis, and showing nearby centers on a map will address this issue effectively. The proximity of the site to other shopping centers and to residential areas is demonstrated dramatically in aerial photographs, and these can also be excellent marketing tools for the agent leasing retail space.

The analog method can be used in conjunction with other approaches. Tracking city or village stickers on automobiles in the parking lot will indicate how many customers come from a particular town or neighborhood and perhaps identify long-distance shoppers. It is also possible to "locate" customers by recording automobile license numbers and obtaining residence addresses from the licensing agency database. Questionnaires mailed at random to households around the site or random consumer interviews conducted over the telephone or in person can yield additional useful information. As indicated previously, customer surveys conducted on site will reveal where customers live and what kinds of merchandise they purchase when they visit the site. Customer surveys can be used to collect specific data about an existing site so the leasing agent can accurately state its current market when approaching prospective tenants and to guide future expansion or renovation of an existing center.

Demographic Profile. A demographic profile is the result of a quantitative study of population size, density, and distribution and a qualitative

F I G U R E   2.1

Data for a Demographic Profile

- Population size, density and distribution
- Projected population growth
- Family size
- Ages
- Level of education
- Household income
- Employment
- Homeownership
- Consumer spending

These and other related data are collected and compiled by the U.S. Bureau of the Census and published annually in a *Statistical Abstract of the United States*. Specific data profiles are also available from commercial sources that tailor an information package to the researcher's needs (see bibliography of resources).

---

evaluation of the lifestyle and spending habits of a specific portion of the population (figure 2.1). The profile relates demographic findings to their impact on retailing.

One of the best ways to appeal to retail tenants is to show them that the potential exists for them to operate profitably at the site. In this respect, the leasing agent can use the demographic profile as a marketing tool. The size of the population and its projected growth is a concrete indication of whether the market is large enough to support the retail site. Current population density and distribution data can be used to demonstrate the location of the property in relation to the largest number of potential shoppers, and future population growth estimates permit projection of sales potential.

Several methods are used for estimating population growth. Census tracts or data from local planning agencies or state data centers will show changes from year to year. The researcher can compute average annual change in population over the previous ten years and apply the rate—a percentage—to future years. Population growth in the trade area can also be estimated in the larger context of the county or state in which it is located by using a step-down approach. When future population growth is projected for the larger area, the ratio of the trade area population to the county or state population is adjusted for each year. The trade area contribution to population growth will remain stable over time, or it will increase or decrease.

Population growth projections are based on the assumption that established patterns will continue from year to year. However, many factors besides normal increases in growth have to be taken into account. New industries or a new school or college may stimulate growth, but a factory shutdown or an economic setback in an agricultural area may lead to a decline.

The ratio between homeowners and renters is also important. Growth or decline in either category may suggest a retail need that the subject property should address more energetically. Similarly, average selling prices for houses and condominiums as well as sizes and rental ranges for apartments will reflect disposable income. This type of information is used to decide which sector of a city or town will be most favorable for a particular type of retail operation. The leasing agent prospecting for an upscale tenant would use a demographic profile to show that a high percentage of people living in the trade area own their homes, a fact that indicates greater financial stability and potentially increased purchases of luxury items. Homeownership can sometimes signal the opposite, however; a high percentage of new homes in an area may indicate that residents are just starting out and have relatively large mortgages and generally less disposable income.

The average size of the family and the average ages of its members can tell the leasing agent a lot about the retail needs of the community. A large proportion of families with young children will require different kinds of merchandise than older couples with no children at home.

In addition, the level of education in the community will influence buying habits. A college-educated population suggests a fairly upscale community, and the leasing agent will take this into account when prospecting for tenants. However, correlations between income and education should be made cautiously. It is often assumed that people with more education have more disposable income, but this is not always true; in a university community, there are many professors and students who have little money to spend on luxury items. Type of education—vocational, technical, professional or graduate—is also important.

A demographic profile also includes information on household income and employment. While property values in an area are suggestive of income level, actual household income figures provide concrete information about the amount of disposable income available for retail purchases. Local trends in median family income can be compared with national and regional trends to determine if the area is lagging behind—or surpassing—other markets in the country. If a household income analysis shows the number of two-income families in the area to be higher than the national average, the leasing agent should proceed with caution. While this can mean that these families have more disposable income for nonessential purchases, it can also mean that the area's economic climate is poor and that both husband and wife must work to make ends meet.

Not only are family size and average income important but also how many people in the family must work to support it and how much each worker earns. The lower the average family income in an area, the greater the portion of family income spent on necessities like food. In a trade area dominated by low-income households, a specialty regional center may not survive, but a neighborhood shopping center with a supermarket anchor might thrive.

The primary sources of income in the area—whether industrial, office, commercial, or agricultural—will also affect the kinds of merchandise customers buy. Working women are a major consideration—especially the number of professional women in the trade area, because their apparel and other needs differ from those of women employed in other capacities.

Estimates or projections of population growth or economic changes in the trade area are crucial to successful leasing of a property because shopping centers are usually built with long-term financial goals in mind. Many communities are constantly shifting both their size and their economic base, and their demographic profiles can change markedly over time. Major shifts in a demographic profile could necessitate a change in the tenant mix of a shopping center, and the agent working on a rehab project or dealing with tenants that are renewing their leases after long tenancies can do a better job if he or she reviews the current demographic data for the center's trade area.

Shopper Profile.   Another important component of the trade area analysis is a profile of the area resident in his or her role as a shopper. This shopper profile gives insight into aspects of the consumer that such categories as education, age, household income, or employment do not cover. It tells why customers shop at a particular store, the quality and price range of what they buy, what needs they have that are not being filled, what media they are most familiar with, what time of day they shop, where they live in relation to the shopping site, and other pertinent details. For the established center, a comprehensive on-site survey or a telephone survey is an excellent method of compiling a shopper profile. Comparable information should be available to the agent leasing a new center through market research firms that specialize in taking surveys and analyzing their results. Data for a center that serves the same general geographic area may apply. Newspapers in particular are a valuable resource. Also, chambers of commerce, retailers' councils, and even some universities occasionally conduct polls and surveys; and their data may have relevance to retail leasing. Otherwise, a specific survey may have to be commissioned.

Surveys can focus on different issues, depending on the type of retail space—a suburban shopping center or a downtown department store, for example—and whether it is already established or in a predevelopment stage. A customer survey at a suburban mall might ask what a shopper intended to buy and what he or she actually did buy, the amount of time spent in the mall, whether the shopper ate there, and how many people he or she shopped with. (Studies have shown that the average shopper in a mall stays 110 minutes and spends $35 per visit.) If the mall is also being used as a community social or cultural center, the survey might include questions about musical or theatrical events recently attended or movies seen at the mall. A survey conducted downtown would ask whether the shopper lives in the city or works there, what method of transportation he or she used to reach the shopping area, and what time of day the consumer shops most frequently. Since shopping at lunchtime is common downtown, the survey might question customers about where they ate lunch, whether it was in a department store or elsewhere, and how much money they typically spend at lunchtime. Events other than shopping also bring people into the city, and the customer might be asked questions about cultural or other events—art exhibitions, concerts, parades, etc. Last but not least, the survey may ask the customer to compare shopping downtown with shopping at suburban malls and to suggest ways to improve shopping at the location in question.

Site Attributes

Once the region, the immediate trade area, and the demographic profile have been examined, the retail center itself is analyzed in depth. The focus of this analysis is on location and topography, accessibility, visibility, the characteristics of the surrounding area, the shape and size of the center, the relationship of the site to major roadway intersections, and any zoning restrictions that might affect commercial buildings. For shopping centers that are already established, such matters as tenant mix, sales volumes, overall management of the property, and anticipated growth are additional considerations.

Location.   A map is a useful tool for looking at a retail store's location in the larger context of the surrounding market. Of concern for any retail site is where it is located in relation to residential areas, schools and college campuses, offices, and neighboring industries. For large centers, location along a heavily traveled route—on the way to or from residential areas or major business sections—is important. A small center should be located near enough to a residential community to constitute a neighborhood store visited on a near-daily basis. A larger center can hope to attract customers from both residential and commercial areas. Good customer interchange among different stores in the trade area is one sign of a well-chosen location. Ideally stores should generate business for each other, and customer traffic should move smoothly throughout the area.

The immediate surroundings of the store or center are also an issue. What is across the street from the retail site and whether commercial areas are clearly separated from residential areas are important points. Adjacent businesses will provide one kind of potential customers, nearby residences another. Also, if there are zoning restrictions in response to environmental concerns, these have to be clearly understood by both owner and potential tenant.

Many residential communities are opposed to new shopping centers, and there may be objections to overcome. If the only access to the new store or center is a residential street with single-family homes, people who live there will likely object to increased vehicular traffic. On the other hand, nearby high-rise apartment complexes and offices will benefit the store by creating more walk-in trade.

Accessibility.   The retail site located on or close to a major thoroughfare will have a better chance of success. Large community centers and regional centers should be easily accessible from interchange points between expressways and freeways. Neighborhood centers should be located on or near through streets.

Whatever its location, the retail site should be easy to enter and safe to leave. This requires provisions for automobiles turning into and out of the center. Left turns require specially constructed lanes or an island, while right turns require deceleration lanes for entrances and acceleration lanes for exits.

Visibility.   A crucial point for all commercial ventures and especially for retailing is visibility. If the subject property is a shopping center, the center's logo as well as the signs of the major anchor tenants should be clearly visible from the street or highway. Studies have shown that people driving 35 miles per hour can easily overshoot the entrance to a parking lot if it is not well-marked. Entrances should have clear, readable signs that are not obscured by construction materials, trees, or other buildings. Sometimes a site that fronts on a highway may be at a disadvantage in spite of its seemingly good location; competing distractions such as other business signs, roadway markers, and neon lights may reduce its visibility.

Shape and Topography.   Another important site attribute is the shape of the retail store or center and the terrain on which it is located. Shopping centers generally are *not* built on sites with shops located on both sides of a street or highway. Such division of a site impedes pedestrian movement, causes confusion in the direction of vehicular traffic flow, and creates a sense of disharmony and disorientation in a place where unity is all-important. (For a more detailed discussion of shopping center configuration, see chapter 6.)

Shopping centers should be regular in shape, with no acute angles, sharp projections, or indentations. There should be sufficient depth to accommodate automobile circulation in the parking lots. Each store should be assured of adequate frontage—another good reason for uniformity of design. Zoning regulations have traditionally required a building-to-land ratio of 1:3. In other words, for every 10,000 square feet of stores, 30,000 square feet of parking, landscaping, and delivery areas were required. Although this 1:3 ratio is still in use, it is expected that the shopping center of the future will be built with a more economical use of land for parking. When a shopping center is part of a property developed for different uses, the overall demand for parking is usually less. Shared parking facilities can reduce the amount of land required for the development and effect a cost savings. (See chapter 6 for a more detailed discussion of parking.)

The terrain should be as level as possible, ideally with no more than a 5 percent slope and good drainage. The site's infrastructure is another concern: well-designed curbs, gutters, sidewalks, and landscaping can make the difference between success and failure. Judicious use of trees, walls, and fences as buffers is often a solution to problems of proximity to residential areas. However, a shopping center should look like what it is. Excessive plantings can reduce visibility as well as increase maintenance costs that are passed along to the retail tenants.

Management.   Prospective retail tenants often judge a property by the development and management team, especially when they plan to lease in an established center. They will be concerned about how well the property is maintained, whether there are good security and waste disposal services, if public areas are kept clean and well-lighted, the lawn is trimmed, the parking lot pavement is smooth, and trash is removed at regular intervals; and—very importantly for large centers—whether there is an on-site manager. A retailer might be wary of leasing in a property that shows signs of wear and tear, which can have impact on sales. Certainly sales performance of the various stores in the center can be measured in relation to average sales performance for similar stores elsewhere in the trade area. All of these concerns reflect on management's ability to maintain the property at a competitive level so that it will increase in value over time.

Competition

A major step in the market research is to examine the property in relation to each of the other competing stores or shopping centers that draw customers from the same trade area. Depending on the nature of the competition, the property will typically draw customers from several different sources:

- Excess population that is a result of growth in the trade area
- Patrons of other stores in the area

Shopping Center Comparison Grid

Center Data	Subject Ctr	Ctr #1	Ctr #2	Ctr #3
Name				
Contact				
Phone number				
Type of center				
Age				
GLA				
Spaces available				
Sizes				
Rent per sq ft				
Sales per sq ft				
Term of leases				
Vacancy rate				
Tenant improvement allowance				
Parking ratio Parking index				

- Consumers who come from other trade areas because the goods offered in the subject store are not available where they normally shop

In order to determine where customers are coming from—or where customers are likely to be lost—it is important to understand the effects of other retail operations in the area. Most stores can expect some leakage either into or out of the trade area. Leakage refers to either (a) sales of the same category of merchandise at stores that are located beyond the trade area, or (b) sales at stores in the trade area that have not been accounted for in the study. Leakage is usually expressed as a percentage.

Maps can be helpful in comparing different stores and centers. Pinpointing the locations of competing retail sites on a map will graphically indicate their distance from the subject center as well as pertinent features of the surrounding terrain that may affect sales at each center.

Pertinent facts about nearby shopping centers—prevailing rents, vacancy rates, total GLA, location and site attributes, age, sales volumes, common area maintenance fees, charges for real estate taxes and insurance,

F I G U R E   2.2 (continued)

Center Data	Subject Ctr	Ctr #1	Ctr #2	Ctr #3
ADDITIONAL RENT Percentage rents				

Net as to:
  Taxes
  CAM
  Insurance
  Management
  HVAC				

Periodic rental escalations				
Operating cost increases				
Merchants' Association				
Type of concessions				
GENERAL CONDITION Visibility				
Location				
Maintenance				
Security				
Landscaping				
Signage				
COMMENTS				
Rating (1 to 5)				

parking ratios and parking indexes, tenant mix, and major tenants—can be compared directly using a grid (figure 2.2). Another method is to rate each center numerically to provide a more objective basis on which to compare it to the subject center. Using the same grid form, ratings might range from "poor" to "excellent" (1 = poor, 2 = fair, 3 = good, and 4 = excellent). Centers can also be ranked first, second, third, etc., among the number being compared or rated on a scale from one (lowest) to ten (highest).

It is important to know what to look for when rating a shopping center. The two most important points of comparison for a potential tenant are location and major tenants. Location is rated not only on the basis of broad categories such as population, income level in the trade area, and retail sales potential, but also on such specific aspects as traffic counts and speed limits at or near each site and the availability of public transportation. For example, a higher speed limit would likely reduce visibility and could impede access, so it would be cause for a lower rating. If a center is located at an intersection, whether traffic flows past the center on the "going-home side" or the site is on a secondary corner is a consideration.

A center with rents that are already at the top of the market would be rated lower because there is less flexibility in negotiations, and a center that has longer leases would be rated lower because it cannot respond readily to fluctuations in the economy. On the other hand, centers with triple-net leases are rated higher than those with gross leases, and centers whose leases have built-in escalation clauses are also rated high. If expenses are lower than market rates, a center is given a higher rating, while a center that grants overly generous tenant improvement allowances is given a lower rating because unusual concessions can signal difficulty in attracting tenants.

Vacancy rates are another consideration for comparison. Generally vacancies should not exceed 4 percent for regional malls or 6–8 percent for smaller centers; sites with vacancy rates exceeding 10 percent would be rated very low. (Vacancy rates vary for different areas at different times. Figures from a 1987 survey by the International Council of Shopping Centers indicate that strip centers with less than 50,000 square feet of GLA had average vacancies of 15 percent, with the rate decreasing to 10 percent for larger centers—200,000 or more square feet; enclosed malls with less than 200,000 square feet of GLA had average vacancies of 10 percent, with the rate decreasing with increasing mall size—to 3 percent for centers with 800,000 or more square feet of GLA.)

Use of a comparison grid should highlight the strengths and weaknesses of the subject property relative to the comparable competition. Whenever possible, established retailers should also be interviewed about their perceptions of a center's strengths and weaknesses. The leasing agent can use this information to determine what factors to emphasize in the leasing effort—the property's positive points—and what factors to downplay. The same data can also suggest to the owner improvements that will enhance the property's value relative to competing sites.

In addition to an assessment of the competing centers as they exist right now, questions should also be raised about their future building plans and about the development of other shopping facilities outside of the trade area. The developer who purchases adjoining or nearby plots of land will also be insured against the encroachments of competitors. Information on competitive centers and competing retailers becomes even more important to the leasing agent as it relates to sales potential.

SALES POTENTIAL

Although market share information is not included in every market survey, these data help developers, owners, and leasing agents determine if a retail property is likely to succeed in a particular location. A new retail center cannot create a new market. Lenders may require a statement of sales potential to ensure that the property will bring a good return on investment and be a profitable venture. In many cases a center's survival will depend on its ability to fill a void left by existing retail properties or to offer products that are merchandised more attractively or are more easily accessible than those offered by the competition, thereby drawing customers away from existing stores. As a result, it is particularly important to determine what share of the market a new retail property will be able to obtain.

The leasing agent should want to know everything about the competing retail sites that can influence the drawing power of the new center—who their customers are, which trade area provides most of their sales (along with income and expenditure figures for the trade areas they serve), how big their tenants are and the different tenants' dollar sales per square foot, and what rents their tenants pay (including the terms of their lease agreements and how tenant improvements and concessions are handled). Based on consumer purchasing patterns and sales volumes for existing retail space, the agent can calculate the sales potential for the entire area. That portion of the overall sales potential that is not already taken up by existing centers is the new property's possible share of the market, along with whatever sales it can successfully take away from its established competitors.

Calculating Sales Potential

The total number of consumer dollars available to retailers for the entire trade area, the *sales potential,* is distributed among the different retail categories (food, women's clothing, men's clothing, books, etc.) based on income and population data. Each retail category is allotted a different amount for overall *per capita expenditure*—how much each consumer spends per year on a particular type of merchandise—as a percentage of income based on historical data and projections. Per capita spending data reflect a combination of several factors—income, occupation, and household size among them. Areas where the population has comparatively high

F I G U R E   2.3

Calculating Sales Potential

Average Income   ×   Population   =   Total Potential Income

$$\frac{\text{Expenditure for Merchandise (by Type)}}{\text{Income}} = \begin{array}{l}\text{Per Capita Expenditure}\\ \text{for Merchandise Type}\\ \text{(as Percent of Income)}\end{array}$$

$$\frac{\$200\ (\text{Apparel Purchases})}{\$20,000\ (\text{Income})} = .01 = 1\% \quad \begin{array}{l}(\text{Apparel Purchase as}\\ \text{Percent of Income})\end{array}$$

$20,000 (Income)   ×   10,000 (Area Population)   = $200 Million (Potential Income)

$200 Million   ×   1%   = $2 Million
 (Potential   (Percent   (Sales
  Income)   of   Potential
                  Income   for
                  Spent   Apparel)
                   for
                 Apparel
                Purchases)

Total sales potential for the area is the sum of the different percentages of income spent for different categories of merchandise. If consumers spend 1% for apparel and another 3.6% on consumer goods generally, the total sales potential would exceed $9 million.

$200 Million   ×   4.6%   = $9.2 Million
 (Total   (Percent   (Total
 Potential   of   Sales
 Income)   Income   Potential)
                  Spent
                    on
                 Consumer
                  Goods)

(See also Figure 2.4.)

---

income, a large percentage of its workers employed in white collar occupations, and relatively small household sizes offer the greatest per capita expenditure potential for department store-type merchandise. The differentiation between these types of goods and so-called convenience goods and services—food, drugs, eating and drinking establishments—has important lifestyle and marketing implications in relation to development of the optimum blend of retail tenant and merchandise types for a given center.

Using income as the basis, population and income data for the primary, secondary, and tertiary trade area zones are projected ten to fifteen years into the future in five-year increments. Past and anticipated future trends in employment and income are taken into consideration. Income is

F I G U R E   2.4

Allocation of the Annual Consumer Income Dollar in 1985

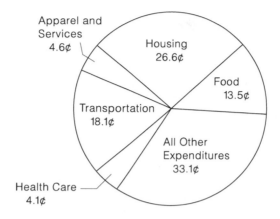

Apparel and Services 4.6¢

Housing 26.6¢

Food 13.5¢

Transportation 18.1¢

All Other Expenditures 33.1¢

Health Care 4.1¢

Prepared from data reported by the U.S. Bureau of Labor Statistics in *Statistical Abstract of the United States: 1988 (108th edition).*

multiplied by population, and sales potentials are estimated as a percentage of projected total income. For example (figure 2.3), if average annual per capita expenditure for apparel today is $200, and per capita income is $20,000, the amount spent on apparel represents 1 percent of the individual's income. Assuming that the individual's income increases to $25,000 in five years and his or her apparel purchases remain at the same level (1%), in five years, per capita apparel expenditures would be $250. If the trade area population is 10,000 today, the total projected income for the trade area is $200 million; apparel purchases representing 1 percent of that amount total $2 million. Sales potential is the sum of the different percentages of income spent for different categories of merchandise as a percentage of the total projected income. Thus, if consumers in the trade area spend an average of 4.6 percent of their total annual income on consumer goods, the sales potential is that percentage of the projected total income for the area (4.6% of $200 million is $9.2 million). Figure 2.4 details average annual consumer spending.

Using per capita expenditure as the basis, the $200 each consumer spends on apparel can be expressed as sales potential by multiplying the dollar amount by the population ($200 × 10,000 = $2 million). Per capita expenditures may be derived by dividing total sales dollars for a category of merchandise by the population—the reverse of the equation just given. Future per capita expenditures for different categories of merchandise can be calculated from past trends and projected levels of inflation. Total sales potential is a function of estimated population growth and projected per capita expenditures, which again should be projected for ten to fifteen years into the future in five-year increments.

Calculating Retail Center Market Potential

Once the sales potential for the general trade area has been determined, it is possible to estimate market share for the specific retail property. The computations should also indicate whether there is room for growth, an important concern for owners and developers.

There are two methods of allocating the portion of the trade area sales potential that a particular retail center will be able to claim for itself. They are called "market share" and "residual analysis," respectively, and application of both methods will ensure accuracy.

The *market share* approach establishes a ratio between the new retail space and the total retail space available in the trade area. The size in square feet of the new store or of the major stores in a new shopping center is adjusted to calculate *effective space*—the amount of space that is capable of drawing customers. The amount of comparable retail space in the trade area is adjusted similarly. The amount of new space is then added to the amount of existing space to form a new total. The percentage represented by the ratio of the new center's effective space to the calculated new total effective space is the new center's share of the market.

$$\frac{\text{Effective Space in New Center}}{\text{Total Effective Space in Trade Area}} = \text{Market Share for New Center}$$

Market share for each trade area zone can be estimated similarly. Multiplying the new center's share by the sales potential translates market share into dollars, and these amounts are usually also projected fifteen years into the future.

EXAMPLE: A developer is planning a new shopping center that includes 420,000 square feet of department store space. Research has shown that there is already a total effective trade area space of 850,000 square feet out of a total available space of 1,000,000 square feet. The effective space represents only 85 percent of the total space because the remaining 15 percent is known to represent sales to consumers who reside outside the trade area. Effective space for the new center would also be only 85 percent of the total square footage: 420,000 × 0.85 = 357,000. Addition of the new property to the minimum total effective trade area already in existence yields a new total: 850,000 + 357,000 = 1,207,000 square feet. Dividing the new store space by the total yields a percentage: 357,000 ÷ 1,207,000 = 29.6 percent—the share of the total effective market the new center can possibly obtain.

Residual analysis uses sales dollars to represent unsatisfied potential in the market. Each competing retail facility is categorized as to specific types of merchandise, and sales are estimated for each category. Such sales data may be found in the *Census of Retail Trade* or *Dollars and Cents of Shopping Centers.* Using projected sales potential for the entire market, and subtracting the effective sales, the remainder is called the residual sales potential—the amount remaining for the new retail store. For example, if the sales potential for apparel in a trade area amounts to $13.5 million and the effective sales in apparel are $10 million, the difference of $3.5 million represents the residual sales potential for which the new store can compete.

Although the formulas for measuring sales potential for a retail center are useful, it is important to remember that the results are only approximate. Many factors have to be taken into account when predicting a store's success. During the first year, a new store is presumed to operate at less than its full potential, acquiring a greater share of the market in subsequent years. Also, because the nature of the market can change significantly in a relatively short time, residual market estimates are only applicable to the first three to five years of operation.

The results of market share and residual analysis computations have to be interpreted with care. A large residual market share usually indicates that a new retail space could succeed because consumers are probably shopping outside of the trade area for items that are not available inside it. However, a small residual market share is not necessarily an indication that there is no market for a new store. A strong new store that is easily accessible and attractively promoted could presumably draw business away from other stores.

Estimates of retailers' sales potentials can be useful tools for the leasing agent and for the owner. If there is a choice between two prospective tenants that are otherwise similar, the one that would generate the larger sales potential would be preferred. However, there are other elements that play a role in a retail property's success.

Store Feasibility and Size

Market share is an important component in determining feasibility, which is an estimate of how much the store must sell on a per-square-foot basis in order to be profitable. The size of a store is directly related to its feasibility. Store size (square feet) multiplied by required sales (dollars per square foot) yields total required sales, in dollars.

Most retailers establish their store size based on what experience has indicated to be the most efficient way to present their merchandise. However, a comparison of required sales and the potential sales the retailer can expect to capture will suggest whether a proposed store should be larger or smaller than originally planned. If a proposed 2,000-square-foot store must have sales of at least $150 per square foot, it has total required sales of $300,000. If its share of the market was estimated to be $300,000 or more, the store would be considered a feasible venture. However, if the estimated market share was only $200,000, the business could not survive. Dividing the market share by the size of the store yields fewer dollars per square foot as potential sales ($200,000 ÷ 2,000 square feet = $100 per square foot). In this circumstance, it might be advisable to consider a smaller space for this store.

In order for a store to be feasible, market share must be equal to or greater than the total required sales. A sales potential that is smaller than the total required sales indicates only a poor chance of survival in the specific marketplace.

Analysis of the sales potential for a retail center is the culmination of the research conducted in the market assessment. It places the retail property in the context of the immediate trade area and in relation to its competitors, enabling its owner and the leasing agent to predict its success. The results of a good analysis should indicate (1) whether the market potential is large enough to support a particular store; (2) how much of this market potential the retail center can hope to capture, given the existing and anticipated competition; and (3) whether estimated sales will cover operating costs and meet required profit levels. The owner will need this information in order to prepare a *pro forma,* the operating model for the retail property. The agent uses the analysis to establish rental rates and formulate a leasing plan.

SUMMARY

Both retailers and developers undertake similar studies when assessing a retail market. Environment is all important for the success of a retail business, a fact to be kept in mind when prospecting for appropriate tenants for a particular site. If the retailer cannot succeed in a given location, the owner of the site will not make a profit either. Adequate cash flow and high occupancy levels are the property owner's goals; they are achieved by establishing appropriate rental rates. Market research should be designed to suit the property at hand. A thorough assessment will include an economic overview of the region, a more specific trade area analysis, an assessment of the various site attributes, a comparison of the subject property with competing retail sites, and an evaluation of sales potential.

Because the regional economy can affect the operation of a retail business, such factors as industry, commercial activity, available labor force, employment data, per capita income, local zoning laws, natural resources, and climate are evaluated. In some instances, national economic issues—and international economic issues—will also play a role in the success of a shopping center or individual retail business.

An effective trade area analysis takes into account the geography of the primary, secondary, and tertiary zones and the location of the site in relation to highways, land features, and the competition. Included in this analysis is a demographic profile reporting population size, projecting future population growth, and characterizing the age, education, income, and spending habits of trade area consumers. Attributes of the site itself—accessibility, visibility, and the various facilities available at the center or store—are also important, and the site is compared with competing centers (or stores) of similar size and function in the area.

Sales potential is important information for retailers and developers alike, especially as it relates to the ability to pay minimum and percentage rents. The retailer's market share is that portion of the total sales potential for the area that has not already been tapped by competing stores. Most retailers know approximately how much they must sell on a per-square-foot basis in order to survive, and potential market share for a new or additional location must equal or exceed that sales requirement if relocation is to be feasible. If a proposed space is not economically feasible for a given retail business, there is little chance of that prospect signing a lease.

3

Establishing Rents for New Centers

Once the site has been positioned within its market, the agent can begin to develop a plan for leasing it. The initial *leasing plan* developed by the owner and leasing agent is an illustration of how the property is expected to look when it is fully occupied and operating. It should demonstrate how all the aspects of the property—amount of space, types of tenants, location, parking, etc.—will function as an integrated whole. One of the most important features of the leasing plan is the rent schedule. Rental rates are influenced primarily by prevailing economic conditions—current rents in the general market, the nature of the competition, and current vacancy levels. The latter are particularly important because market rents may be affected by overbuilding. The different rental rates and tenant improvement allowances for comparable properties in the trade area are scrutinized to ascertain current market conditions as one begins to price rents for the subject property. *Comparable properties* is a key concept in rent pricing, and location and tenant mix should be evaluated carefully when selecting properties as "comparables."

The owner's financial goals also play a role. While leasing agents usually have little to do with the development process, their work requires basic knowledge of ownership structures, property evaluation, and financing techniques and an understanding of how these elements are related to revenue. Various owners' and developers' investment philosophies may differ substantially. A developer may want to maximize loan dollars while an equity partner may want to maximize cash flow. *Net operating income (NOI)* is one factor used in establishing the value of a property. In order to sustain a property's value, a certain amount of rent has to be generated. Rents priced solely on the basis of rates in effect at comparable properties may not always afford the developer an adequate return on investment because newer properties will almost always have proportionately higher financing and construction costs. Each property, owner situation, and market is different.

Many financial institutions require proof of substantial returns before lending money on the property. Thus the type of loan an owner or developer obtains will have an effect on rental rates, and the leasing agent should know how to evaluate the adequacy of the rent schedule in relation to debt-service requirements. (Shopping center development financing as such is described in appendix B.)

The general rental rate established for the property is the average amount of income per square foot of GLA per year that the rentable space must generate in order to meet the expenses of operating the property, service the debt it carries, and provide the owner with a profit. This *base rent* is adjusted for each individual store or space on the property, based on the size and location of the store or space, the amount of the center's operating expenses that are allocated to it, the type of business that will use the space, and the retailer's expected sales volume.

Not to be forgotten is the tenant's perspective—what the prospect is willing (or able) to pay. Rent is just one of several *occupancy costs,* which include prorations of expenses for the center as a whole (insurance, real estate taxes, and utilities, as well as maintenance, management, and marketing fees). Retailers generally try to keep their occupancy costs as low as possible. Those that pay a large percentage of their total sales toward rent and other occupancy costs will more than likely have difficulty staying in business. A high proportionate occupancy expense requires that a retailer sell merchandise at an abnormally high markup, have little competition, and have an optimum location in an area where average income is high.

THE LEASING PLAN

Two types of leasing plans are commonly used in leasing retail space. One is part of a marketing package that is used as a prospecting tool to attract tenants and includes demographic data for the property, a site plan, and other pertinent information about the store or center. The components and function of this type of leasing plan are described in greater detail in chapter 5.

The second type of leasing plan is used as an in-house planning tool. Prepared before the construction of a new store or center or prior to any renovations on an existing property, the purpose of such a plan is to target potential tenants, define the tone of the property or site, and project optimum rental revenues. In creating a leasing plan for a new property, the information from the market assessment is used to determine which types of tenants should be included in the center, where to locate them, and what rents to charge. On the other hand, a leasing plan for an existing center may recommend changes in tenant mix and tenant location based on changes in the buying habits of consumers in the market and on each tenant's contribution to the profitability of the center.

The size and scope of the leasing plan prepared by the leasing agent will depend on the type of store or center being leased and on the owner's needs and goals. However, certain basic components are usually part of every in-house plan. The layout of the property is important. Each tenant space should be shown in proportion to the actual size of the property, allowing some flexibility to suit tenant needs. Details to be included are:

- Types of tenants (types of merchandise)
- Names of signed tenants that fit the types
- Results of analysis of the data generated in market research
- GLA requirements of individual tenant types
- Tentative locations of prospective tenants in the property

Other points that may be included are the GLA of individual stores, with frontage and depth measurements for each store space; dimensions for the entire center, including common areas, and the GLA of the center as a whole; the anticipated parking space count and ratio, and rates of percentage rent for each tenant. All of this information will be useful to the leasing agent and other in-house personnel who become involved in the leasing process. Some types of information, however—percentage rents, for example—would not be carried forward into any leasing plan that is to be shared with prospective tenants.

Recommendations with respect to tenants should include the types of retailers the leasing agent believes will generate the best possible tenant and merchandise mix and thereby the most income for the center. For a new property, the owner and the leasing agent identify specific uses for specific spaces and decide what portion of the whole center will be devoted to each merchandise category, taking into account both the total GLA available and the typical store size needed for each type of retailer. Using this information and the market research data on trade area needs and competitive stores, the leasing agent projects how much of the center should be made up of women's apparel stores, eating and drinking establishments, bookstores, etc. (table 3.1).

For an existing center, the focus should be on both current and prospective tenants and on changes that could profit the center as a whole. The leasing plan can recommend renewals for tenants whose leases will expire shortly, or it may suggest replacements for tenants whose sales are

T A B L E   3.1

Comparison of Shopping Center Composition (Percent GLA)

Tenant Classification	Super Regional	Regional	Community	Neighborhood
General Merchandise	7.1*	13.0*	35.9	7.1
Food	3.6	9.8	16.7	34.3
Food Service	8.5	7.0	5.1	7.6
Clothing and Accessories	31.9	26.6	7.4	4.5
Ladies' Wear	19.3	16.6	4.3	2.6
Children's Wear	1.0	0.9	0.5	0.4
Men's Wear	5.8	4.3	0.9	0.5
Family Wear	5.8	4.8	1.8	1.0
Shoes	9.0	7.3	1.9	1.1
Home Furnishings	3.1	1.8	2.2	2.7
Home Appliances/Music	3.8	3.0	1.9	1.7
Building Materials/Hardware	0.2	0.9	2.7	2.7
Automotive	0.6	0.1	0.9	1.3
Hobby/Special Interest	4.6	3.8	2.1	2.1
Gifts/Specialty	6.9	5.5	2.3	2.3
Jewelry	3.0	2.7	0.7	0.5
Liquor	0.2	0.3	0.5	1.3
Drugs	2.8	3.8	5.1	10.0
Other Retail	4.2	4.0	3.8	4.5
Personal Services	2.6	2.7	3.8	8.3
Recreation/Community	4.3	3.4	2.8	1.6
Financial	2.0	2.7	2.1	3.7
Offices (Other than Financial)	1.5	1.5	1.9	2.7
Total	100.0	100.0	100.0	100.0

*Figures for super regional and regional shopping centers *exclude* department stores.

From data reported in *Dollars and Cents of Shopping Centers: 1987* (Washington, D.C.: ULI—the Urban Land Institute, 1987). Used with permission.

FIGURE   3.1

Example of Leasing Plan

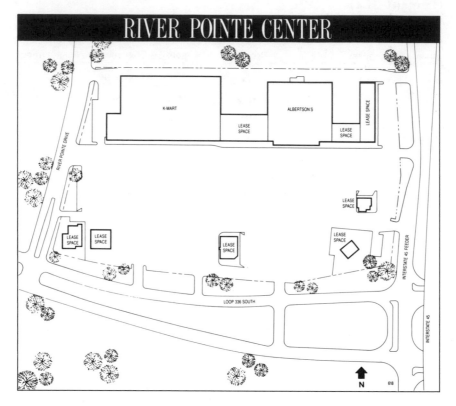

Store layout portion of a marketing leasing plan for River Pointe Center in Conroe, Texas. (See appendix C for complete leasing plan.) Reproduced courtesy of Weingarten Realty.

not as strong as they could be. It should also identify categories of compatible retailers whose sales volumes are traditionally large. In general, prospects for either new or existing spaces should be evaluated carefully to determine how they will fit into the established center.

The in-house leasing plan may be generally regarded as a "wish list" for the owners and developers, showing the form the retail site could take when fully leased and operating. The plan may be changed many times before all negotiations are concluded. In the meantime, however, it serves as a necessary foundation from which to begin prospecting for tenants and negotiating leases.

There is no one way to prepare a leasing plan. A picture of the leasing plan can be as simple as a drawing that shows only relative sizes and posi-

F I G U R E   3.2

Example of Leasing Plan

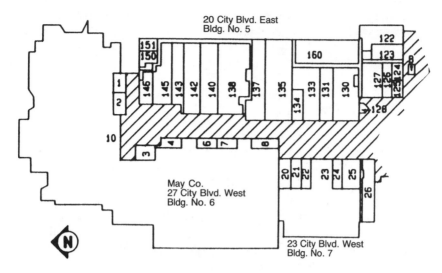

Retail Building No. 6

Store	Sq Ft	Merchant
1	863	U.S. Post Office
2	831	Rock Party
3	790	Cafe Metro
4	750	Golden Square and
		Accessories
6	640	Wild Tops
7	697	Parklane
8	910	The Shoe Trend
10	160987	May Company

Retail Building No. 7

Store	Sq Ft	Merchant
20	1298	General Nutrition Center
21	1062	Sunshine, The Natural
		Alternative
22	1180	Good Looks Beauty Supply
23	15460	United Artists Theater
		(6 screens)
24	885	
25	1798	Ashly Jewelers
26	3257	Chuck Balboa's Labels

Part of the leasing plan for The City Shopping Center in Orange, California, showing locations of store spaces for buildings 5, 6, and 7 and listing square footages and tenants for buildings 6 and 7. (A complete version of this leasing plan appears in appendix C.) Reproduced courtesy of Tishman West Management Corporation.

tions of individual spaces, or it may be a more-detailed drawing that indicates the square footage of each store and the locations of various equipment and facilities. Figure 3.1 shows part of a marketing leasing plan for River Pointe Center in Conroe, Texas (location of store spaces). The complete plan includes a listing of demographic data (trade area population, median family income), retail expenditures in the trade area, traffic counts, and impending road improvements along with a map of the area showing the center in relation to the city of Conroe. This type of leasing plan is suitable for handing or mailing to prospective tenants. Figure 3.2 shows a portion of the leasing plan for The City Shopping Center in Orange, California, with store locations and square footages for stores in two of the three buildings represented. (A picture of the complete center layout along with a listing of tenants in all occupied spaces is also shown in appendix C.) This type of leasing plan would be used primarily by the leasing agent. An even more detailed in-house plan might include rents and pass-through proration percentages.

TYPES OF RENTS

Rent schedules used in retail space leasing can be complex. Each retail site requires its own individually designed rent schedule. There is no single method that will work for every retail site. Usually retailers will have an idea of the rents they expect to pay, and the owner will have expectations of a level of rental income before the negotiation process begins. Information on market rates and terms will be available to both.

Rents are commonly stated in retail leases in one of three ways— minimum or guaranteed rent, percentage rent, or a combination of the two. Retail space leases in shopping centers commonly require that the tenant pay a portion of the expenses of maintaining the property as a whole, and these pass-through expenses are often regarded as "additional rent." If operating expenses are *not* passed through directly, they are normally computed into the base rent. Therefore, the leasing agent must also know how to compute additional charges into the basic rent and how to compute rent increases from year to year. The experienced leasing agent knows which types of rental arrangements are appropriate for a particular property and how to employ them to the advantage of both owner and tenant.

Minimum or Guaranteed Rent

The *minimum rent,* sometimes called *guaranteed or fixed-minimum rent,* represents the rent that is usually paid in regular monthly installments and is not dependent on sales volume. It can be based on market rents, which are determined by comparing rents from similar properties. However, the market rate is only a starting point for the negotiation process; the market rate is usually adjusted for the type of retail site, the owner's financial objectives, and the needs of the individual tenant.

Minimum rental rates vary from one geographic area to another and may vary with the age of the center. A new property may have larger financial commitments to meet, and this will be a consideration in establishing its rents. On the other hand, an existing center may sustain higher rents than a new center can command simply because of its being successfully established and well located. Size and type of store or center also make a big difference, as does location. A community center in a suburb will charge different rents than a strip center in an inner-city neighborhood, and their rents will differ from those charged for a freestanding store space downtown.

The amount of the minimum rent often depends on other parts of a lease as well. If the tenant is expected to pay the owner a percentage of its retail sales, the minimum rent may be negotiated somewhat lower to reflect this fact. On the other hand, minimum rent may be negotiated higher to compensate for the owner's investment in tenant improvements (tenant improvement allowance).

Minimum rent offers advantages for both the owner and the tenant. It assures the owner a level of income that does not depend on the tenant's sales volume or vary with fluctuations in the tenant's income. It guarantees the tenant a set amount of rent to be paid for the duration of the lease, an amount which can be budgeted for specifically. For these reasons, minimum rent is nearly always a part of a standard retail lease. Also, because the future is unpredictable, adjustments to the minimum rent may be provided through an escalation clause.

Percentage Rent

Retail leases often include clauses that call for the tenants to pay the owner a percentage of their gross sales in addition to the minimum or base rent, although actual payment of additional rent based on gross sales is not all that common. Whether percentage rent is called for or not, many owners require that tenants report their gross sales.

There are several ways to compute *percentage rent.* The two most commonly used methods are described below. The first is based on a percentage of gross sales as the rent amount, with a guaranteed minimum rent to be paid; the second provides for a specific fixed rent plus a percentage of gross sales over a stated dollar amount as "additional rent."

When a tenant pays percentage rent with a guaranteed minimum rent, the lease might state that the tenant will pay 5 percent of gross sales with a minimum annual rent of, say, $60,000; it will usually also require payment to be made in equal monthly installments—in this case, the rate would be $5,000 per month. The volume of sales required to oblige payment of percentage rent is called the *breakpoint,* which is the annual minimum rent divided by the percentage rent rate.

$$\frac{\$60,000 \text{ (Annual Minimum Rent)}}{.05 \text{ (Percentage Rent Rate)}} = \$1.2 \text{ million (breakpoint)}$$

In this example, gross sales would have to exceed $1.2 million in order for percentage rent to be due. Thus, if sales were $1.25 million, the amount of additional rent due as percentage rent ($2,500) would be computed as follows:

Gross Sales × Percentage Rent Rate = Total Rent Due
Total Rent Due − Minimum Annual Rent = Percentage Rent Due

$1.25 million × .05 = $62,500
$62,500 − $60,000 = $2,500

Because minimum rent is paid monthly, the lease may require computation and payment of percentage rent on a monthly basis as well.

$$\frac{\text{Annual Rent}}{12} = \text{Monthly Minimum Rent}$$

$$\frac{\text{Monthly Minimum Rent}}{\text{Percentage Rent Rate}} = \text{Monthly breakpoint}$$

$$\frac{\$60,000}{12} = \$5,000 \quad \text{and} \quad \frac{\$5,000}{.05} = \$100,000$$

On this basis, percentage rent for a year might work out as shown in table 3.2. Note that the accumulated percentage rent paid does not equal the annual percentage rent computed earlier. Adjustment for this discrepancy is discussed later.

The amount of gross sales at which the percentage rent equals the minimum rent is referred to as the *natural breakpoint*. Most retail lease references will be to this natural breakpoint. However, some leases may be negotiated to include an *artificial breakpoint*—a dollar amount of gross sales that is higher or lower than the natural breakpoint (figure 3.3).

Occasionally an artificial breakpoint may be negotiated—as a specific compromise regarding tenant improvements or as another concession. A retailer may have to make more extensive improvements to a shell space than the normal tenant improvement allowance, if any, would cover. The retailer may also be sure that the sales volume will support a higher minimum rent to "finance" the extra improvements through the center owner. In which case, the owner may agree to the larger tenant improvement expense and *lower* the breakpoint so that the retailer will begin paying percentage rent on a smaller sales volume. In this way, the owner is gradually repaid for the cost of the improvements without changing the tenant's minimum rent. However, if an owner is unwilling or unable to pay for extra tenant improvements, the retailer may offer to absorb the cost of the improvements over the course of the lease term and request a *higher* breakpoint as compensation (figure 3.3). The preceding percentage rent calculations determine whether and how much percentage rent is due

T A B L E   3.2

Percentage Rent on a Monthly Basis (Example)

Month	Gross Sales	5% of Gross Sales	Percentage Rent Due*
January	105,000	5,250	250
February	100,000	5,000	——
March	99,000	4,950	——
April	125,000	6,250	1,250
May	101,000	5,050	50
June	102,500	5,125	125
July	98,500	4,925	——
August	101,425	5,072	72
September	99,500	4,975	——
October	101,250	5,063	63
November	107,500	5,375	375
December	109,325	5,466	466
TOTAL	$1,250,000	$62,501	$2,651

*In this example, percentage rent due is *in addition to* $5,000 minimum rent per month (as stated in the text).

F I G U R E   3.3

Artificial Breakpoint

Minimum rent = $1,000/month
Percentage rent = 5% as overage

$$\frac{\$1,000}{0.05} = \$20,000 \text{ (natural breakpoint)}$$

To LOWER sales volume for percentage rent, set artificial breakpoint at $15,000:

$20,000 − $15,000 = $5,000 extra income subject to percentage rent
$5,000 × 0.05 = $250 extra rent paid by tenant

In this case, the owner benefits because percentage rent is paid sooner.

To RAISE the sales volume for percentage rent, set artificial breakpoint at $30,000:

$30,000 − $20,000 = $10,000 sales *not* subject to percentage rent
$10,000 × 0.05 = $500 percentage rent savings to tenant each month

In this situation, the tenant benefits because percentage rent payment is delayed.

An artificial breakpoint is set higher or lower than the natural breakpoint in order to accommodate negotiated compromises such as payment for improvements.

when the percentage rent is tied to the minimum rent, which is paid regardless of any other charges.

The second type of percentage rent does *not* relate directly to minimum rent. For example, a lease might state that the tenant will pay a minimum rent of $12,000 per year plus percentage rent in an amount by which 2 percent of gross sales exceeds $100,000. Here, the minimum rent is $12,000, paid in monthly installments of $1,000. Percentage rent is related solely to gross sales. In other words, the retailer pays the owner 2 percent of gross sales over $100,000 per year—on $120,000 annual gross sales, percentage rent would be $400. As a reference point, the "breakpoint" as demonstrated earlier would be $600,000 (annual rent of $12,000 divided by the percentage rate of .02). Clearly minimum rent and percentage rent are not related in this situation.

Occasionally, a lease may be negotiated such that the tenant pays *percentage rent only,* with no minimum rent. This is extremely rare and is likely to be used when it is difficult to keep a space filled—a distressed property—or if an owner's investment is comparatively small and he or she is willing to take a risk on a tenant starting a business or struggling to maintain a business during hard times. A percentage only rent may be requested by a major tenant in a good negotiating position. The owner who accepts such a rental arrangement hopes that the sales volume will provide a substantial income, but there is no assurance that this will occur. Certainly this latter arrangement would not be desirable for a new development where the rent established in pre-leasing to major tenants is a determining factor in the financing of the project.

Retailers that pay a straight percentage rent occasionally negotiate a decline in the percentage rate as their sales volume increases. This is a way to limit the amount of percentage rent to be paid. An example is shown in figure 3.4. A supermarket with annual sales of $18 million would pay $270,000 rent per year if percentage rent were 1.5 percent; with a declining percentage rate, the rent would be substantially less.

The opposite situation sometimes is negotiated—for some specialty stores or for amusements or rides in a theme center—and leases call for percentage rents that increase as sales increase. If a retailer does business on both a wholesale and a retail basis and thus applies different markups to different types of merchandise, the lease may reflect two different percentage rates.

No matter how percentage rent is to be computed, the percentage rate is agreed upon during lease negotiations and often depends on the nature of the retailer's business and the typical sales volume for that category of goods. Supermarkets frequently have low percentage rents (commonly 1–2%) because they sell large volumes of goods at low markups, and even a small portion of their gross sales will yield a large amount of percentage rent. On the other hand, jewelry stores might have percentage rents that

F I G U R E   3.4

Declining Percentage Rents

Flat percentage rent:
    gross sales = $20,000,000/year
    percentage rate = 1.5%
    percentage rent = $20,000,000 × 0.015 = $300,000

Declining percentage rent:
    gross sales = $20,000,000/year
    percentage rate = 1.5% on first $10,000,000 = $150,000
                      1.25% on next $5,000,000 = $62,500
                        1.0% on all sales over $15,000,000
  $20,000,000 − $15,000,000 = $5,000,000 × 0.01 = $50,000
  Total rent on declining basis = $262,500
  Savings to retailer = $37,500

A declining percentage rent is negotiated by retailers whose high sales volume assures a large percentage rental payment under any circumstances. The declining rate reduces the percentage due as the total sales volume increases.

---

range from 5 to 10 percent because they typically have high mark-ups. Some examples of percentage rent rates are given in table 3.3 (page 62).

Percentage rent is normally collected in arrears on a monthly basis. In other words, percentage rent on January sales is due in February. However, payment is often arranged on an annual or quarterly basis for larger tenants. Typically owners will "annualize" the retailer's total sales volume and total rental payments at the end of the year. When the lease calls for annual adjustments, cash refunds are sometimes given if the dollar amount is small; but it is more common for an overpayment to be credited to the retailer's account to offset future minimum rent payments, tenant charges, or percentage rents.

Other, less popular, ways to calculate percentage rent include (1) as a specific percentage of gross sales with a *maximum* rent and (2) as a percentage of profits or net sales.

The question of whether percentage rents are worthwhile has been debated for some time. Some owners choose to avoid the issue by simply charging higher minimum rents. On the one hand, the extra income can be a welcome addition to the owner's cash flow. On the other hand, it is difficult to collect percentage rent in some cases, and sometimes the amount is very small. Among small businesses, it can be easy to misrepresent gross sales or hold back percentage rent from time to time. Some shopping center owners rarely see percentage rent from their small-business tenants. Similarly, retailers that operate two or more different locations can easily claim that the bulk of their sales occurred in the other

T A B L E 3.3

National Percentage Lease Ranges

Type of Store	%	Type of Store	%
Art shops	5–10	Grocery stores (chain)	1–4
Auto accessories stores	2–6	Grocery stores (convenience)	1–6
Barber and beauty shops	1–10	Jewelry stores (costume)	5–12
Book and stationery stores	2–10	Leather goods	4–8
Candy stores	5–10	Liquors and wines	1–6
Department stores	0–3	Men's clothing stores	3–10
Drugstores (chain)	0–5	Optical shops	3–10
Drugstores (individual)	2–6	Radio, TV, hi-fi stores	2–7
Dry cleaners and laundries	4–10	Restaurants	4–10
Fabric (yard goods) stores	3–7	Restaurants with bar	5–10
Furniture stores	2–8	Women's dress shops	2–7
Gift shops	6–10	Women's shoe stores	3–8

Percentage rate ranges are for selected store types from data compiled and reported annually for 66 retail categories in 16 cities nationwide in *Buildings: The Facilities Construction and Management Magazine*.

Reproduced with permission from *Buildings* 83(1):54–58, January 1989. ©Copyright 1989 Stamats Communications, Inc.

outlets. National chains, on the whole, are less likely to conceal their sales receipts. Misrepresentation can be minimized by conducting regular audits of tenants' sales records and tax reports. This is an excellent management practice; but a good audit can cost more than the amount owed, and audits may not be feasible for every tenant. The lease should state that the owner retains the right to audit, and if an error of more than 2 percent is found, the tenant is responsible for paying the cost of the audit.

Many owners and agents know if a retailer is reporting honestly after comparing its sales results and inventory levels with those of other stores. Significant misrepresentation can prompt an owner to cancel the tenant's lease and replace the tenant with a competitor. When this occurs, other retailers in the center quickly get the message and report their sales honestly.

In any case, the retail space lease should contain a clear definition of what both owner and retailer understand *gross sales* to mean. Usually it means *all* goods and services sold on the premises, with certain exclusions—sales taxes, credits and refunds, returns to suppliers, and transfers between stores. Retailers may also want to exclude such items as credit card service fees (bank charges), employee discounts, gift certificates, alteration and delivery charges, vending machine receipts, and sales of lottery tickets, to name a few. The decision to exclude specific items depends on the kind of deal the owner and retailer are able to negotiate. Because they can become a point of contention, specific exclusions should be carefully delineated during the lease negotiation process and stated in the lease document. Also, the lease should require all tenants to submit sales reports to the owner so that the economic health of each tenant can be monitored. This reporting requirement may be difficult to negotiate, however—especially if the tenant is not required to pay percentage rent.

OTHER PAYMENTS IN ADDITION TO RENT

Whether a lease calls for payment of minimum rent, percentage rent, or both, most retail tenants also pay something toward the overall costs of operating the property. Specific tenant payments for operating expenses are always separate from rental rates, but the base rent of a property may be influenced by how these expenses are handled. Exactly what a given tenant will pay for is stated in the lease.

When tenants pay a percentage of the property's operating expenses each month, the property manager usually allocates monthly charges uniformly—based on the annual budget; adjustments for actual costs are made at year end. Tenants that pay for operating expenses have some form of *net lease*. There are several types of net leases, each depending on how much of the owner's costs are passed through to the tenant. In a single net lease, the tenant pays only for real estate taxes on a pro rata basis. In a net-net lease, the tenant pays for real estate taxes and insurance costs; maintenance costs remain the owner's exclusive responsibility. With a net-net-net or triple-net lease, the tenant is responsible for a pro rata share of all the property's expenses, including common area maintenance, although roof and structural repairs may remain the owner's responsibility. In most cases, however, maintenance of the tenant's premises is the tenant's responsibility. The triple-net lease is the most common type for shopping centers.

Charges for operating expenses are in addition to minimum and percentage rents and are individually specified for each tenant, generally based on that tenant's proportionate share of the property's GLA. In some leases, operating expenses may be defined to include a specific percentage (5–15%) for administrative and overhead expenses, which may include management fees. Contributions (dues) for a merchant's association or marketing fund are also prorated and included in the "additional rent" charges.

With any type of net lease, the base rent should reflect the fact that

T A B L E   3.4
Consumer Price Index—January*

	1989	1988	1987	1986	1985	1984	1983	1982	1981	1980	1979
U.S. City Average	**362.7**	**346.7**	**333.1**	**328.4**	**316.1**	**305.2**	**293.1**	**282.5**	**260.5**	**233.2**	**204.7**
Chicago Metro	363.0	344.4	334.3	326.3	315.1	305.2	294.0	275.4	258.9	230.3	199.7
Los Angeles Metro	368.2	351.2	335.1	326.8	313.0	299.1	285.6	285.6	259.4	232.6	199.6
New York Metro	367.2	350.7	331.6	323.1	308.4	297.3	282.6	268.5	249.4	226.1	202.9
Philadelphia Metro	363.0	344.6	327.7	320.3	306.3	294.4	282.1	275.7	253.2	227.2	202.3
Boston Metro	375.0	349.0	333.2	327.1	309.4	297.3	286.8	274.0	256.4	227.3	201.6
Anchorage	290.7	288.5	286.7	287.1	278.3	271.5	257.6	253.0	240.1	218.2	198.1
Denver Metro	382.4	372.2	361.1	364.4	350.6	343.5	327.5	305.4	277.3	247.3	216.2
Portland Metro	339.1	327.8	317.2	321.3	306.8	295.1	286.6	288.4	266.4	244.6	211.7

Base year = 1967 = 100; CPIs for these eight metropolitan areas are published every January; Boston is reported bimonthly; Denver, Anchorage, and Portland are reported semiannually.

NOTE: New base year 1982–84 was adopted in January 1988, and CPI statistics are currently being reported using both base years beginning with 1988. This table includes only selected cities for which CPI data are collected and uses only the 1967 base year to show the changes over the 10-year period indicated.

Reproduced with permission from the March 1989 issue of *Commercial Lease Law Insider*, a monthly newsletter, page 10. Published by Brownstone Publishers, Inc., 304 Park Avenue South, New York, NY 10010 (212) 473-8200.

specific overhead expenses have not been included in it. Theoretically, the more costs that are accounted for in separate charges, the lower the base rent will be. However, the total rent paid should be within the market's range.

There are some situations in which the owner does *not* pass through any of the operating expenses: Insurance, taxes, common area maintenance (CAM), heat, ventilation, and air conditioning (HVAC), and any other incidental costs related to the upkeep of the property remain solely the owner's responsibility. In these cases, higher minimum or percentage rents may be charged as compensation, and the lease is referred to as a *gross lease.* Straight gross leases are rare, although they may be used where the market favors the tenant; or they may still be in effect in older buildings with established long-term leases. Sometimes major anchors with considerable bargaining power will ask for—and receive—gross leases. They may also be used in downtown buildings that have difficulty attracting retail tenants.

ESCALATION OF RENTS

Most owners cannot accurately predict what their expenses will be in the future, especially with changes in the market and the economy. Inflation alone would debilitate a site if there were no protections for the owner who holds a long-term lease calling for fixed-minimum rates. Because of this, some long-term leases include an escalation clause calling for regular increases in the minimum rent. (Older leases do not always have these provisions.) Leases for anchor tenants may call for rents to increase every five years while those for ancillary tenants may require annual increases. The escalation clause permits the rent to be adjusted to accommodate changes due to inflation. Adjustments for inflationary changes may be based on the Consumer Price Index (CPI), especially during the initial lease term. The CPI, published by the U.S. Department of Labor, Bureau of Labor Statistics, measures changes in prices of food, clothing, shelter, transportation, medical services, and other items over a period of time. It is computed monthly or bimonthly for most standard metropolitan statistical areas (SMSAs), and the CPI for the nearest SMSA would be used in a given situation.

Representative CPI values for January are shown in table 3.4. Numbers in the column for each year represent percentage increases from the designated base year, which has a set value of 100. Using the first year of the lease term as the designated starting year, the rent increase is computed for each succeeding year based on the difference between the CPI for the current year and the CPI for the preceding year. The difference between the two CPIs is divided by the CPI for the earlier, and the result multiplied

FIGURE   3.5

Rent Adjustment Using the CPI*

	Beginning of Lease (January 1987)	First Rent Adjustment (January 1988)	Second Rent Adjustment (January 1989)
CPI = 333.1		346.7	362.7
Change in CPI		13.6	16.0
Percent Increase[†]		4.08	4.61

*CPI values are for month of January only (see table 3.4); base year 1967 = 100.

[†]Computed by dividing the amount of the increase by the previous year's CPI and multiplying by 100.

For a tenant whose rent was $1,000 per month when the lease began in January 1987, the monthly rent would have increased to $1,040.80 in January 1988 and to $1,078.88 in January 1989. The amount of each increase is computed by multiplying the monthly rent by the next year's percentage increase and adding that amount to the current rent.

346.7 (1988 CPI) − 333.1 (1987 CPI) = 13.6 (Change in CPI)
13.6 (Change) ÷ 333.1 (1987 CPI) = .0408 = 4.08 (Percent Increase)
$1,000 (1987 Rent) × .0408 (Percent Increase) = $40.80 (Rent Increase)
$1,000 (1987 Rent) + $40.80 (Increase) = $1,040.80 (1988 Rental Rate)

---

by the monthly rent yields the new rental rate. An example using the U.S. city average CPI for January is shown in figure 3.5.

Tenant and property owner may also agree to periodic increases in the fixed-minimum rent that do not depend on a measurement of inflation. Such increases are usually stated as a percentage. (Because percentages are tied to dollar volume, using them provides some protection against inflation.) Options for lease renewals may guarantee increases in rents. Minimum rents may also be increased incrementally, escalating stepwise at regular intervals.

ESTABLISHING RENTAL RATES FOR SHOPPING CENTERS

Shopping center owners are concerned primarily with (1) maximizing occupancy levels at the highest possible rental rates and (2) increasing sales for all their tenants so that the largest amount of percentage rent based on tenants' sales income is paid to the owner. Careful planning is required to establish adequate rental rates that will both yield a profit for the owner and be acceptable to the tenant. Because each tenant in a shopping center pays a different rent, all the different rents must be balanced in such a way that they produce the desired overall income for the center. Established rents should yield the greatest income for the owner commensurate with the highest occupancy rates.

Tenants that have large space requirements—department stores, supermarkets, etc.—pay significantly less rent per square foot than those whose space requirements are smaller. On a square-foot basis, large spaces can cost less to build than small ones. Also, there are comparatively few large space users, which limits the demand or competition for these spaces. The lower rent per square foot paid by major or anchor tenants is justified by the demand for the goods they sell. Their drawing power enhances ancillary tenants' sales as well. Even paying lower rates per square foot, these tenants may provide the greatest proportionate share of the property's rental income simply because of their large size.

Determining Market Rents

In establishing rental rates, a major consideration is the economic status of the trade area and the market within which the retail property will be competing. The results of the market survey will help the agent determine *market rents*. The trade area analysis and the demographic profile indicate the economic strength (purchasing power) of the community, the locations and types of competition, the variety of industries and businesses (employers) in the area, and especially the rents being paid for retail space in the market.

The *laws of supply and demand* also influence market rents. If the available retail space exceeds the number of prospective tenants, the area is considered *overbuilt,* and rents may be set below established market rates as owners compete with each other for tenants. If there are more tenants looking for space than there is space available, the area is considered *underbuilt,* and rental rates will usually favor the owner who will have no trouble finding prospects to pay higher rents. If supply and demand are approximately equal, there will be a sufficient number of available tenants, and rents for the market will probably be stable. *Demand for retail space rarely exceeds the supply.* An area with a higher than average occupancy level will attract new developers, and the additional space they create will lead to a lowering of demand.

High vacancy rates or a poor location may force an owner to offer concessions. In a slow market, a lower base rent may attract tenants and lower the natural breakpoint at which percentage rent would apply, thus increasing the chances that percentage rent will be due. The agent who uses this strategy should try to combine it with a short-term lease so that, if market conditions improve, rents can be raised when the lease expires. Many tenants resist signing short-term leases; however, some tenants prefer short-term leases so they won't be committed for a long period if they discover that they have chosen a poor location.

While a lower base rent may be acceptable for short-term leases, it can be detrimental for long-term leases. Any change in the overall base rent will alter the rent structure in every lease for the center, with long-term effects on the owner's income. Occupancy levels at the retail property may be higher when the established rent is lower than the market rent, but less income will be generated and the value of the property will be reduced. For these reasons, owners prefer not to lower the rent. Instead, they may offer other concessions such as a period of free rent or a larger tenant improvement allowance, either of which may satisfy the tenant without seriously affecting the income from the property. The leasing agent should always establish rental rates and lease terms with future trends in mind.

Adjusting Rental Rates for Individual Spaces

Once a fair market rent is established for a shopping center, that rent can be adjusted for each space and each individual tenant. The final rental schedule will consist of the *base rent* with adjustments for a number of specific factors such as

- Store size and dimensions (frontage, depth)
- Pro rata share of common operating expenses allocated to the space
- Type of tenant
- Type of center
- Location of the space in the center (proximity to anchors or parking, visibility, etc.)
- Condition of the leased space
- Market need or demand for the retailer's merchandise
- Tenant's projected sales volume
- Other variables.

Use of different variables to adjust the base rent is a common practice when designing a rent schedule, and the variables used have differing importance. In some centers, signage, glass frontage, and visibility from the street may be of greater importance than other factors. Elsewhere, the fit of a tenant's merchandise with the tone set by the anchor tenant may receive proportionately greater consideration. The agent's job is to design a leasing plan that will identify the most desirable tenants and to create a rent schedule that will be acceptable to both owners and prospective tenants.

Store Size.   The amount of space to be occupied is a primary consideration because it is used as the expressed basis for payment of minimum rent—per square foot. It is also the basis for computing the tenant's pro rata share of common area expenses and other operating charges, which will be based on the floor area.

The floor area of each site in the shopping center must be measured accurately because it is used to set the ratio of each tenant's space to both the common area space and the total (or gross leasable) area of the entire

FIGURE   3.6

Measurement of Ground Floor Store Area

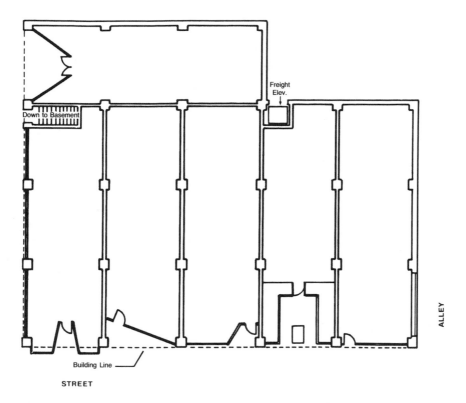

The standard method for measuring store area in buildings fronting on a street (as depicted here and described in the text) is used most often for retail spaces in office buildings. Store spaces in shopping malls are measured slightly differently.

Reproduced with permission from *Standard Method for Measuring Floor Area in Office Buildings* (ANSI Z65.1, 1980)—Secretariat—Building Owners and Managers Association, 1201 New York Avenue, NW, Washington, DC 20005, 202-308-BOMA; 1990 Standard publication date—March 1, 1990.

shopping center. For shopping malls, the GLA of individual spaces is measured from the outside of exterior walls to the center of demising walls—the walls between adjacent tenants.

A similar method is applied to stores that front on streets or occupy spaces in office buildings or mixed-use developments. This standard, established by the American National Standards Institute and published by the Building Owners and Managers Association International (BOMA), is depicted by the drawing in figure 3.6 and stated as follows.

The number of square feet in a ground floor Store Area shall be computed by measuring from the building line in the case of street frontages, and from the inner surface of corridor and other permanent partitions and to the center of partitions that separate the premises from adjoining rentable areas. No deduction shall be made for vestibules inside the building line or for columns or projections necessary to the building. No addition shall be made for bay windows extending outside the building line.

Operating expenses are passed through based on the size of the tenant's floor area compared to the gross leasable area of the entire shopping center. If the GLA of the center is 250,000 square feet, and one tenant occupies 2,500 square feet, the tenant's space represents 1 percent of the center's GLA—computed by dividing the tenant area (2,500 sq ft) by the total GLA (250,000 sq ft) and multiplying by 100. Thus, that tenant's pro rata share of pass-through expenses is 1 percent. A store that occupies 1,250 square feet of space in the same center would pay only 0.5 percent. These percentages are applied to the total monthly costs for parking lot, landscape, and common area maintenance (CAM), etc., and charged to each tenant accordingly. In some instances, department store anchors choose to maintain their own common areas, and they are not charged additional rent for the upkeep of other common areas within the center, or they pay very low annual amounts. When anchor tenants maintain or own their own stores, the anchor store area is normally excluded from the calculation of the total GLA used to compute nonanchor tenant's pass-through expenses; and any contribution by the anchor is deducted from the total operating or CAM costs before they are prorated among non-anchor tenants. The method used to calculate proration of operating expenses is always stated in the lease.

Also related to size are the specific dimensions of the space—its width and depth. Width is often the sole indicator of store frontage. Many retailers want to maximize this dimension because a large frontage offers greater opportunities to display merchandise directly to passersby and thus attract more customers.

Store depth—the distance from the back wall to the main thoroughfare—is also important for the proper display of merchandise within the store. Depths of 50–60 feet are standard; stores this deep are considered desirable though their location would determine whether they are considered prime space. In spaces with a greater than average store depth—between 70 and 90 feet—merchandise is visually removed from the customer; these spaces are less likely to generate as high a sales volume per square foot as spaces with less depth and are usually considered secondary. Depths in excess of 90 feet reduce visibility; merchandise at the back of the store cannot be seen without going deep inside. Excessive depth also lessens the desirability of spaces where the store width does not off-set this disadvantage. For most ancillary spaces, store depth will be greater than store width or frontage. Large stores with depths greater than 60 feet—those occupied by major and anchor tenants in particular—are proportionately wider. However, a disproportionate ratio between depth and width can lessen the desirability of the space.

Type of Tenant.   Rents for smaller store spaces vary with the type of merchandise being sold. For example, candy and nut shops occupy very small spaces, but they pay very high minimum rents compared to an apparel store, for example. This is because they have a large sales volume at a high markup. Candy and nuts are usually purchased on impulse, so these shops are located in highly visible areas where shopper traffic is heaviest. Being located in such "prime space" is another consideration in setting the rents for this type of tenant.

On the other hand, major tenants in shopping centers—large department stores, supermarkets—usually pay base rent at a lower rate per square foot than smaller or ancillary tenants. There are two reasons for this disparity: The overall construction cost of a large building is sometimes lower than the per-foot construction cost for a small space. Far more important, however, is the fact that anchor tenants generally negotiate from a position of strength.

As has been noted earlier in this chapter, it is also possible for department stores to pay percentage rent only and no base rent. However, percentage-only rents are not commonplace, especially in new shopping centers where it is not only desirable but necessary to have all tenants—including anchors—pay a minimum rent. Lending institutions usually will not finance a new development unless there are advance lease commitments from key tenants, meaning guaranteed rental income. Therefore, it is to the owner's or developer's advantage to attract an anchor tenant that will pay minimum rent, even if it means offering a lower per-square-foot rate. Anchor tenants are important to shopping centers because they are big advertisers capable of drawing large numbers of customers, and their commitment to the center will speed the leasing of space to ancillary tenants.

Location within the Center.   The store's geographic location in the shopping center is a major consideration in the assignment of rent. Tenant spaces located at outside corners, at the front of the center, and near major anchor tenants all typically rent for higher rates because they are considered prime space. Kiosks—small, freestanding retail structures positioned in the mall or common area of a shopping center—are also considered prime space. Spaces located on the main mall between anchor

FIGURE   3.7

**Sources of the Income Dollar of U.S. Community
Shopping Centers**

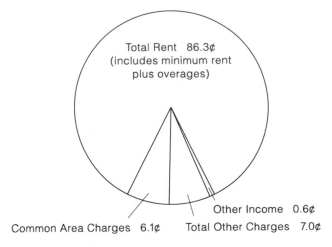

Total Rent 86.3¢
(includes minimum rent
plus overages)

Other Income 0.6¢

Common Area Charges 6.1¢   Total Other Charges 7.0¢

From data reported in *Dollars and Cents of Shopping Centers: 1987* (Washington, D.C.:
ULI—the Urban Land Institute, 1987). Used with permission.

tenants are not considered prime but are still desirable from the perspective of the tenant. These spaces usually rent for above-average rates but
not the same high rates assigned to prime space. Spaces located off the
main mall are considered secondary and are generally assigned rental
rates that are lower than those for prime or more-desirable spaces. Likewise, second-floor and basement spaces usually rent for less than first-
floor spaces. Spaces at the ends of secondary malls or in inside corners
have the least visibility and, consequently, the least shopper traffic; therefore they command the least rent.

Condition.   Another factor related to the space itself is the condition in
which it is rented to the tenant. New store space is frequently leased as a
shell; it may have a ceiling, side and back walls, a storefront, a wood or
concrete floor, and roughed-in utility outlets but is generally considered
unfinished. Shell space usually will not command as high a rent as a space
that has been or will be completely finished, although the difference in
rent may not be significant. On the other hand, a new tenant in a space that
was previously occupied may have to incur the cost of demolition to reduce the space to a shell state before building to its own store specifica-

FIGURE   3.8

Allocation of the Expense Dollar in U.S. Community Shopping Centers

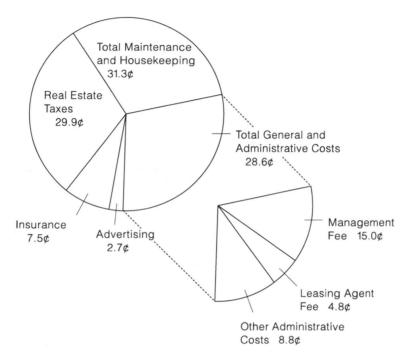

From data reported in *Dollars and Cents of Shopping Centers: 1987* (Washington, D.C.: ULI—the Urban Land Institute, 1987). Used with permission.

tions. The amount of "improvement" to the so-called shell space is what affects the rent.

EFFECTIVE RENT

To this point, the discussion has focused on the diversity of factors that are considered in pricing rents for retail space. Rents comprise nearly all of the income that accrues to the center (figure 3.7), and it is this income which is disbursed on a continuing basis to pay for the costs of operating the center (figure 3.8). It is this ongoing relationship between income derived from rents and the expenses of operating a shopping center that makes it so important to know where every dollar is coming from and where it is being spent.

As has been stated repeatedly, the base or minimum rent is adjusted and negotiated for each tenant. If operating expenses are not passed through to the tenant, they must be factored into the minimum rent that the tenant pays. Also factored into the base rent is the standard tenant improvement allowance, if offered by the owner. These considerations lead to a *higher* base rent per square foot of GLA. When operating expenses are passed through to the tenant on a pro rata basis, the base rent per square foot may be *lower* to reflect this. When percentage rent is paid as *overages* —in other words, computed on gross sales and reduced by the amount of minimum rent paid—the confident expectation of large sales volume as a base for percentage rent may lead to negotiation of a lower base rent for that tenant. Any negotiated concessions (free rent, additional tenant improvement allowance, etc.) may affect a tenant's base rental rate as well.

The bottom line is the amount of rental income the owner actually receives from the tenant each month. This *effective rent* is the total rental income derived from the space for the entire term of the lease after it is divided into equal payments over the term of the lease. A simple example would be an initial period of free rent to compensate for the time needed to finish a 1,000-square-foot shell space. The lease may call for minimum (base) rent of $15.00 per square foot per year for a period of three years. A three-month period of free rent does not change the rental rate stated in the lease, but it does change the effective rent the owner is paid.

Lease Term = 3 Years (3 months free rent)
Base Rent = $15.00 Per Square Foot
Store Size = 1,000 Square Feet of GLA

Area (GLA) × Base Rent = Total Annual Rent
Total Annual Rent × Lease Term = Total Rent Due

1,000 Square Feet × $15.00 Rent = $15,000 Annual Rent
$15,000 Annual Rent × 3 Years (lease term) =
    $45,000 Total Annual Rent

$$\frac{\text{Total Annual Rent}}{12} = \text{Monthly Minimum Rent}$$

Monthly Minimum Rent × 3 Months (free) = Amount of Free Rent

$$\frac{\$15,000}{12} = \$1,250 \text{ (per month)} \times 3 = \$3,750 \text{ Free Rent}$$

Total Rent Due − Free Rent =
  Effective Rental Income on the Full Lease

$45,000 − $3,750 = $41,250

$$\frac{\text{Effective Rent}}{36} = \text{Effective Monthly Rental Income}$$

$$\frac{\$41,250}{36} = \$1,145.83$$

In the example given above, the effective monthly rent was reduced from $1,250 to $1,145.83. (On a square-foot basis, the rate of $15.00 has been reduced to $13.75.) The tenant ultimately benefited in the amount of $104.17 each month (or $1.25/sq ft). If this difference is not compensated in some way—negotiation of a lower breakpoint for percentage rent, for example—the owner has effectively lost this amount as income each month of this tenant's lease. The concept of effective rent should be kept in mind when any concession is negotiated.

SUMMARY

Pricing rents takes place before leasing is begun. Lending institutions and other financial backers require a statement of the property's value before investing in a new store or center, and this information is dependent for the most part on rental income. Establishing rental rates is a good way of projecting the property's potential income. The rental schedules are usually incorporated into the general leasing plan, which also includes a physical layout of the property and suggestions for tenant mix and placement.

Several different rental structures can be used for retail space. The minimum or guaranteed rent—the amount the tenant will pay every month—is usually based on current market conditions or competitive rates. Percentage rents are another standard feature of the retail lease. They may be based on a percentage of the retailer's annual gross sales or, more commonly, on the excess over a certain volume of sales. That sales volume, called the breakpoint, may be the minimum rent divided by the percentage rental rate (the natural breakpoint); or, in some instances, it may be negotiated and artificially set lower or higher to accommodate tenant or owner. Occasionally a retailer with a very large sales volume will negotiate a declining percentage rent, with the rate decreasing as the amount of gross sales increases. In some situations, an increasing percentage rate may be appropriate. Percentage rents are most often used in combination with a minimum rent; however, some owners favor abandoning percentage rents altogether and charging higher minimum rents to protect them from the loss of potential income from percentage rents that may not accrue.

Leases may be net or gross. With a net lease, the tenant pays for some or all of the operating expenses of the property on a pro rata basis. With a gross lease, the owner is responsible for all expenses, including insurance, property taxes, and common area maintenance charges. Most shopping centers use net leases, although in older centers or in areas where retail tenants are in high demand, gross leases may still be found.

In a shopping center, rents are adjusted for individual store spaces based on their size and location. Individual rents are also based in part on the type of merchandise the retailer offers (potential market and sales volume) and the prospective tenant's negotiating power (financial strength and track record). Because an anchor tenant's presence is crucial to a shopping center's success, its base rent per square foot is often substantially lower than the average base rent per square foot set for the site.

There are no hard and fast rules for rent pricing. Although market rates may approximate the optimum rent, many factors contribute to differences among rents within the same trade area or from store to store within a shopping center. Owners may have to offer concessions to counteract high vacancy rates or attract tenants that will be an asset to the site. In general, lowering rent as a concession will effect a long-term reduction of the property's income. More generous tenant improvement allowances or a few months' free rent during construction are more suitable concessions to offer. (Other types of concessions and the agent's role in negotiating them are discussed in chapter 8.) However, all concessions that affect the amount of rent actually paid will alter the effective rent the owner receives as income. This is the bottom line and the reason that the rent schedule must be constructed so carefully in order to maximize the rental income from the property as a whole.

Tenant Mix

The combination of retailers selected for a particular center can mean its success or failure. Even before the center opens, a lender may be more willing to finance it if a sufficient proportion of the executed leases indicate tenant creditworthiness that justifies the risk. After the center has opened, a successful blending of retailers will generate traffic and maximize sales for all the tenants.

The relationship between the number and percentage of types of stores in a shopping center and their location within it is called *tenant mix*. Tenant mix is influenced by many factors—the type of shopping center; its location, size, and anchor tenant or tenants; the demographic profile of the trade area, and consumer needs. A super regional center will have a different tenant mix than an urban neighborhood center. A single center located in a rural community and serving a large trade area may support a wider range of merchandise, while a more focused or fine-tuned approach to tenant selection may be required if a new center is planned for an area that is already saturated with retail operations. Generally speaking, the larger the scale of the development, the greater the choice of tenants; but large centers sometimes face more complicated problems in creating a balanced tenant mix. In neighborhood centers, where the choice of tenants is more limited, tenant mix as such may be less important. Each type of center usually has a list of merchandise classifications and tenants that are considered indispensable to its success.

CLASSIFYING TENANTS

Market segmentation can be used as a means of identifying prospective tenants that probably would not benefit from leasing space at a particular retail site. Segmentation of a given market is done by classifying retailers on the basis of several characteristics—type of store, store size and operational requirements, and type of merchandise sold or services rendered.

Generally the type of center is defined by the major or anchor tenant or tenants. Because anchor tenants generally set the tone for the shopping center, it is usually desirable to group other tenants in a way that reflects the type of anchor with which their business is associated. Grocery stores, department stores, and discount stores all attract different kinds of ancillary tenants. If a center is being renovated, the effect of existing tenants on any newcomers has to be weighed, and vice versa. Certain types of retailers are more compatible than others.

The desirability of a particular retailer as a tenant is also guided in part by the retailer's potential sales volume, customer draw, and ability to pay high minimum and percentage rents. These factors are the top priority in trade areas where high rents are the norm and above-average sales performance is critical for the retailer's survival. (Financial considerations are an important part of qualifying prospective tenants, as discussed in chapter 5.)

On the other hand, the retailer will want a good reason for locating at the site. A toy store will not be interested in a trade area with a concentration of young single people, and a drugstore may not want to compete where three similar stores already exceed the area's needs.

In order to match the space with a suitable tenant, the needs of both property owner and retailer have to be considered. Type and size of store, type of merchandise and its targeted consumer, and prospective tenants' potential to succeed financially will all have an impact on the profitability of a particular shopping center.

Type of Store

Shopping center owners and developers distinguish between two basic types of tenants—anchor and ancillary. Typical *anchor tenants* in large centers are department stores or supermarkets. While no major shopping center can survive without such anchors, most of a center's profits can come from the smaller businesses that occupy the spaces adjacent to or surrounding them. Leasing agents who are beginning their careers usually do not negotiate leases with anchor tenants; most of their efforts are devoted to leasing the ancillary spaces. *Ancillary tenants* are often classified on the basis of ownership—chain stores, franchises, or independent operations. Each of these types has its place in a well-balanced shopping center.

Anchor.   Certain types of anchor tenants have become standard for certain types of shopping centers. Super regional centers usually include three or more major department stores, each occupying 100,000 or more square feet of GLA. It is not uncommon to have five or six anchor tenants in such a center. A regional shopping center will have at least one anchor tenant (and preferably two or more) that occupies 100,000 square feet of GLA. Such anchors are usually full-line department stores that have strong national or regional reputations, and whose images and prices are generally in line with both the economic environment in which the shopping center is located and the purchasing power of its potential customers.

A community center may have a discount store, a variety store, or a hardware and garden store as an anchor. Although junior department stores used to be successful in this type of center, they are being replaced by off-price outlets. Full-line department stores usually do not anchor a community center. However, many department stores are now opening smaller stores that offer a limited array of merchandise, and such spin-offs may be suitable for community centers. Supermarkets are excellent anchor tenants for neighborhood centers, especially when they are combined with drugstores.

Discount anchors promote both hard lines such as auto parts, appliances, and electronics and soft lines such as apparel and shoes. A relatively new type of center, the off-price center, is completely tenanted by retailers that offer discount items; it may have several large discount anchors rather than just one. In size and tenant mix, the off-price center may be compared with the larger community center.

A group of food stores may replace a more traditional anchor. Such cluster anchors can be found in specialty centers which may have restaurants or food courts as key tenants, with movie theaters or other entertainment complexes supplying major traffic. Some specialty centers have succeeded without any so-called anchors because the bulk of their traffic consists of tourists who are attracted by a unique selection of gift shops and an ambiance.

National and Regional Chains.   *Chain stores* are multiple retail outlets operated under centralized ownership and management. A chain can consist of a few stores in a small geographic area or hundreds of stores nationwide. Merchandise in all the chain's outlets is usually identical. A corporate headquarters controls all business functions of this type of retailing operation, and each outlet has standardized, specific requirements regarding size and space. Many larger chains have regional representatives who are responsible for locating new space and representing the chain during negotiations.

Retailers that operate multiple outlets in several states are considered *national chains*. They can range from large department stores—Sears, Roebuck & Company; Montgomery Ward—to variety stores such as Woolworth, all of which have a presence in shopping centers nationwide. National chain stores are the most frequent choice for anchor tenants in a shopping center because their well-known names and good credit ratings will enhance the reputation of the center. Ancillary tenants may also be national chains; many "name" apparel shops, bookstores, jewelry stores, and card shops can be found in shopping centers nationwide.

Regional chain stores have multiple outlets located primarily in one major section of the country such as the Southeast, New England, or the Pacific Northwest. Their local drawing power makes them ideal shopping center tenants in their respective regions. There are also *local chains* that operate several stores within a single metropolitan area. Sycamore Specialty Stores in the Midwest and the Linen Barn in the East are examples of regional chains; Dominick's Finer Foods in the Chicago metropolitan area would be considered a local chain.

Franchises.   The *franchise* operator (franchisee) invests money in the business and takes care of all the operating expenses at a single location. The franchisor provides management training, national advertising, and assistance with recordkeeping, for which it receives a royalty fee from the franchisee. Fast food restaurants such as McDonald's or Arby's are typical franchises, but gas stations, hotels, and other service companies are also franchised. Franchisors are always looking for new outlets, and they offer numerous opportunities to lease space in different types of shopping centers.

Independent Stores.   Individually owned businesses that have only one or two locations in the same city are considered independent. These unique entrepreneurial enterprises—referred to in the past as "ma and pa" operations because they were generally small and family owned—were once the backbone of American retailing. They can still provide variety and color in a shopping center and often give it a competitive edge.

Independent stores typically occupy less space than most chain stores. Often they have strong followings that can benefit both the center owner and the other retailers. It should be kept in mind, however, that while independents may add variety to a tenant mix and help create a unique character for the center, they also have to be monitored carefully during their early years of operation in the center. New independents often suffer business losses their first year or two because of inexperience or poor management. To reduce the risk for the center, any new businesses that lease space in a center should be offset by tenants that have been in business awhile. The need to grow may lead independent businesses to seek space in larger shopping centers; for many independents, however, the chances for their success are greater in neighborhood or community centers or in business areas that have individual storefront spaces. When a new business is recruited as a tenant, its chances of being successful in the location are greater if the agent takes more care in developing financial information and works with the prospect to determine more precisely what the store is going to be (see chapter 5).

Temporary Tenants. It takes time to establish the right tenant mix, and *temporary tenants* can give an immediate boost to a shopping center as well as enhance the existing tenant profile. They can fill a gap by providing goods that permanent tenants might not supply; or they can lend a festive atmosphere to a holiday promotion, encourage impulse buying, and add variety and novelty to the center's standard merchandise lines and overall decor. Temporary tenants are often seasonal businesses. They help increase traffic during peak times and sell goods that people tend to buy on impulse or only during certain holidays.

Temporary tenants commonly operate in kiosks, which are small, free-standing booths or stalls set up in a center's common area. They pay higher rents per square foot and lower overhead (operating expense pass-through) charges than permanent tenants, in return for which they have high visibility and locations in the busiest areas of a mall or shopping center. An alternate temporary location is a pushcart attractively painted and decorated with banners, ribbons, canopies, etc. Although a specialty center like Faneuil Hall Marketplace in Boston may have thirty-five to fifty temporary tenants at any one time, most regional or community centers strictly limit the number of such tenants that can be operating at a given time. Too many kiosk or pushcart businesses make a center seem overcrowded and can distract customers from the permanent tenants.

Sometimes a temporary tenant will occupy a vacant store space, maintaining the owner's cash flow until a permanent tenant can be found. Temporary tenants may also serve as a means of testing sales of a new kind of merchandise an owner wants to introduce in a center. On this basis, the successful temporary tenant can become a valuable permanent addition to the shopping center.

The merchandise offered by temporary tenants should complement both the tone of the center and the types of goods offered by the permanent tenants, without detracting from the latter's sales. Figure 4.1 lists examples of generally acceptable types of merchandise for such temporary tenants. Not listed there are the range of seasonal items that relate to specific holidays (Christmas, Easter, Halloween) and can be the focus of special sales for most of the permanent tenants in the center as well.

Kiosk and Pushcart Tenants' Merchandise and Services

Candy	Photofinishing, film, flashbulbs
Costume jewelry	Pottery
Flowers	Prepackaged food gifts
Fruit and nuts	Rubber stamps
Greeting cards	Shoe shining
Hand-crafted items	Souvenirs
Keys	Stuffed animals
Leather goods (small)	T-shirts
Newspaper and magazines	Ticket Sales (entertainment)
Personalization services (engraving)	Tourist Information
Photocopying and fax services	Toys and novelty items

Normally the income from rents paid by temporary tenants goes directly to the owner along with other tenants' rent. Temporary tenants are subject to base and percentage rents and other charges under a regular lease. In some centers, however, temporary tenants occupying kiosks or carts in the common area may do so under a license agreement, with the licensing fee paid to the merchant's association which has jurisdiction over the promotions in the common area. The revenue from the licensing fees is then used to help promote the center and improve the traffic for all stores. This latter arrangement is one that benefits all the retailers in a center. Permanent tenants will note that the licensing income provides additional funding for promotions—from which they benefit directly—and they will likely encourage the association to bring in temporary tenants. If temporary tenants generate substantial funds, the owner's contribution to the merchant's association can be reduced—a direct benefit to the owner.

Temporary tenants become permanent tenants even if they only occupy permanent kiosk-type space. Because of the prospect of permanency, shopping center owners often regard temporary occupancy as a trial to see if the individual retailer's goods appeal to customers on a regular basis. Temporary tenants that are questionable or unacceptable should be avoided.

Size and Operational Requirements

It is important to find the best possible tenant for a particular space, and different types of businesses have different space and operational requirements. Therefore, tenants are also classified on the basis of the size of their operations and their suitability for the space that is available in the shopping center. A furniture store will require a large amount of floor space for display as well as space for storage. A supermarket requires a large amount of adjacent parking that encourages a quick turnover of spaces. Both of these types of businesses need loading docks and adequate trash facilities.

Although individual retailers within each category have different-sized stores, there is usually a range of standard space requirements for each type of business. Retailers operating in a space that is too large or too small for them are less likely to succeed.

Department Stores.   Department stores may be full-line, limited-line, junior, or discount operations. Full-line department stores carry so-called mass merchandise—housewares, furniture, appliances, apparel, books, toys, etc. They usually anchor regional and super regional shopping centers. Some large "department" stores offer only limited lines of merchandise. They may sell linens and housewares (soft goods), for example, but not furniture and major appliances (hard goods). Junior department stores offer predominantly soft goods. Discount department stores may be chain stores, freestanding factory or manufacturer's outlets, or off-price stores. Junior and discount department stores commonly anchor community centers.

A full-line department store in a super regional center may occupy 60,000 to more than 200,000 square feet of GLA, with national chain stores being slightly larger (median 150,000 square feet) than local chains (median 80,000 square feet). Department stores in regional centers range in size from 50,000 to 180,000 square feet of GLA. Junior department stores that anchor community shopping centers occupy 18,000–80,000 square feet of GLA. Discount department stores that anchor community centers are slightly larger (25,000–100,000 square feet of GLA). (The GLA of different types of department stores that can anchor super regional, regional, community, and neighborhood shopping centers is shown in table 4.1.)

Full-line department stores require a large parking area that is accessible to customers from the building's entrances. In addition to display space for merchandise, they have to have loading docks and freight areas, trash bins or compactors, and they often require basement storage—plus space for stock rooms, offices, an employee lunchroom, public restrooms, and possibly a small restaurant or cafeteria for shoppers. They may also need rooms for staff meetings and personnel training. Spin-offs from large department stores that operate as subsidiaries have gained in importance. Most often these are small apparel operations. In the long run, they can provide more business for a leasing agent than a full-sized store will. Junior department stores have operational requirements similar to those of full-line department stores, although they generally have smaller freight and loading dock requirements because they do not offer large-sized hard goods. Discount department stores reduce their overhead by using sales

T A B L E   4.1

Gross Leasable Area (GLA) of Department Stores

Type of Center	Tenant	Median	Range of GLA in Sq Ft
Super Regional	Full-Line	131,602	60,000–230,510
	National Chain	149,730	68,337–230,510
	Local Chain	80,240	49,534–191,592
	Junior	20,149	2,856–43,264
	National Chain	12,232	2,856–31,916
	Local Chain	22,327	7,930–76,500
	Discount	28,557	—
	National Chain	28,557	—
Regional	Full-Line	93,600	50,232–180,832
	National Chain	95,129	48,198–181,949
	Local Chain	85,924	53,604–135,617
	Junior	23,475	4,818–70,308
	National Chain	21,600	3,476–51,610
	Local Chain	25,015	—
	Discount	72,900	14,000–118,701
	National Chain	50,000	—
Community	Junior	45,684	18,000–79,845
	National Chain	50,618	18,288–81,550
	Local Chain	30,000	15,000–67,200
	Discount	55,500	24,916–99,349
	National Chain	62,989	25,000–102,433
	Local Chain	40,000	7,319–80,155
	Independent	38,000	—
Neighborhood	Junior	12,000	—
	National Chain	10,529	—
	Discount	22,320	—
	National Chain	24,000	—

From data reported in *Dollars and Cents of Shopping Centers: 1987* (Washington, D.C.: ULI—the Urban Land Institute, 1987). Used with permission.

areas as storage space. Nonselling space is often reduced to as little as 10 percent of the entire GLA, while regular department stores will use from 20 to 40 percent of their GLA for storage and operational functions. Discount department stores usually require a wider, more open type of building; but many of the design elements they request depend on their particular image and type of customer.

Apparel Stores. Apparel stores sell men's, women's, and children's clothing, shoes, and accessories. Store size is determined from the line of merchandise and the type of chain operation. Large chains have specific requirements that they will communicate to the leasing agent through their leasing representative. National chains selling women's clothing and shoes generally require larger store spaces than do national chains selling men's clothing and shoes (table 4.2); but among local chains, the converse is true—those selling men's clothing and shoes usually have the larger space requirements. Shoe stores require less space generally, and those selling men's shoes tend to have the smallest spaces—presumably because the variety of styles and colors they stock is smaller; women's shoe stores must carry more selection possibilities.

Drugstores.   Drugstores may be small, freestanding pharmacies located among neighborhood shops and occupying as little as 650–1,200 square feet of GLA, or they may be full-service drug and sundry stores that anchor a shopping center. They may be combined with supermarkets or include small cafeterias or restaurants. At the low end of the size scale, a traditional drugstore in a neighborhood center may occupy 6,000–10,000 square feet of GLA if it is part of a national chain, 3,000–9,700 square feet if it is part of a local chain, or 1,800–8,000 square feet if it is an independent store. At the high end of the size scale, the so-called super drugstore occupies more than 10,000 square feet of GLA, and outlets for national chains can be as large as 26,000 square feet while local chain outlets average 14,000 square feet. (Some drugstores in power centers occupy 50,000 square feet of GLA.) Super drugstores often take the place of variety stores, offering housewares, hardware items, magazines, toys, and even foodstuffs.

Other Chain Stores.   Several types of stores have special operational requirements because of the types of merchandise they carry. House and garden shops, often part of chain variety stores or super drugstores, have seasonal requirements that may include outdoor display areas or a greenhouse-type arrangement that can be used for other purposes in off seasons. Showroom or catalog stores need room for display if not for sales, and they require 2,100–70,000 square feet of GLA.

Toys, books, sporting goods, furniture, audio and video products, craft supplies, and electronic equipment are other types of merchandise sold by chain stores in shopping centers. While specific requirements vary with the type of merchandise, spaces occupied by these chains have been *decreasing* in size over the years. Smaller store spaces are a way to reduce operating costs. Less rent, a smaller inventory to maintain, and fewer sales personnel can make an operation more profitable.

Supermarkets and Grocery Stores.   Probably the smallest type of food retailer is the convenience food store occupying less than 6,000 square feet of space in a strip center and operating as a local or neighborhood gro-

T A B L E 4.2
Median GLA of Apparel Stores

Super Regional	Sq Ft GLA	Regional	Sq Ft GLA	Community	Sq Ft GLA
Ladies' Ready-To-Wear		Ladies' Ready-to-Wear		Ladies Ready-To-Wear	
National Chain	3,179	National Chain	3,717	National Chain	3,900
Local Chain	2,530	Local Chain	3,338	Local Chain	2,909
Ladies' Shoes		Ladies' Shoes		Ladies' Specialty	
National Chain	1,617	National Chain	2,015	National Chain	2,800
Local Chain	1,447	Local Chain	1,325	Local Chain	1,800
Ladies' Specialty		Ladies' Specialty		Family Shoes	
National Chain	2,550	National Chain	2,720	National Chain	3,050
Local Chain	2,309	Local Chain	2,080	Local Chain	2,400
Men's Wear		Men's Wear		**Neighborhood**	
National Chain	3,000	National Chain	2,720	Ladies' Ready-To-Wear	
Local Chain	3,276	Local Chain	4,900	National Chain	4,000
Men's and Boys' Shoes		Family Shoes		Local Chain	2,400
National Chain	1,260	National Chain	3,307		
Local Chain	1,784	Local Chain	2,999		
Family Shoes					
National Chain	3,123				
Local Chain	3,531				

From data reported in *Dollars and Cents of Shopping Centers: 1987* (Washington, D.C.: ULI—the Urban Land Institute, 1987). Used with permission.

cery store. The conventional supermarket has a median GLA of about 23,500 square feet; it may be part of a neighborhood shopping center and often leases space in an already existing or remodeled building. The *superstore,* also found primarily in neighborhood centers, is larger still— from 30,000 to 60,000 square feet of GLA. A combined supermarket and drugstore can occupy as much as 60,000 square feet of GLA (the average is 50,000), and the trend toward ever larger supermarkets continues, with spaces larger than 80,000 square feet being sought. In addition to space for display and sales, stores that sell food require stock rooms, refrigeration, and freight and loading dock areas. This is particularly true for supermarkets.

Restaurants and Fast Food Services. Freestanding restaurants in a shopping center require easy access from the mall area as well as adequate parking. They also require kitchens, extra wiring and plumbing, and special sanitation services. Restaurants serving liquor are generally larger than those that serve food only, and they may require extra space for bars, bar stools, etc. A sit-down restaurant serving liquor in a regional or super regional center can range in size from 1,900 to 8,500 square feet. In a community or neighborhood center, restaurants serving liquor are usually smaller (1,400–7,600 square feet).

Many restaurants do most of their business in the evening and on weekends and holidays. These hours may not always be compatible with regular shopping hours in enclosed malls, so special provisions have to be made for customer access and for operation of the common areas. To provide for access, restaurants that are expected to stay open later than the mall proper can be located where they can have one entrance to the mall and another to the outside. If mall services are extended to accommodate restaurants, common area pass-through expenses may have to be prorated differently for tenants that operate after hours.

Freestanding fast food operations may require as little as 400 or as much as 3,800 square feet of GLA. In some instances, clearance for a drive-up window and movement of automobiles to and past it may be a consideration. However, each of the major chains and franchises has different leasing stipulations. Most fast food facilities require special parking arrangements and building designs, and these may be at variance with the overall design of the center. No matter what type of food service is provided in a shopping center, well-designed sewer lines and adequate provisions for garbage disposal, pest control, and general sanitation are required.

Food Courts. Most super regional, regional, and specialty malls have some sort of food service. More and more these are *food courts* designed to attract shoppers with a variety of fast food offerings. There is a tendency

T A B L E   4.3

Median GLA of Principal Food Court Tenants in Super Regional and Regional Shopping Centers

Super Regional	Median GLA (Sq Ft)	Regional	Median GLA (Sq Ft)
Chicken	890	Sandwiches	1,250
Pastries	830	Pizza	615
Deli	794	Mexican	586
Seafood	740	Hamburgers	546
Soup/Salads	725	European	532
Hamburgers	710	Potatoes	525
Mexican	700	Oriental	515
Pizza	696	Ice Cream	488
Steak	640	Hot Dogs	461
Ice Cream	630		
Drinks	627		
European	617		
Oriental	604		
Doughnuts	600		
Potatoes	595		
Hot Dogs	588		
Cookies	541		
Yogurt	541		
Popcorn	535		
Sandwiches	528		

From data reported in *Dollars and Cents of Shopping Centers: 1987* (Washington, D.C.: ULI—the Urban Land Institute, 1987). Used with permission.

to cluster the food shops around a common seating area, which may be centrally located or used as a draw to an otherwise "slow" wing of the center. The size of the food court will vary with the size of the center, but the open space should accommodate about thirty-five seats for each food court vendor. The individual food stands are generally small (400–1,300 square feet of space). Table 4.3 shows median GLAs for principal food court tenants in super regional and regional shopping centers.

Food courts are sometimes operated as a single concession by one individual who coordinates the different menus and oversees the business of the individual food stands. In this type of setup, there may be only one central kitchen, supply area, and cold storage room. However, most food courts are comprised of separate fast food operations, each having its own kitchen, although several vendors will sometimes share larger kitchens. Each stall should have its own exhaust system, but a tray-washing area or conveyor belt may be shared by the entire court. Food courts also require extra trash removal and maintenance services and adequate facilities for daily deliveries of food. The usual seating arrangement is tables with chairs or benches, although some larger centers landscape the area with plants or fountains in an effort to set or enhance a particular theme for the food court.

Service Tenants.   Dry cleaners, barbers, beauty parlors, shoe repair services, tailors, laundries, and similar service tenants cater to customers' personal needs. Although they are most often part of a neighborhood or community shopping center, some service tenants do lease space in regional and super regional centers. Strip centers with easy visibility from the street are popular locations for service stores whose square footage requirements are minimal: A shoe repair store in a neighborhood center will occupy about 700 square feet of GLA, a dry cleaner about 1,500, and a barber shop about 650. Because convenience is their primary attraction, service tenants require highly accessible parking. Table 4.4 lists the median GLA of personal service tenants in neighborhood, community, regional, and super regional shopping centers.

Type of Merchandise

Stores are also classified on the basis of the kinds of merchandise or services they offer. There are four general categories of merchandise that are commonly identified and referred to as *GAFO*.

G   General merchandise (hardware, kitchen appliances, dishes, etc.)
A   Apparel (clothing, shoes, accessories, etc.)
F   Furniture (sofas, chairs, beds, major appliances, etc.)
O   Other (food, toys, books, etc.)

Figure 4.2 is an expansion of GAFO to indicate specific merchandise types included in general categories.

Other Classification Factors

The main classifying factor for retail tenants is type of goods sold. Price line, product image, and the type of customer likely to be drawn to the

T A B L E   4.4

Median GLA of Personal Service Vendors (in Square Feet)

Tenant	Neighborhood	Community	Regional	Super Regional
Barber				
National Chain	——	——	——	——
Local Chain	648	689	——	1,090
Independent	612	680	704	728
Beauty				
National Chain	1,200	1,400	1,100	1,146
Local Chain	1,247	1,200	1,232	1,415
Independent	1,184	1,350	1,170	1,322
Cleaners				
National Chain	1,682	1,917	——	——
Local Chain	1,500	1,500	1,500	1,536
Independent	1,470	1,500	1,980	1,500
Formalwear Rental				
National Chain	——	——	1,319	1,201
Local Chain	——	2,200	——	975
Independent	——	1,240	——	930
Health Spa				
National Chain	4,476	4,800	——	——
Local Chain	3,200	4,217	8,449	——
Independent	2,440	2,850	——	——
Key Shop				
National Chain	——	——	240	397
Local Chain	——	——	——	195
Independent	——	——	——	153
Laundry				
National Chain	——	——	——	——
Local Chain	2,238	1,600	——	——
Independent	1,750	1,600	——	——
Photocopy				
National Chain	——	1,159	1,110	1,091
Local Chain	——	1,000	——	1,071
Independent	——	1,100	——	450
Shoe Repair				
National Chain	——	——	——	350
Local Chain	700	——	——	521
Independent	744	510	720	550
Travel Agent				
National Chain	——	——	——	900
Local Chain	1,200	1,000	895	765
Independent	1,160	900	700	755

From data reported in *Dollars and Cents of Shopping Centers: 1987* (Washington, D.C.: ULI—the Urban Land Institute, 1987). Used with permission.

FIGURE   4.2

Retail Tenant Classifications

General Merchandise
Department store
Discount department store
Junior department store
Showroom/catalog store
Variety store

Clothing and Accessories
Bridal shop
Children's wear
Costume jewelry
Family wear
Hosiery
Jean shop
Ladies' ready-to-wear
Ladies' specialty
Leather shop
Maternity
Men's wear
Uniform shop

Shoes
Athletic footwear
Children's shoes
Family shoes
Ladies' shoes
Men's and boys' shoes

Home Furnishings
Bath shop
China and glassware
Curtains and drapes
Cutlery
Floor coverings
Furniture
Lamps

Home Appliances and Music
Computer/calculator
Gourmet cookware
Musical instruments
Radio, video, stereo
Records and tapes
Sewing machines

Gift and Specialty
Books and stationery
Cards and gifts
Luggage and leather

Hobby and Special Interest
Arts and crafts
Bicycle shop
Cameras
Coin shop
Game store
General sporting goods
Hobby
Toys

Food Service
Restaurant without liquor
Restaurant with liquor
Cafeteria
Fast Food
Cookie shop
Doughnut shop
Ice cream parlor
Muffin shop
Pretzel shop
Sandwich shop
Yogurt shop

Food
Supermarket
Convenience market
Bakery
Candy and nuts
Delicatessen
Health food
Specialty foods

Hardware
Home improvements
Paint and wallpaper

Personal Services
Barber shop
Beauty shop
Dry cleaner
Film processing
Formal wear rental
Health club
Key shop
Laundry
Photocopy and fax service
Shoe repair
Travel agent
Video tape rentals
TV and appliance repairs

Financial Services
Automated Teller Service
 (ATM)
Banks
Insurance
Real estate
Savings and Loans

center by a particular retailer are all additional factors in classifying retail businesses. Goods themselves can be further differentiated as fashion or convenience items, classifications that can influence the distance customers are willing to travel to purchase them. *Destination purchases* are those items a customer will make a special trip to buy. For example, furs or sporting goods will draw customers from a greater distance than will grocery and cosmetic items. Chewing gum, pantyhose, cigarettes, and magazines—items bought at the spur of the moment by customers who are usually on their way to another store—are *impulse purchases*. Food service also varies with image and price line: A sit-down restaurant requires a clientele with both time and money to spend, while a fast food operation can be sustained by customers in a hurry who may have less money to spend. Within each of these broader categories, there are other, more subtle distinctions as well.

Many of the final decisions about tenant selection will be based on the type of shopping center the owner is planning. Some established department and chain stores have created a niche for themselves and appeal to a particular segment of the consumer market. They enjoy customer loyalty. They know who their customers will be at a given time and how much those customers are likely to buy. The issue to be resolved is whether the shopping center as a whole will cater to the customers that a particular store will attract. If demographic studies indicate that consumers in the center's trade area are looking for a different type of merchandise, a business like this would not be the optimal choice for tenancy.

Certain retailers have a higher profile than others. They advertise more extensively, are better known among consumers generally, and are considered leaders in their particular fields. Typically these high-volume businesses are very much in demand. That demand, coupled with their usually strong credit ratings, gives them a strong position from which to negotiate lease terms, including lower per-square-foot rental rates. The fact that large retailers occupy large store spaces from which they generate large sales volumes means the income to the center from their rents will be similarly large. The business they attract to the center will generate sales for the other tenants and thus enhance their ability to pay rent, including percentage rents. If the cost of development in the trade area drives up market rents, the tenant's ability to pay a substantial rent may become a top priority.

DETERMINING TENANT MIX

As indicated in chapter 3, the leasing plan is a guide to identifying suitable retailers and defining an appropriate tenant mix for the particular center. The goal should be to create synergism among the retailers. *Synergism* is the beneficial effect of the individual retailers upon each other as they operate within the center as a whole. For an enclosed mall, it is important to create an overall image that is recognized by its customers as unique and not an exact replica of every other shopping center they have ever seen. In a neighborhood or community shopping center, image and uniqueness are less important than having a viable mix for that location. A shopping center gains character over time, but the initial choice of tenants can set it on the path to success from the day it opens. Two important guidelines

FIGURE   4.3

Creating the Ideal Tenant Mix

- Number and GLA of individual spaces (leasing plan)
- Space allocation based on merchandise categories (type and size of center, trade area data, anchor tenants)
- Anchor tenant selection (type of merchandise, price lines, image, customer loyalty)
- Competition (presence or absence of specific retailers and/or types of merchandise)
- Community needs (met and unmet)

will help create an optimum tenant mix: (1) the GLA of the shopping center and the percentage of this GLA to be devoted to certain merchandise categories, and (2) the compatibility of selected tenants. The point to be avoided is the one at which repetition of retailers—for example, the number of shoe stores—becomes category overkill. Sometimes the tenant composition of competing malls and strip centers can guide decisions about depth and breadth of merchandise, keeping in mind that regional, community, neighborhood, convenience, and specialty centers each work best with different groupings of tenants.

Finding the right group of tenants requires some research. The leasing agent has to know how many spaces in the subject center are to be leased and how big they are, how much square footage should be devoted to each category of merchandise, the anchor tenant in the subject center, the most popular chain stores and franchises in the trade area, merchandise categories that are lacking in the trade area, and the needs of the community (figure 4.3).

The leasing plan is the source for information on GLA, although individual tenant units may not remain as they were first planned. Depending on the negotiating power of a specific retailer and the financial capabilities of the center owner, an individual space may be expanded or redesigned to suit a particular retailer's needs.

The space devoted to specific categories of merchandise depends on the type and size of the shopping center, characteristics of the trade area, and the preferred anchor tenants. Various rules of thumb apply: Some professionals recommend 60 percent of the units in regional malls for fashion retailers, 20 percent for gift and leisure retailers, 15 percent for restaurant and food retailers, and 5 percent for service tenants. (See also table 3.1.) Merchandise prices also have to be considered. The question here is one of range and how broad or narrow to define it. Comparatively high-priced merchandise appeals to one part of the market while comparatively low-priced merchandise appeals to another. The diversity and overall mix should work well to meet the needs of the immediate trade area.

Many other issues influence the types and proportions of merchan-

FIGURE   4.4

**Ancillary Retailers Typically Associated with
Grocery and Fashion Anchors**

Grocery Store Anchors	Fashion Anchors
Beauty and barber shops	Art galleries
Card and gift shops	Audio and video
Drug stores	Bookstores
Dry cleaners	Bridal shops
Electronics stores	Jewelry stores
Fabric stores	Kitchenware stores
Florists	Luggage shops
Liquor stores	Shoe stores
Newsstands	Toy stores
Optical stores	Tuxedo rental shops
Tanning and health spas	Women's, men's and children's apparel shops
Video rentals	

dise categories within a particular shopping center. Anchor tenants play a major role in establishing tenant mix because specific types of ancillary tenants seem to be commonly associated with particular anchor tenants (figure 4.4), and these groupings actually define the type of center that results. The types of retailers in the trade area and in competing shopping centers—and their comparative success in the marketplace—can be a powerful influence. The leasing agent has to learn what works (or doesn't work) in those centers, how and why (or why not) the tenants in centers similar to the subject center are compatible, and whether the area is saturated with certain types of retailers.

Certain retailers naturally complement each other's business while others, when combined, naturally detract from each other. In general, shopping centers should strive for a good mixture of both competing and noncompeting businesses. In large centers, it is common to lease space to several retailers that sell the same type of goods. Assuming there is enough traffic at the site, competition is not necessarily a disadvantage for similar businesses because consumers are more likely to shop at a center where they are offered a greater selection. Competing businesses generally result in an overall increase in traffic flow. Grouping related businesses—men's clothing, shoes, and sporting goods; women's clothing and shoe stores; and children's clothing and toy stores—increases the volume of sales for each of them. Service-oriented businesses such as hair dressers, shoe repair shops, and tailors are also compatible. Grocery stores, butchers, delicatessens, bakeries, and candy stores make good neighbors, too.

With so many national chains seeking space, regional shopping centers from coast to coast are beginning to look like carbon copies of each other. If an agent makes a conscious effort to lease a certain percentage of a center's space to small businesses from the area, that shopping center will have a distinctive tone. Although smaller businesses often pose a greater risk for shopping center owners because they lack the staying power of chain stores, these retailers add an air of novelty and excitement for which there is no substitute. The suitability of such businesses to a particular center will depend on the center's size and the retailer's potential to succeed in it. Common tenants for different types of centers along with their varied space requirements are indicated in table 4.5 and below.

- *Super regional and regional centers.* Very large shopping centers draw customers from a wide trade area and therefore often appeal to a broader economic base. Retailers that function best in these centers offer different grades and types of merchandise at varied prices. The differences in tenant mix between super regional and regional centers are minor. Although fashion retailers are predominant, both regional and super regional centers include a large variety of ancillary shops. Because of their larger size, super regional centers may have a slightly wider selection of stores than regional centers and a greater number of stores offering one particular category of merchandise. Regional centers commonly include bank service centers and optical chain stores, perhaps because these centers are often located closer to residential communities that do not have these services readily available. Either of these businesses might occupy a freestanding space outside the main building. Super regional or large regional centers may also reserve a certain portion of their GLA for recreational or community use.
- *Community centers.* These centers usually serve the needs of a specific community rather than drawing customers from a larger trade area. Often they are anchored by junior department stores, discount stores, or variety stores—occasionally by a supermarket. Ancillary tenants can represent most merchandise categories, although there are usually fewer stores in each category in community centers than in regional centers. In this type of center, too many competing stores tend to detract from each other's business rather than contribute to customer traffic. Stores that offer personal services— beauty shops, barbers, travel agents, dry cleaners—are generally successful ancillaries in community centers.
- *Neighborhood centers.* Anchored by supermarkets or a combination supermarket and drugstore, neighborhood centers are meant to fill the everyday needs of consumers living within the immediate area. Typical ancillary tenants offer food or food products and personal

T A B L E   4.5

Median GLA of Tenants Most Frequently Found in Shopping Centers (in Square Feet)

	Super Regional	Regional	Community	Neighborhood
General Merchandise				
Department Store	155,106	93,600	——	——
Discount Dept.	——	——	55,500	——
Junior	——	——	45,684	——
Food				
Superstore	——	——	36,699	——
Supermarket	——	——	24,928	23,500
Health Food	——	1,650	——	——
Candy and Nuts	666	660	——	——
Food Service				
Restaurant with Liquor	4,608	5,000	4,000	3,200
Restaurant without Liquor	——	——	2,905	2,250
Fast Food	773	796	1,700	1,931
Drugs				
Super Drugstore	——	——	13,292	13,280
Drugstore	——	——	——	6,000
Specialty and Gifts				
Toys	3,547	——	——	——
Cards and Gifts	2,404	2,667	2,532	2,310
Books	3,370	3,125	2,385	——
Clothing				
Ladies' Ready-Made	3,567	3,600	2,900	2,000
Men's Wear	3,000	3,000	3,000	——
Jeans Shop	2,869	3,000	——	——
Ladies' Specialty	2,309	2,375	2,000	1,630
Shoes				
Family	3,125	3,270	2,872	——
Ladies'	1,562	1,774	——	——
Men's and Boys'	1,267	1,268	——	——
Jewelry	1,290	1,250	1,400	1,200
Appliances				
Records and Tapes	2,500	2,400	——	——
Radio, video, stereo	2,454	2,295	2,083	——
Liquor	——	——	——	2,500
Personal Services				
Cleaners	——	——	1,500	1,500
Videotape Rentals	——	——	——	1,268
Beauty Salon	——	——	1,280	1,200
Travel Agent	——	——	——	1,200
Barber Shop	——	——	——	650

From data reported in *Dollars and Cents of Shopping Centers: 1987* (Washington, D.C.: ULI—the Urban Land Institute, 1987). Used with permission.

services: Delicatessens, bakeries, florists, tanning centers, video sales and rentals, shoe repair services, and liquor stores are all compatible in a neighborhood center. The breadth of merchandise offered depends on the size of the center and the trade area it serves. Generally these centers have few if any apparel stores, although the fast pace of the working mother in today's society is encouraging apparel stores to locate in neighborhood centers. This is a convenience for the working mother who does not have time for the regional shopping center experience.

- *Specialty centers.* Off-price centers include a variety of stores that offer discounted merchandise; often the retailer is the manufacturer or its representative. A discount center may be anchored by a discount department store, with a mix of ancillaries that offer discounted merchandise. Tourist-oriented centers do well with boutiques, arts and crafts shops, jewelry stores, gift and souvenir shops, gourmet food stores, and apparel or other stores offering goods that consumers might not be able to find near home or in an ordinary shopping center. Restaurants or food vendors are good tenants for most specialty centers.

Tenant Compatibility

Good tenant mix is important to achieve a shopping center's maximum potential. Poor placement of tenants or poor choices of retailers result in less compatibility. Prospects will seek out centers that have a good mix. The result of a poor tenant mix is far reaching. Among the problems that must be overcome are (1) poor traffic for the center as a whole, (2) poor or confused image for the center, and (3) weaker sales for everyone—but mostly for the stores that do not fit. For example, locating a coin-operated laundry next door to an automotive parts store in a strip center could lead to problems related to both image and parking: A customer changing oil or repairing his or her car in the parking lot while waiting for clothes to dry in the laundry creates a mess and uses more than one parking space.

The leasing agent should always strive to create the best possible tenant mix. Generally, this means being selective in choosing individual retailers in order to find the tenants that can do the most for the "idealized" mix. One way to visualize an ideal tenant mix is to consider the center as a single department store where all the individual shops are departments in it. Key questions in this regard are whether the shops as a group are compatible with each other and, most especially, whether a consumer would be likely to shop at most of them. Any retailers that do not fit these objectives should not be considered further.

Guidelines for establishing an ideal tenant mix for a specific center can be developed directly by the agent by the following methods.

- Watching demographic changes in the area
- Observing the compatibility of tenant mixes in competing centers
- Evaluating sales of existing tenants
- Talking to the whole spectrum of tenants in a center to find out what does and does not work
- Reading trade journals to find out what is happening elsewhere

Sometimes the problems of a less-than-ideal tenant mix are not discovered until after a shopping center has been open for a while. However, a center that has been established for years can have its dominant merchandise changed radically as individual spaces are re-leased again and again, diluting the original concept. Even in re-leasing, the leasing agent should devote a lot of time to evaluating the market, determining what types of merchandise or services are needed in the area at the present time, and then seeking the best possible tenant replacement.

Early clues to problems of poor tenant mix are low morale among tenants and difficulty in promoting the center as a whole because its market cannot be defined clearly. The response to this is action. Relocating tenants within the center may be a satisfactory solution. Moving tenants out and replacing them with retailers that are a better fit with the developed image for the center may be a necessity. This latter may mean buying out an existing tenant's lease to expedite the change.

Market conditions are a consideration as well. In a slow market, where vacancy levels are high, tenant "mix" may have to be compromised in favor of establishing occupancy and generating rental income. If a less-than-ideal mix must be chosen, the agent should be certain at least that the selected retailers do not compete directly with existing tenants. Another outgrowth of a slow market is a tendency among specialty retailers to broaden their merchandise lines to increase sales. Changes in merchandise offerings have to be monitored so that the variety sought for the center as a whole does not disappear because most of the retailers are offering the same wide array of goods. No shopping center can survive as a collection of "general" stores.

SUMMARY

Tenant mix is the result of selecting different retailers for a particular shopping center. Appropriate tenant groupings and the percentage of each merchandise category that will be represented in the center are determined on the basis of the type of center, its location and size, and trade area demographics—as well as the major anchor tenant. The search for the right tenants is a three-step process—first, development of the leasing plan with the idealized allocation of specific spaces by store type; then segmentation of the market to classify retailers in the area by their characteristics; and, finally, selection of retailers from the different categories in order to create a balanced mix.

Classification of stores depends on several factors:

- *Kind of store* (national chain, regional chain, independent operation). Many shopping center developers seek to balance the ratio between chain stores and independent operations. Temporary tenants boost shopping center sales and add variety to the permanent tenant composition. The decision to use a larger percentage of local retailers versus national retailers or to lease common area spaces to kiosks and pushcarts usually depends on the size, scope, and image of the shopping center itself.
- *Space requirements.* Full-line department stores require more GLA than junior and discount department stores. Chain stores often have standardized GLA requirements to be met; national chains usually require the greatest amount of space. Apparel retailers, drugstores, personal service vendors, and restaurants vary in size from center to center. Certain tenants will also require special operational features (food services have to have refrigeration, for example).
- *Type of merchandise.* What will work best in a particular shopping center depends on that center's size and the trade area it serves. The acronym GAFO indicates the major classifications—general merchandise, apparel, furniture, and other. Merchandise is also categorized by price and product image.

Ancillary tenants should be compatible with anchors. Past experience has indicated that grocery store anchors work most successfully with drugstores, liquor stores, barbers, newsstands, and dry cleaners, among others. Fashion anchors are best supported by jewelry stores, women's and men's apparel stores, bookstores, and similar types of tenants. Tenants that naturally complement each other—women's clothing and shoe stores, for example—work well together. The type of center also influences tenant choice. Three or four shoe stores can compete successfully in a regional center, whereas a community center might have only one. Neighborhood centers usually concentrate on food and personal service vendors rather than fashion tenants.

Tenant selection should also address community needs. Merchandise categories that are lacking in competing centers are possibilities to consider. If there are numerous outlets of the more popular chain stores in the trade area, it may not be able to support another outlet. A good tenant mix will help each tenant maximize sales and will be attractive to lenders, developers, and consumers alike.

Compatibility as a factor in tenant mix becomes even more important when the agent is re-leasing space in an established center or when vacancy levels are high. A poor tenant mix can drive customers away in the best of times; a good tenant mix will draw customers to the center regardless of changes in the market.

5

Prospecting

The process by which the leasing agent seeks out specific retailers to become tenants in a shopping center is called *prospecting*. The search for tenants usually expands over time. One source will lead to another; referrals, business contacts, and other brokers will contribute to an agent's growing list of prospects. Next the agent assesses the desirability of each prospective tenant for a retail space by evaluating that retailer's business history and fiscal stability, a process called *qualifying*. Not every prospect is suitable for space at a particular site; usually only a small number of prospects are qualified for each available space, and only one can rent it.

As a result of effective prospecting, retailers find out whether a particular site will meet their needs, and agents gain in-depth knowledge of the target market and are better equipped to qualify prospective tenants. There is no substitute for prospecting.

LOCATING PROSPECTS

Prospecting develops the agent's ability to handle a wide variety of contacts and to adapt selling techniques to different situations. There are two important ways of locating prospective tenants—by promoting the retail space itself and by actively canvassing for tenants. Together, these two methods will help the agent lease the space as quickly as possible.

Promoting the Retail Space

In order to attract prospective tenants to new or existing retail space, the space and the center as a whole have to be promoted. A major decision regarding such promotion is which aspects of the property to emphasize to the target audience. Different features of a property will appeal more to one type of retail business than to another. The agent has to determine what will interest the particular prospects he or she is seeking. A variety of media are available for promoting retail space, each having specific impact and disadvantages.

Signage. Building signs are one of the best and most important ways to both advertise the property and attract business for the agent's firm. Most center owners will permit an agent to erect a sign on the property identifying the leasing agency and sometimes the owner as well. Properties being developed erect signage before construction begins. This can and should include the leasing agency in addition to the developer, the architect, and the owner.

Signs should be easy to read, with large letters that are readable by people in cars and some distance away from them. Signs should be upright, perpendicular to traffic flow if possible, and maintained in good condition. Signs are intended to attract phone calls, so the amount of information on them should be kept to a minimum—the fact that the property is available or the number of square feet to be leased, an availability date (especially for a new property) and, most important, whom to call. The agent's name, company, and telephone number should be included. Occasionally a sign may suggest a use for the property such as "ideal for restaurants." This is more common where a previous tenant had built in special fixtures that were not removed when the premises were vacated. Signs erected at shopping centers may name a major anchor tenant in an effort to attract specific ancillary tenants. In all circumstances, the contents of signs are the property owner's discretion, but the agent should encourage adherence to the basic principles of clarity and brevity. Size and placement of signs may be regulated by local laws or ordinances.

Outdoor Advertising. Billboards convey concise messages in a relatively limited space, and their message is exposed to a wide range of potential tenants. However, billboard advertising is expensive, and the form may be more suitable for new or expanded shopping centers than for single spaces or freestanding stores. The best locations for such signs are intersections, highways, and transportation depots near the property. The size and content of billboard advertising is influenced by the volume and speed of traffic passing the sign. Generally, billboard copy should do little more than announce that space is available for lease and provide a number to call. The agent or the development company should be named only when that is a selling point in itself.

Other types of outdoor advertising include exterior store signs, decorated barriers on construction sites, paintings on fences and sides of buildings, and window displays. "For Lease" signs posted on construction sites, along with a rendering of the center and the names of major stores and various shops that will be opening there, are commonly used. While these types of advertising would not be the main thrust of the leasing campaign, they can be used effectively as part of a larger promotional program.

Leasing Brochures and Flyers.   Occasionally a direct mail campaign will be undertaken, using inexpensive flyers or fact sheets. Generally, "mass" mailings are not economically feasible, even for major shopping centers; telephone canvassing can be more effective. However, a direct mail campaign may be useful if an agent is seeking a definite type of retailer to fill a specific niche in the tenant mix of the center, and there are several possible prospects to be approached.

A formally printed brochure can be an effective leasing tool for a large shopping center. It can include detailed information about the property, the development company, and the leasing agency, in addition to maps and photographs of the property, relevant traffic and consumer statistics, and demographic data. Content and design of the brochure will depend on both the audience and the message. Color printing and drawings showing people in a finished shopping area add to the impact as well as to the expense of brochures. Such a brochure is particularly useful as a reference tool for prospective tenants. It can be included in the leasing information package provided to prospects or mailed out with a note as follow-up to a face-to-face or telephone contact. Brochures can also be used as a prospecting tool when mailed to a select group of retailers along with other promotional pieces, or they can be used as a way of generally advertising the development company's retail portfolio. When leasing a community or neighborhood shopping center or a small site in a retail strip in an urban area, there is little need for a glossy brochure. (Appendix C includes an example of a leasing plan that is a brochure.)

Promotional Letters.   Another good way to reach prospective tenants through the mail is with personalized letters. These are usually addressed to a narrower market than a brochure mailing would be. Personalized letters can be produced efficiently on a word processor or computer. Minimally they merge a standard form letter with individual addresses and salutations, and it is possible to program specific additions or changes to the body of the letter for greater individualization and impact. A general letter should be short and conversational, describing the property and urging the reader to respond by calling the agent. A more specific letter would focus on features or aspects of the site that the agent expects will appeal specifically to a particular prospect. Although letters can be mailings by themselves, they are usually most effective in conjunction with site submittal packages or as follow-up to other promotional activities. For some applications, letters can be comparatively expensive, especially when greater individualization is required. However, the personalization itself can be an important part of the impact.

Trade Publications. Advertising in trade publications is another way to send the message that new retail space is available. This can be targeted more or less specifically based on the particular publication used. *Women's Wear Daily* and *Restaurant News* are examples of periodicals that reach large numbers of retailers in a specific retailing category. Other publications such as *Stores* (published by NRMA), *Chain Store Age Executive, Shopping Center World,* and *Monitor* (formerly *National Mall Monitor*) are addressed to a wider audience, which includes the entire spectrum of retailers in addition to shopping center development and management personnel. The leasing agent should keep in mind, however, that trade advertising is not a substitute for canvassing. In general, it is a way to target national rather than local retailers. Its best use is to supplement other promotion rather than as a major campaign in itself.

National Meetings and Conventions. Agents leasing large properties should especially consider attending the annual conventions of the International Council of Shopping Centers (ICSC) and the National Retail Merchants Association (NRMA). ICSC sponsors dealmaking sessions each fall as well as local and regional "idea exchange" meetings. These and other shopping center-related gatherings are opportunities for the leasing agent to meet developers, property managers, marketing directors, and fellow brokers whose experience and expertise can provide valuable insights into the leasing business.

Retailers' conventions and other national meetings are potential promotional opportunities, although these gatherings are attended by leasing agents less often. Each season, buyers for large department stores and small retailers themselves attend conventions where manufacturers present their new merchandise. These conventions are usually classified by the types of goods or services they represent, such as the United Jewelry Show, the Greeting Card Association convention, the National Housewares Manufacturers Association exposition and trade show, the National Boutique Show, and the International Fur Show. Some trade shows repeat in one location while others convene at a different location each time. So-called market weeks are held in New York, Dallas, Los Angeles, and other major cities several months before a new season to give retailers a look at new lines of merchandise. Attending these conventions affords the leasing agent an opportunity to meet the retailers or retail franchisors that attend these meetings. The hope is that they will remember the agent's firm when they are relocating or expanding in the future.

Community Involvement and Business Entertainment. Local real estate boards, property management associations, and financial institutions—even service organizations like the Rotary Clubs—are interested in commercial projects and their impact on the local economy. One can generate and foster goodwill by guiding tours of stores and shopping centers or making speeches about retail space before community groups. Such activities provide a subtle form of *institutional advertising* that develops name recognition without reference to leasing as such.

Personal contact with prospects increases communication and develops trust, both of which facilitate business deals. Working side by side with retailing people on committees and planning boards offers the leasing agent a way to develop business contacts directly. Socializing with business contacts can help the agent build up his or her clientele as well as expedite leasing a specific property. Entertaining should be a pleasure for both agent and prospect. Among the many opportunities for business entertainment are lunch or dinner meetings that allow discussion of business in a relaxed, congenial atmosphere without other distractions. Such opportunities often occur in the context of a convention or other type of gathering, and the sharing of a meal provides a way to personalize a meeting. Breakfast meetings, refreshments after work, or small parties are other possibilities. The agent can also offer tickets to concerts, sporting events, or the theater. Not every form of entertainment will be suitable for every client, however—personal preferences and individual tastes have to be taken into account. The objective of the entertainment and its cost are also important considerations because of changes in the income tax laws regarding business expenses.

In addition to activities involving prospects, the agent should maintain social contacts with other real estate professionals who can provide referrals. Membership and active participation in professional organizations enhance an agent's skills and credentials while providing professional and social interaction with individuals who are having similar experiences. There are a number of real estate organizations whose activities are related to leasing, including the Institute of Real Estate Management (IREM) which has numerous local chapters. The Urban Land Institute (ULI) and the International Council of Shopping Centers (ICSC) are organizations whose activities focus on development, leasing, and management of retail properties.

Canvassing

Canvassing involves contacting local retailers or representatives of national and regional chains in an effort to interest them in relocating or expanding to sites that the agent represents. There are primarily two types of canvassing—telephone and personal. Both allow the agent to acquire information about lease expiration dates, expansion plans, and competitive sites. Although canvassing is often time-consuming and does not usually produce immediate results, it does expand an agent's network of contacts and helps qualify prospects for future listings.

Resources.   When canvassing, an agent should use as many available resources to locate potential tenants as possible. Both *Chain Store Guide— Directory of Leading Chain Stores in the United States* and the *Retail Tenant Directory* list categories of merchandise and the names of individual retailers within those categories. They also show the number of outlets each retailer operates and the name of each company's leasing contact in the area. *Crittenden Retail Space News* is a weekly newsletter that tracks retailers' leasing activities with lists of contacts for items reported in each issue. These references are most helpful to the agent interested in leasing space to a national or regional chain store. *Leasing Opportunities,* published annually by ICSC, lists retailers seeking space as well as centers with space to lease. As a guide to local businesses, the yellow pages of the telephone directory will provide the agent with an overview of the trade area market. Local business news publications (for example, *Denver Business Journal*) and locally published directories such as *The Retail Guide to Metro Denver* and *Manhattan Retail Space Market* are more specific sources for leasing prospects. Newspaper ads for sales and promotions by local retailers not only suggest prospects but also demonstrate the image and merchandising styles of different stores.

One of the best methods of locating prospects is word of mouth. Retailers in a downtown area will probably know about other businesses that are looking for new locations; likewise, tenants in an established shopping center will have definite ideas about retailers whose presence would help increase their own trade. Members of the business community and others involved in activities related to retailing will know which retailers are looking for space to rent. People involved in planning commercial buildings, owners or managers of large department stores, and real estate developers are other good sources. Both the chamber of commerce and the utility companies have contacts with local retailers, and financial institutions and mortgage bankers are in a position to know about contract negotiations and plans for expansion. Other possible resources are people who regularly do business with retailers—stationery suppliers, signmakers, wholesalers, store fixture and display manufacturers, etc. Agents can assume that prospects referred to them will be reliable tenants because they are already known to the referral source, and prospective tenants will likely be more accessible to an agent who comes to them through a mutual acquaintance or business contact.

F I G U R E   5.1

Referral Source Card

Person _____Title _____

Firm _____

Address _____City _____

State _____ Zip _____ Phone _____

Spouse Name _____Children _____

Interests _____

Prospect Reference(s)	Contact Date	Results Achieved

Referral Source Contact Notes (include contact dates)

Referral sources are important contacts to develop, and the agent should keep track of individual referrals and successful leasing outcomes that result from them. Figure 5.1 is an example of a form that can be used to keep track of information about referral sources. The top part of the form provides space for the agent to record the contact's name, business title or position, company, and telephone number as well as personal information about his or her family and interests. (The latter can be useful in maintaining future contacts with the individual.) The middle portion of the form can be used to identify specific prospects referred by the source along with notes about the results of approaches to them. There is also space to note when the agent spoke to or met with the referral source and the outcome of those contacts. Whether this type of information is recorded on a printed form or written on cards or stored in a computer, it is a reminder to the agent to keep in touch with such contacts.

Skillful canvassing takes practice and experience. The agent has to be prepared for rejection because many more prospects will be canvassed than can actually become tenants. Even though several canvassing calls may be required to generate a tenancy, the calls themselves can be beneficial. The agent gains experience dealing with retailers' representatives along with added insight into the market. The agent will find out the types of retailers currently operating in the market, their space requirements, and their financial status—as well as lease expiration dates, which can help the agent plan future leasing activities if the information can be obtained.

Ultimately, canvassing is an excellent way of enhancing the agent's reputation—as a professional and as a knowledgeable business contact. Leasing agents work hard at building a network of referral sources. Once this network is established, the leasing firm will generally be sought out by prospects who have heard of the firm's success by word of mouth.

Cooperating with Other Agents.   Maintaining open communications with other leasing agents and agencies in the area is another way to locate prospective tenants and keep up to date on market conditions. Such cooperation can be both internal (within the same leasing firm) and external (outside the firm), with the cooperating agents sharing information about good sites and possible tenants. Agent cooperation can multiply the effectiveness of a leasing campaign because more people become involved in matching prospects and available spaces. However, only a small percentage of retail leasing transactions result from cooperative endeavors.

Agent cooperation can take several forms. An agent may have been showing space to a particular prospect for some time without success. For one reason or another, the various locations do not suit the client's needs. However, the agent knows another agent who has a listing for a location that might be suitable. The first agent contacts the second agent, makes an appointment, and the two of them meet the prospect at the site. If the prospect decides to lease the space, the two agents will split the commission. Conversely, the second agent might have initiated the cooperation because he or she was having difficulty leasing a specific space and knew that the first agent represented a prospect who was difficult to place in the right space. By constantly thinking of ways to match a prospect's needs with available space, the leasing agent can increase the chances of earning a commission in a soft market and, as a result, close more deals.

Retail spaces are often few in number, yet most of these locations are easily visible—vacant store fronts really stand out—and leasing agents in the community can quickly learn when new vacancies occur. In fact, it is difficult to keep vacancies a secret. In general, the brokerage community is small, and agents operating within a certain area often know each other by name. A good reputation in the community is important for the agent who intends to benefit from cooperation. Agents whose practices are unscrupulous or who refuse to sign cooperation agreements are to be avoided. Leasing agents who enter cooperative arrangements should define the terms of their cooperation with written agreements and always maintain the highest professional standards. (Broker cooperation agreements were discussed in chapter 1, and an example is included in appendix A.3.)

Telephone Canvassing. Telephone *canvassing,* sometimes referred to as *cold calling,* is a necessary preliminary to personal canvassing. The aim of the telephone conversation should be to determine whether the prospect is interested and to arrange a personal interview at another time.

A prospective tenant is more likely to respond favorably if the agent who calls is well-informed and seems genuinely interested in that particular retailer's business. "Cold" calling never means unprepared. Before actually making a call, the agent should know as much as possible about the retailer's business, its space requirements, and its financial status. (The latter can be found in annual reports from large companies.) To sell the prospect on the site, the agent has to be prepared to show facts about local and national market conditions, standard rental rates, and the status of competitors, most of which can be compiled from the market analysis performed earlier (see chapter 2). Ideally, the agent should be able to recommend a space on the basis of the prospect's potential ability to do more business at that location. A good match between consumer demographic data for the trade area and the customer profile of the prospect's business is key to this. When canvassing by telephone, technique is extremely important. A good speaking voice and the ability to listen carefully and patiently are required. Usually the first person the agent will talk to is a secretary or a receptionist. However, the agent's efforts should be directed to the leasing decisionmaker in the company. The agent's firm will usually have a master list of the names of real estate managers for large national retailers. If there is no listing for a particular company, the agent can usually obtain this information by calling their switchboard and asking for the real estate department or for the person responsible for real estate decisions. When approaching a small company, the agent will most likely be dealing directly with the president who handles all business transactions, including real estate. Among local or independent retailers, the owner of the store is usually the person to contact. If the person the agent wishes to talk to is not available, the agent should leave a message or call again later. Messages left should include the caller's name and the name of the leasing firm, but specific information about the retail site need not be given. In speaking to the decisionmaker, the agent should get straight to the point. The object of the call is to set up an appointment, not to undertake a leasing transaction. The discussion should be as general as possible but focused to create sufficient interest in the property that the prospect will want to discuss more specific details in person.

Telephone canvassing is not a casual activity; it is a professional discipline. The professional leasing agent sets goals for a number of telephone

F I G U R E   5.2

Prospect Card

Name of Store _____

Address _____Phone _____

Type of Merchandise _____

Min. Frontage _____GLA Req'd (min-max) _____

Location Req. (mall, strip ctr, CBD, etc.) _____

Date Needed _____Rental Range $ _____per sq ft

Anticipated Sales Volume: _____

Special Needs:

Information About Current Operations:

Store size _____(sq ft)   Sales per sq ft _____

Rent per sq ft _____per Month? _____ per Year? _____

Percentage Rent _____Pass Throughs (Amt) _____

Number of Stores _____Years in Business _____

Sales Volume in Other Locations _____

Principal Contact (Owner, Real Estate Mgr) _____

Banking Institutions _____

Credit Report _____Net Worth $ _____

Indication of Interest _____Negotiations Started _____

Lease Terms Proposed:

Comments:

Date of Contact	Person Contacted	Space Shown	Rate Quoted	Results

calls to complete in a day and establishes a definite time to make those calls so that there will be as few distractions or interruptions as possible. A record should be kept of each call, noting the information gained about current rental rates, lease terms, and expiration dates; the time and date of any appointments made; and an appropriate time to call back, if necessary. These notes can be used later to determine how successful the canvassing campaign has been.

Once the agent begins to identify specific prospects, the information gathered about each prospect has to be available for ready reference. Notes made during canvassing will be used later to screen prospects for follow-up and to determine how well they match with specific space that is available. The agent should use a prospect card (figure 5.2) or its equivalent to record detailed information about each and every prospect contacted. The prospect's space requirements, special needs (separate storage, etc.), current rent paid, and credit information are among the many facts that will be reviewed in the screening process and will be important to negotiations. (Prospecting record keeping is described in more detail in appendix D.)

A more sophisticated approach to cold calling is *telemarketing,* direct telephone promotion that relies on lists available for sale from list brokers. Ideally a telephone campaign should be focused on specific types of merchandise and retailers, and lists of chain stores and franchises in different retail categories are available. Some lists are further categorized by financial status of the retailer or by geographic location (address, zip code). Lists also may be *qualified* (updated) or *unqualified.* The latter are less expensive but are also less likely to be accurate. Investment in these kinds of lists is not justifiable for all properties so telemarketing as such is not always a viable approach. Telemarketing is more popular in office leasing than in retail leasing because the numbers of sites and potential tenants justify the expense and effort.

The Personal Visit.   In the initial stages of leasing, much time will be spent talking to potential tenants in their places of business, making new contacts and generating interest in both the retail site and the leasing firm. Personal canvassing is part of the process of assessing the prospect's suitability for the retail space being offered. If a prospect does seem suitable, arrangements can be made for a second interview or a tour of the retail site.

The first step in personal canvassing is to plan a specific route. Businesses closest to the retail site may be among the most promising prospective tenants. Beyond them, the agent can expand the route in concentric circles, eventually covering the entire trade area. Traveling beyond the trade area itself, the agent can seek out retailers whose success in one location could justify expansion into a "new" territory by setting up an additional store in the center the agent represents. It is also important to budget enough time for each canvassing call. Thirty to forty-five minutes is usually sufficient for an initial meeting; less time may not permit the agent to convey the necessary information, and more time may intrude on the prospect's busy schedule. If a prospect seems interested in extending the meeting, the agent should be flexible enough and adequately prepared to do this. It should be remembered, however, that an appointment for a second meeting will permit preparation of an information package that has been tailored for the particular prospect.

Proper timing of the call is also crucial. Often the success of prospecting depends on the agent's ability to determine when a potential tenant will be receptive to a canvassing call. Calls can be scheduled in advance of lease expiration or renewal dates, and that information can be obtained in advance when canvassing by telephone. If the agent knows a prospect's current lease will expire within, say, six months, a visit should be scheduled as soon as possible; a prospect whose lease expires a year in the future can be targeted for contact at a later date. Timing is important, not only for the agent who wants to lease a space quickly but also for the prospect who must make a decision to move and then prepare to do so. A calendar will help the agent keep accurate records of prospects' lease renewals and structure canvassing activities efficiently.

Preparation for the canvassing call requires careful observation of the prospect's current location, including the building, the neighborhood, and adjacent businesses. This will help the agent identify features that are lacking at the prospect's present location and likely be sought at a new location—in other words, which features of the new retail site to emphasize.

Mastery of the art of asking questions will maximize the amount of relevant information obtained from the prospect during the meeting. Good questions are *open-ended;* they invite more than a simple "yes" or "no" response. Examples are questions that ask "what," "how," and "why," and are geared to the prospect's specific situation. Not only the questions but the manner of asking them will establish the agent's level of professionalism and experience. Asking well-chosen questions and learning to listen carefully to the prospect's responses are important components of personal canvassing.

The agent's ultimate objective is to present the retail site in as attractive a light as possible. Models, drawings, photographs, and even videotaped presentations can be brought to meetings to give prospective tenants a clearer idea of the actual or anticipated appearance of the property. Portable presentations are especially valuable when preleasing a retail property that is still under construction. Retailers are more likely to lease space in a property still under construction if they can visualize the finished site.

What the retailer wants to know is whether relocating or expanding will be to its advantage. The agent answers this challenge by describing the features or characteristics of the property and indicating the benefits that are expected to result from these features. Each site will have a specific attraction for an individual prospect, and the agent has to determine in advance what this attraction might be. Location is paramount, and demographic data that will support sales expectations are very important. Except for major tenants, features and benefits attributable to location and trade area market are likely to be the best selling points. The leasing agent can stimulate a retailer's interest in a property and increase the chances of leasing space in it by selecting features of the site that will appeal to the retailer as a prospective tenant and translating those features into specific tenant benefits.

Site Visit.   Showing the retail site is a major step in prospecting. Generally the agent will show only a few sites or spaces that have been carefully chosen to interest the prospect. A junior department store requiring 30,000 square feet of GLA usually will have fewer choices than a women's shoe store requiring only 2,500. When size requirements are smaller, the agent can show several spaces with areas that are within 500 to 1,000 square feet of the prospect's stated GLA preference. However, there may be only one or two possible spaces to show a retailer with large space requirements, and the selling point for those spaces may have to be their adaptability. If the agent is leasing space in a new center or in one that is undergoing renovation, it is acceptable to show the site under construction. However, the agent who is leasing spaces at more than one center should show prospects at least one site that is completely finished.

   If a prospect is a national chain store or a business that will occupy a large space, it is appropriate to mail a site presentation packet before the tour. This collection of facts about the property derived from the market survey should be tailored to the anticipated needs or desires of the individual prospect. The materials may be presented as a book or portfolio with a photograph of the property or some other appropriate illustration on the cover. The cover should also name the agent and the site and, for new properties, the development company. A special touch is to name the prospect as well.

   The contents of the presentation packet will vary with the size of the property and the degree of detail that is necessary. Standard items include:

1. Demographic data for the trade area, including per capita expenditures for different retail categories (especially those of or related to the prospect)
2. Area maps, aerial photographs, architectural drawings, or photographs of the building and neighborhood showing the site in relation to its surroundings

3. A map of the shopping center site, drawn to scale, showing various access routes and parking lot layout and accessibility
4. Distances and driving times between key points on the map and the retail site
5. Availability of public transportation
6. Traffic counts for main thoroughfares and streets that feed into them
7. Pedestrian counts in urban areas (divided into numbers of men, women, and children if appropriate)
8. The gross leasable area (GLA) of both the site and the individual spaces, as well as the size of the property as a whole
9. The numbers of parking spaces planned for each type of tenant (parking ratios, parking index)
10. Which retailers, if any, have already committed to lease there
11. All features of the property other than the retail space itself—common areas, movie theaters, health clubs, etc.
12. The estimated completion date (if the project is unfinished) and construction details such as interior finishing standards that may affect tenants

Future tenants will also be interested in the types of utilities provided at the site and in other details that can affect their businesses—landscaping, lighting, sidewalks, parking facilities, etc. They may also want to know if any new highways are being planned nearby or if existing highways are likely to be widened or otherwise altered. These details can be indicated on maps or site plans included in the package.

Such an elaborate site presentation packet may not be necessary—or practical—for showings of multiple sites to a prospect whose business is relatively small. Instead, the prospect should receive an individualized fact sheet for each property so that comparison of different ones can be facilitated. Basic demographic data about the trade area should be included, along with other pertinent information such as zoning laws and traffic counts and a description of the property itself.

The agent should plan the route to be taken to and through the site and prepare a checklist of the features to be covered during the tour. The tour should show off the neighborhood to its best advantage. Half a day is usually sufficient for showing several retail sites; however, the tour should never be rushed. Prior timing of the drive to the center and a walk-through of each site will establish minimum time requirements. If the visitor represents an out-of-town regional or national chain, the agent may wish to provide a map showing the locations of competitors, major highways with access routes, and other pertinent data that may be pointed out enroute.

The shortest, most direct route to the property is advisable when time is limited. However, if the prospect has the time, the drive can be extended through the surrounding area. The approach to the site itself is also important: Right turns being easier to make, the property will appear more accessible if entered via a right-hand turn.

Once at the property, the prospect's attention should be focused on the site's unique features and benefits. The representative of a national chain may be interested in the atmosphere of the site and general business conditions, while local or independent retailers may already be familiar with the area and are likely to concentrate more on the space itself. Prospects will likely ask questions about neighboring tenants or special features, such as storage space or employee parking, and all prospects will be interested in the anticipated tenant mix.

Although specific rental rates and possible concessions have to be discussed eventually, it is best to avoid mentioning rents during a site visit. Even indicating a range of rates can lead to difficulties because a prospect will want the rent to be at the lower end of the range, and that may not be the actual rent for the space leased. Nor should promises be made regarding tenant improvements or other allowances. What the agent can talk about are market rents in the trade area or concessions that are granted at comparable sites so the prospect will be better prepared to compare the agent's site-specific data favorably.

To encourage the prospect to compare different sites and their available spaces, the agent should ask specific questions. Instead of an open-ended question, "What did you think about the first location?" an agent might ask, "Do you think the parking lot at the first location would accommodate your volume of customers?" Throughout the site visit, the agent should listen closely to the prospect's observations and comments in order to identify the prospect's priorities.

Telephone follow-up of the tour is an important means of maintaining contact with the prospect. In the first post-visit call, the agent should cover any additional information requested by the prospect during the tour and not available at that time. In subsequent calls from time to time in the future, the agent should ask how the decision-making process is progressing. The prospect should be encouraged to commit to a lease within a certain period. This can be done by asking for a date when space is needed or how long it will take to set up operations in a new location. A prospect might be told that in order to open a new store by June 1, a lease should be signed by April 15 so that any improvements to the space can be completed in time. Prospects can be helped to refine their choices by reiterating aspects of each space they were shown and pointing out how specific features will enhance their business. Prospects may also have to be counseled regarding financial arrangements.

Follow-up by mail is also appropriate. A letter citing the different properties and spaces shown to the prospect and inviting comments or return visits serves two purposes—(1) to highlight for the prospect the distinctions among the various spaces shown, and (2) to formally document the showing to a particular prospect. The documentation is important in case there is any question about the agent's role at the time the commission is determined.

Careful planning combined with advance assessment of each prospect's needs will yield profitable results from the site tours. The agent will have a better chance of closing a deal if the prospect senses that the agent is sincerely committed to finding a suitable location and willing to listen to the prospect's concerns.

QUALIFYING RETAILERS

Once a retailer is identified as a serious prospect, the agent assesses the retailer's overall desirability as a tenant for the site. This process is called *qualifying*. The retailer that presents a clear, consistent, recognizable image from marketing to selling will generally do well. Services offered by a store also indicate a retailer's potential success. The retailer with a reputation for respecting customers and paying attention to their needs will do more business and have bigger profits. Above all, the prospect must be financially capable of supporting a new or additional retail operation.

By investigating a retailer's sales performance, credit rating, expense structure, and general business history, the agent can assess the prospect's potential in a specific location. In dealing with small businesses, personal qualifications—business experience and knowledge, motivation to succeed—are also important considerations. This process of narrowing down the list of prospects is especially important when dealing with independent or local businesses, whose operators may be eager to relocate but not necessarily in an economic position to do so. Only the most highly qualified prospects should be retained on the list.

Determining Prospect Desirability for a Retail Property

Matching locations and suitable prospects is part of the retail leasing agent's goal. The store concept must mesh well with the tenant mix of a particular center and meet specific customer needs. The tenant has to be compatible with the image the shopping center is expected to convey. Compatibility can be assessed by reviewing various elements of the retailer's operations.

Promotion and Merchandise Presentation. The successful store conveys a distinct message to the public through both its merchandise and the way it packages and presents that merchandise. Whether a retailer is trying to attract women who are interested in designer clothes or appeal to teenagers who follow fashion fads, a retailing theme should be evident in every aspect of the business. Customers should be able to recognize an image and know what they can find in that retailer's store.

A visit to a current store location will demonstrate how merchandise is displayed. Clothing should be fresh, in good condition, and neatly folded or hung. Shelves in a supermarket should be well-stocked and inventory checked regularly to make sure the store always has popular items on hand. A department store with large windows should have imaginatively designed displays that show new merchandise attractively. Store fixtures—counter space, glass cases, lights, carpeting, etc.—should be harmonious with the store's image, enhancing the merchandise presentation and creating an aura of customer comfort. Packaging of a product and the manner in which it is displayed significantly influence the consumer to buy. A modern, high-tech decor is more appropriate for a computer center than for a bridal shop.

The leasing agent has to learn the retailer's attitudes and policies regarding promotion and advertising. Consumer advertising is related only indirectly to the leasing agent's concerns, yet it has a significant impact that can be measured in the form of percentage rent—in other words, whether and how much percentage rent a retailer will pay. Generally, the more money and time devoted to advertising, the more profitable a business will be. Retailers spend an average of 2–2.5 percent of their gross sales on promotion, more if a store is new in a market or relocating to a totally different one. The promotional effort should be cohesive and consistent, from the sign on the store's exterior to the logo on its shopping bags.

The type of promotion is just as important as the amount of money spent on it. The successful retailer understands the target market and skillfully directs advertising toward it. A supermarket or drugstore might offer coupons in local newspapers or mail booklets of coupons to consumers in the trade area. Conversely, a furrier will advertise in fashion sections of newspapers or send catalogs to a special mailing list. Creative promotional programs indicate that the retailer takes pride in its merchandise and wishes to present it in the best way possible. Fashion shows, cooking demonstrations, and contests are among the more successful ways to attract shoppers and draw attention to an individual store. Seasonal and holiday-related promotions further reflect strength of commitment.

Customer Service.   The way a retailer treats its customers is another form of promotion that adds to the overall image of a store. In qualifying a prospect, the agent should note what services are available to customers and the extent to which they influence a customer's decision to shop there.

Credit services are common. Large retailers frequently offer their own credit cards in addition to accepting major bank credit cards. Many stores offer layaway plans and installment financing as well. The convenience of buying on credit will attract customers to a store and often encourages them to spend more freely.

Allowing customers to return merchandise promotes good will. Return policies should be posted at the point of purchase or near the merchandise as well as printed on sales receipts.

Some department stores offer alterations on both women's dresses and men's suits, shoe repairs, lessons in the use of appliances, and advice of a professional interior decorator. Supermarkets may offer delivery services, although this is not as common as it once was. For shoppers who are unable to leave their homes, a shopping service may be available. Retailers that cater to the career woman may have a wardrobe coordinator on staff. Large department stores and catalog stores may offer computerized shopping services or video directories. Bridal gift registration and delivery of furniture and appliances are other services frequently extended to customers. Whether such services are free or there is an additional charge should be clearly stated in the store's promotional materials.

The caliber and kind of customer services offered define a retailer's niche in the market. The agent must evaluate whether the retailer fits in with the center's customers and other retailers. A prospect may offer services that clash with the center's image.

Store Hours.   Today's shoppers have little time for leisurely shopping trips. They tend to shop after work or during lunchtime but make major purchases on weekends, often on Sundays. Stores that are open weekday evenings and Sunday afternoons offer a welcome convenience. Within a shopping center, all stores should maintain the same hours, with extended hours for holiday shopping. Freestanding stores should arrange their hours to suit the needs of shoppers in the area. Convenience grocery stores that stay open all night are the exception. Some major grocery chains feature 24-hour operations, and restaurants with liquor licenses may be open past midnight in some areas; but direct customer access to them precludes other stores in the same center having to maintain comparable hours.

Personnel.   Sales clerks and store managers should reflect the image of the store and serve customers to the best of their ability. The way personnel are dressed and groomed, their knowledge of the merchandise, the method in which they handle difficult situations such as dissatisfied customers or returns, and their style of selling contribute to the store's image and success. All personnel should be properly trained by the retailer. Sales people are the prospect's representatives to the public. Their performance can make the difference between success and failure of a retail venture.

Housekeeping.   A clean, well-kept store is more likely to attract customers than a dirty one and indicates that the owner or manager takes a strong interest in the way the store is operated. Floors should be swept, vacuumed, or mopped daily, and there should be sufficient room between display racks for customers to move freely. Merchandise should be folded neatly or displayed on hangers, and objects on counters should be arranged in an orderly fashion. Employees' uniforms should be clean and well-pressed, and their dressing rooms should be fresh and free of clutter. Trash should be disposed on a regular basis. Restaurants have to pay particular attention to housekeeping and garbage disposal because unsanitary conditions readily develop where food is prepared. (Local jurisdictions normally require that restaurants pass an inspection by the health department in order to operate.)

Business History and Fiscal Stability

A prospective tenant should have a business history that indicates a potential to succeed in a new location. A retailer's financial strength, credit rating, sales performance and profit margins, expansion plans, and overall business reputation are investigated as part of the qualification process. An independent store owner's personal qualifications should be examined as well because they, too, play a role in successful retailing. Also to be considered is the amount of time required for relocation and set-up to open a new store. It is important to remember that large national chains generally have established reputations and credit ratings. The same information may not be as readily available for small, independent operations. Because of this, the latter may require careful monitoring during their first few years in a new location.

Financial Strength.   Prospects should be asked to submit a financial statement outlining the income and expenses of the business during the most recent year of operation, including gross sales, taxes, and net profit. Loan obligations or other outstanding debt financing should also be listed. Retailers should willingly discuss their financial situation as it relates to leasing at a new location because financial strength is an important consideration in lease negotiations with the property owner. However, some prospects may be reluctant to provide information about finances or other relevant aspects of their businesses because of concerns that competitors or others may be able to use it to advantage. All such information should be considered confidential and treated as such, and each prospective tenant should be assured of this confidentiality up front.

Another important factor is how long the prospect has been in business, both at the present location and at any previous locations. The longer a business has been in operation, the stronger a tenant it will be.

However, newcomers should not be ruled out. Financial success is more important than the number of years in business. If a women's clothing store has generated enormous profits within two years by capturing a new share of the market, it is certainly healthier financially than a clothing store established in the same market for fifteen years and operating at a steady loss. The older business may no longer be viable, or a new location could revive it. On the other hand, a very new business can be successful early and overexpand without justification. *Each prospect has to be evaluated individually.*

Usually a new business or one that has relocated will not show a profit for several months. Yet the prospective tenant must be able to support the business in the meantime; this means carrying both inventory costs and general expenses, including rent, employee wages, taxes, insurance, etc. Any outstanding debt should be questioned, and a prospect's cash balance should be verified. The owner of the retail space will want to know if the prospect has sufficient funds available to cover security deposits, tenant improvements, new furnishings, and additional inventory.

Credit Rating. Dun & Bradstreet issues a directory listing credit ratings and, in some cases, detailed financial profiles for individual companies. Many large chain store operations are included in that list, and those with a *triple-A rating* are the most desirable tenants in any project. To ensure stability and attract strong ancillary tenants as well as customers, shopping centers are usually anchored by at least one store with a triple-A rating.

Obviously not every tenant in a shopping center will be rated triple-A, but each prospect's creditworthiness has to be verified. In dealing with a small business or a first-time retail tenant, the leasing agent should ask for at least two credit references in addition to references from a former landlord. Calls to suppliers or utility companies will reveal how retailers pay their bills and whether they do so on time. If the prospect is operating a franchise, the agent should find out whether the franchisor is reputable and whether it provides proper training and adequate support for its franchisees. Less-experienced operators should be able to demonstrate to the agent that they can make sound financial plans. Plans for future expansion are a good indication that the prospective tenant is serious about retailing and financially healthy enough to support a new location.

If a prospect's financial statement shows an adequate profit and a reasonable expense structure without excessive debt, and if the present store is well-stocked and customers are buying the merchandise, then that retailer is probably qualified economically for a retail space lease. Conversely, inability to secure references from a previous landlord or refusal to disclose financial information is cause for concern, as is a history of frequent moves. In fact, evidence of tampering with sales records or discrepancies in record keeping would be a sufficient reason to discontinue negotiations.

Reputation. Although there are many different stores within a retail category, there is usually one that stands out from the rest with a name that is easily recognizable to customers. The agent who is looking for a tenant to provide considerable customer draw should not overlook the importance of an established identity in the field of retailing. If the prospect has a certain following within a particular trade area, it is important to determine whether that customer loyalty will extend to shopping at the new location. Some of the prospect's existing stores may have better sales than others, and the reasons for this difference should be explored.

Sales Performance. A retailer's overall sales performance (volume of sales, market share, and number of different store locations) is important. The question is whether the volume of sales a prospect can generate will be commensurate with the volume needed to operate profitably at a new location. A business that has a good selling record in relation to debts and other obligations is more desirable as a tenant than one that does not. The key factor is the ratio of income to debt. A retailer may have a high gross income but a low net revenue because too much is paid out up front to service debts.

Each type of business has different profit requirements; supermarkets operate on a low markup and have to sell almost twice as much per square foot as a shoe store in order to make a reasonable profit. The prospect's current sales per square foot can be used to assess whether the new location will have a positive impact on sales performance. If the new location will yield fewer dollars (lower sales) per square foot than the current location, a move may not be feasible. The agent will also want to verify that merchandise turnover at the prospect's store is sufficient. Stock turnover (discussed previously in chapter 1) refers to the rate at which inventory is converted into sales within a certain period. Generally speaking, the fresher the stock, the more likely it is to sell. Monthly inventory records or operating statements provide a clear indication of stock turnover. However, such records may not be available to the agent. Small businesses may not even generate such data. A visit to the prospect's store a few weeks after the first visit will reveal how quickly stock is turned over. Customer traffic can be readily observed, and physical inspection will show whether a retailer's inventory is adequate and appropriate. Dust on shelves and merchandise clearly signals slow turnover, as do expiration dates that have passed. Large spaces between hangers on clothing racks indicate that inventory is inadequate. Stock turnover is an important measure of a retailer's sales performance. It is a reflection of how well the retailer understands the target market and how to sell to it.

Timing the Store Opening. Although not directly related to business history, it is important to clarify when the retailer will open for business in a new location. If it normally takes two months for a retail business to be fully operational and a prospective tenant will require four months to finish out its space and set up for business, a leasing agent should think twice about offering a lease to that particular prospect. New shopping centers rarely are fully leased at the time of opening; but there is usually an official opening day, and ability to meet that deadline for opening can be an important consideration. Timing of openings to be ready for holidays and heavy sales times demonstrates marketing savvy and a knowledge of consumer shopping habits. Because timing is crucial, the agent should ask prospects about the types of improvements they intend to make at the new location and how long they expect it will take to complete them.

Other Stores and Growth Plans.   In assessing a large retail business, the leasing agent should ask about other store locations and plans for expansion. One indication of a retailer's strength is its ability to operate multiple stores. On the other hand, a shopping center's business can be weakened if a retailer has another outlet located too close to the center; in fact, some retail leases do not allow a tenant to open a new store within a certain distance from the store covered by the lease. (Specific lease clauses are discussed in detail in chapter 7.) The leasing agent should also ask about the volume of business at other existing stores for comparison with the projected sales potential for the new store.

Personal Qualifications.   Not every prospective tenant will be a chain operation with a large staff, a widely known reputation, and published financial statements. A good prospect list will include independent and individually owned businesses, and such prospective tenants should not be judged solely on the basis of business finances. Certain personal attributes of a business owner contribute to success in retailing and are reflected in the individual's motivation, enthusiasm about the business and about its relocation, plans for future expansion, and generation of new ideas for promotions or merchandise display. Intelligence, good communication skills, and salesmanship are additional personal qualifications for success, along with practical knowledge of budgeting and finance, ability to manage people effectively, and understanding of the needs of the consumer marketplace.

Another factor to consider is experience in the business world. Entrepreneurs can be welcome tenants if their goods or services fit the desired tenant mix. However, they will have to be qualified carefully. An individual's skill at making candles at home does not necessarily translate into business acumen, whereas a woman who wants to open a sweater boutique and has previous experience as a buyer of women's clothing in a large department store might be an excellent prospect. In other words, relevant experience can contribute to success; an idea that is merely novel or fashionable may fail to materialize if not packaged properly.

Although the business owner is usually the only individual whose personal qualifications are evaluated, there are certain exceptions to this "rule." For example, if the person opening a haute cuisine restaurant is not a qualified chef, it would be appropriate to verify the credentials of the individual hired as the chef. Anyone leasing space from which to provide professional services—opticians, doctors, lawyers—should have the appropriate qualifications to do so.

SUMMARY

Prospecting, the process of locating, pursuing, and evaluating suitable retailers for a particular space or shopping center, is one of the most important activities of leasing. Without it, no business would be generated. Over a period of time, the leasing agent or the agent's firm may have gained a strong enough reputation that active prospecting is no longer necessary. However, most of the beginning agent's energy will be expended in contacting prospective tenants and others in the retailing business.

Prospecting has two distinct components, both of which can take place simultaneously in the leasing campaign. One is promotion of the retail space itself. The content and cost of a promotional program depend on the size of the property and the type of tenants to be attracted. Signage is one vehicle that works for nearly all types of retail space. For shopping centers with large advertising budgets, direct mail promotion can be effective. Involvement in community affairs, real estate associations, and planning boards, as well as participation in social activities that offer opportunities to network, establish the leasing agent's presence. Attendance at shopping center and retailing-related conventions affords opportunities to make contacts and gather information about retailers' plans for relocation and expansion.

Active canvassing is the other component of prospecting. The method used depends on the type of business the agent is interested in attracting. If the space to be leased is small and the agent's office is located in a retailing district, the agent can simply walk from store to store and approach store owners or managers directly. When leasing space in a large shopping center or dealing with national chain store retailers, the telephone can be used to explore interest in expansion or relocation and to schedule a personal visit. Whatever methodology is employed, the agent has to be prepared to make many calls in order to obtain a single signed lease.

When serious prospects emerge from the canvassing campaign, they can be given a tour of the retail site or sites, and the agent should be prepared to answer the prospect's questions about the retail property and about the trade area. A presentation package can be developed from market survey data and given to prospects prior to the visit. Follow-up by telephone is necessary and appropriate.

Throughout the canvassing effort, the agent is qualifying prospects, eliminating those that would not be suitable tenants. A prospect's suitability is evaluated on the basis of financial background, merchandising policies, current and projected sales volume, and business history. Business practices such as customer service policies and personnel training programs are also relevant issues. When the leased space is in a shopping center, an important consideration is whether a retail business will fit in with other, established retailers—the tenant mix.

Opening a new store or relocating a business is a difficult and challenging venture, moreso for small-scale retail operations. To be successful, a retailer must also demonstrate financial skill, personal drive, and an understanding of the consumer market. Qualifying is the process whereby the agent selects the best possible tenant for a particular space.

6

Shopping Center Design and Tenant Placement

The design of a new shopping center is influenced by both the topography of the property and the types of tenants that will occupy it. Where one retailer is located in relation to the other tenants can affect not only that retailer's business but also the success of the center as a whole.

In designing a shopping center, architects consider the size of the site, its terrain, and the owner's plans for its development. Tenant selection and placement within the center often reflect structural considerations related to size and configuration. The interrelationship among rental rates, ownership profit, and retailer sales performance changes as the size or shape of the center or of an individual space is changed.

Flexibility in store design is crucial. It is certainly present in the new shopping center space that has proliferated in recent years. In order to compete effectively against such new retail developments, older centers are being rehabilitated and revitalized, and this has become an enterprise in itself. It is often more economical to rehabilitate an existing center than to build a new one because most new centers must absorb the high cost of land, pay start-up expenses, and exist on limited income until stabilized occupancy is achieved.

Many elements must come together in the design of a shopping center so that individual spaces can be leased to the best possible retail tenants. These include:

- Flexibility of store design
- Store size (frontage, width, depth)

- Store visibility
- Pedestrian flow
- Parking

For enclosed malls, other common design considerations are a unified theme, length of the pedestrian mall, and placement of food courts. Access for tenants to move merchandise in and out may require provision of double doors or additional (rear) entryways.

The impact of center design is far-reaching. The formal leasing plan lists proposed space allocations, rental rates, specific merchandise lines, and retail tenants based on the physical design of the center. Design will also affect tenant signage, which is very important to all retailers and especially to those leasing space in strip centers. Limitations on interior space construction and even allowable merchandising practices are other elements of the leasing plan that can be affected by the center's physical design.

COMMON ISSUES IN SHOPPING CENTER DESIGN

The architect has two goals: (1) to maximize the desirability of the retail space and (2) to minimize the amount of space that is not used directly for selling purposes. High construction costs challenge the designer to create attractive space at minimum expense. The objective is to have shoppers feel comfortable physically and psychologically. To accomplish this, entrances and exits must be easily accessible, and common areas must be spacious (but not cavernous) and well-lighted. Pedestrian walkways must be wide enough to accommodate groups of shoppers but not so wide that they lose the effect of being able to see shops on both sides of a mall. Shopping center developers work to create a sense of unity by having all storefronts, signage, common areas, and windows of the center share a common design. This is done by integrating the different aspects of the individual retail spaces—size, lighting, display, store depth, layout, visibility, etc.—into one cohesive and functional structure. Also, because a consumer's decision to shop at a particular store or center may be determined by the availability of parking, parking lot design is often as crucial as store design.

Over the years, shopping centers have evolved from the simple, traditional linear shape of the shopping strip to a variety of building forms that are designed to enhance land coverage and retail performance as well as customer flow. Shopping malls (as opposed to strip centers, which generally have all stores open to the outside) are usually enclosed. In such an enclosed mall, issues of form and function are even more relevant. In order for a mall to operate as profitably as possible, its design has to suit its type and size. Malls can be single- or multilevel, built new on open land or developed within renovated structures such as historical buildings, warehouses, and factories. They often feature landscaped common areas, food courts, pedestrian walkways, escalators and elevators, and large parking lots, all of which will contribute to the leasing plan for the shopping center.

Most leasing agents handle retail space that is a finished product as far as design is concerned. Occasionally, however, there may be opportunities to lease retail space that has yet to be developed. In the case of the leasing agent who works for the developer of a new center, the leasing effort may begin long before there is constructed space to show. The design itself may exist only on paper. Ultimately, design will affect the leasing effort in many ways. The type of center and the location of a given space in it will determine visibility, which affects desirability, which ultimately affects rental rates. Other design considerations relate to the tenant's perspective; these include the center's potential to attract customers and the individual retailer's space requirements.

Store Design

Retail space design emphasizes visibility and the connection between display and sales. The design aspects of individual store spaces that are most relevant to the leasing effort include size, frontage (including display capability), depth, visibility, accessibility, and general layout. The leasing agent must be able to (1) effectively communicate specific facts about the structure and layout to prospective tenants and (2) explain how all parts of the center will function together to create a workable whole.

The architectural design of the shopping center should reflect the center's function as a single entity composed of separate but interconnected parts, with unity of design and structure stressed not only in such features as landscaping and building materials but also in storefront decor and signage. Each tenant should be assured maximum frontage and visibility for the space leased, and all stores should be easily accessible from any part of the center. The developer and the architect plan how the objectives of the center are to be achieved structurally. Typically about 25 percent of the land at a shopping center site is covered with buildings. This includes *freestanding buildings* constructed separately, close to the street. The selection of retailers to occupy these outlying spaces will depend on the overall tenant mix of the center. Common areas (including parking lots) usually cover 65–75 percent of the land.

Size.   Store size is often determined by the projected sales per square foot of a particular prospective tenant. A neighborhood bakery may be very successful in a 900-square-foot space; but move it to 1,800 square feet of space, and it may not have sufficient sales to be able to support the increased occupancy costs. Thus, a minimal space may be preferable to one that is too large for a tenant to justify based on its sales records. Often a smaller store space is more manageable for the tenant. Most shopping centers today are built with numerous small store spaces. A similar trend is also seen in department stores, where small theme boutiques centered around a particular type of merchandise or a specific designer brand name are replacing the more traditional arrangements of merchandise. The ability to offer variety in this way can be more significant for the retailer than the actual amount of space.

Structural flexibility is particularly important for the future of a center. Rehabilitation of established properties is becoming a commonplace, and the structural design should accommodate capability to enlarge or reduce individual spaces. Lease terms also require flexibility so that the owner can retain the right to relocate a tenant in a different space if necessary. Given the more compact store architecture of newer developments, economical use of space is especially vital. Store frontages can be varied without sacrificing the individual retailers' selling space by building large stores so that they overlap (or form an "L") behind small ones.

Store Frontage and Display.   The front of the store is the first thing a customer sees, and it can influence the customer's decision to shop there. Because of this, the prospective tenant is understandably concerned with the display opportunities of the storefront of a particular space. Each storefront should also fit with the overall design of the shopping center architecturally while at the same time presenting the specific image of the individual store. Storefronts should be designed for maximum visibility to pedestrian traffic. If they face a street, as in a strip center, they should be visible to automobile traffic as well.

Among the many factors that influence the use of store frontage for display are the geographic location of the shopping center, the location of the individual space within the center, the climate in the area, and the type of merchandise being offered. Window or display space is not mandatory for every type of retail business; different retail operations have different display needs. A cosmetic or jewelry store, for example, can get by with less window space and rely on signs advertising specials, whereas a women's apparel shop has to have room for mannequins. A chain store of any size will usually have specifications for storefront design, and its specifications may suit one particular space better than another. Time has also altered perceived display requirements. Supermarkets once had all glass storefronts; today they often have solid fronts that offer no view of the interior. A solid front wall permits storage of products against that wall without the backs of the shelves being visible from the outside. Perishable goods which once were commonly displayed in store windows last longer if they are kept away from sunlight. In this case, space that was once considered necessary for display or visibility has become vital for storage. Also contributing to this change were the need to conserve energy and the desire to prevent vandalism.

In enclosed malls, the open storefront has replaced the large show windows of the downtown department store. One advantage of this arrangement is the greater flow of traffic in and out of the store. Another is a wider area for display of goods. Instead of limited window space, the entire width of the store can be used, allowing for a greater variety of display possibilities. However, many apparel stores larger than 2,000 square feet of GLA are returning to more limited access and display windows because they permit a better development of the store's image inside as well as provide better security.

Depth.   Store depth refers to the distance from the front window wall to the back wall. As with excessive floor area, excessive depth can be detrimental to success. Store depths may range between 40 and 120 feet. However, a 120-foot depth is too great for a store with an area smaller than 8,000 square feet; a depth of 110 feet is the maximum for a 7,000-square-foot site. Most small stores occupy 3,000-square-foot or smaller spaces with preferred depths of 75–80 feet. Stores this size with depths greater than 80 feet are usually difficult to lease. In particular, if depth is disproportionate to width, the store's contents are visually removed from customers and an effect of peering through a tunnel is created. Greater store depths may be more easily tolerated in malls because the excess depth may be required to accommodate delivery access and storage space on the same level as the display and selling areas. Strip centers, on the other hand, are often designed for rear-access delivery; and additional store depth is not required. Although the structure itself may have an apparent uniform depth, individual spaces can be designed with varied depths by positioning shallower spaces so that they overlap freight access for a larger space.

Store Width.   Store width is related to both frontage and depth. Most retail spaces have a fixed width of window or display space. Store widths in a shopping center have to be controlled so that each tenant has a reasonable amount of frontage. In enclosed shopping malls, store widths of 30–40 feet are common, with an average about 33 feet. This allows for comfortable pedestrian flow patterns inside the spaces and prevents overcrowding. Stores of this width are easily visible from both sides of the mall walkway. In strip centers, widths of 20–25 feet are common for stores up to 65 feet deep with widths of 30–35 feet for stores 85–100 feet deep.

Retailers tend to prefer stores with as much width and as little depth as possible in order to maximize exposure. From the developer's viewpoint, however, assuming that the same sales volume can be achieved for a given amount of floor space, it is usually preferable to design stores narrow and deep rather than wide and shallow. With depth as the flexible dimension, a greater number of individual stores can be built between anchor tenants, particularly in an enclosed mall.

Tenant Shell Space.   In a brand-new center, most ancillary tenants lease what is called a *shell space*. In enclosed malls, this usually includes a certain frontage on the mall, three unfinished stud walls separating it from other stores, an unfinished slab floor, a roof but no ceiling, a rear door, and incoming utilities. In smaller centers, the tenant is usually responsible for all improvements except for the slab and storefront. In order to allow greater flexibility in leasing configurations, inside walls are not constructed initially. Tenants generally provide their own wall and floor coverings, lighting fixtures and any special wiring, interior decorating, storefronts and closures, furnishings, shelving, counters, displays, and other interior improvements. However, in some locales retail spaces may be built out to near completion so that the retailer has only to provide wall and floor coverings and specific display fixtures for its business. Many strip centers also build out stores at the time of initial construction because (1) it costs less to build out all at one time and (2) local tenants often have neither the funds nor the experience to finish the space themselves.

It is common practice to offer ancillary tenants an improvement allowance to install items necessary for their particular business. This is often stated in the lease as the cost of specific improvements up to a limited dollar amount per square foot. A tenant improvement allowance is sometimes a point for negotiation of concessions—some tenants may negotiate for more money for improvements or for a period of free rent. Restaurants, for example, often have special design requirements that necessitate a greater allowance. (Negotiation of tenant improvement allowances is discussed in more detail in chapter 8.)

The way build-outs are handled varies from one locale to another and depends on the type of center where the space is being leased. Once a space has been built out for an initial tenant, it is usually re-leased in "as is" condition. Theoretically, the next occupant benefits from the previously installed improvements. However, some shopping centers (mostly regional centers) require a minimum investment by the new tenant to assure that the space is upgraded and gets a new look. This investment may be based on a total amount ($50,000 minimum) or stated on a per-square-foot basis ($50 per square foot).

Build-to-Suit.   Major tenants themselves often have substantial input into design. In new centers, the commitment of anchor tenants such as department stores or supermarkets is essential—both to obtain financing and to attract ancillary tenants—and anchor tenants are consulted about their requirements before construction begins. Some anchors prefer to own and construct their own buildings. They may purchase the land for their stores outright, or lease it (a ground lease). Otherwise, anchors may negotiate a *build-to-suit* arrangement with the developer, who agrees to construct the store to the anchor's specifications. Even in a build-to-suit arrangement, the exterior of the building may have to conform to the overall pattern of the shopping center or mall; however, an anchor tenant has greater flexibility than an ancillary tenant in regard to interior design. A developer is usually willing to pay the extra cost of customized construction because (1) the anchor is expected to attract customers to the center, presumably in large enough numbers to make it worthwhile, and (2) without the anchor the center cannot be developed at all.

Mall Length

An enclosed regional shopping center designed in a straight line may have too great a distance between anchor tenants or appear too monotonous to the shopper. A mall that is extremely long can seem like a tunnel, which can inhibit pedestrian movement and reduce visibility of individual stores. The impression of excessive mall length can be overcome in part by staggering the storefronts, having some protrude into the mall either as a block or on an angle, although this tactic must be used cautiously because it, too, can reduce visibility of individual stores. Creative use of other visual elements (banners hung across the width of the mall walkway, judiciously placed mirrors, varied colors or patterns of floor coverings) can also modify shoppers' perceptions of excessive mall lengths.

Similarly, a strip center that is overlong and not imaginatively designed can be boring to look at from the street. A more visually inviting image can be created by introducing varied roof lines and staggered storefronts.

Pedestrian Flow

Width as well as length of mall walkways influences pedestrian flow. Widths ranging from 30 to 40 feet are common, with expansions to 60 feet in areas that form courts or other special areas. Often the width of the mall and the height and treatment of the ceiling are interrelated. The layout or shape of an enclosed mall can be used intentionally to direct people away from the center of the walkway and toward the storefronts. A court or other widened area open to the walkway often encourages shoppers to change direction. Pedestrian flow can also be directed by strategic placement of kiosks, seating areas, escalators, plants, fountains, and sculptures, as well as some types of stores (fast food).

Open versus Enclosed Malls

More and more large shopping malls are enclosed because the climate in many regions prevents people from shopping comfortably all year round in an open-air center. After dark, the enclosed mall presents a much more inviting interior—that of a lighted, protective cocoon rather than a dark, cold open sky. The retailer's sales potential is enhanced in enclosed malls because storefronts are open to the walkway without doors or windows, providing more space for display. The storefronts are protected after hours by metal grills or locked sliding doors. Merchandising possibilities in enclosed malls are endless. So-called sidewalk sales and promotional entertainment become feasible in any kind of weather. In fact, the advantages of enclosed malls are so obvious that developers have renovated older open "malls" by enclosing them and increasing the amount of leasable space. However, neighborhood and strip centers—small centers generally—still work best if all stores are open to the street and parking lots. These centers rarely have a unified theme, and each store may set its own hours of business although the owner may establish a general time frame.

Shopper Conveniences

In a large shopping center, anything that makes shopping more convenient is an advantage. Public telephones and ample washroom facilities are standard features of most enclosed malls. Many regional centers have one or more information desks manned by well-informed staff who can direct shoppers to specific stores. Stationary directories (signs) or electronic directories (computers) also benefit shoppers. Storage lockers, newsstands, and a local post office branch are found in some regional malls. Parents with infants or toddlers appreciate stroller rentals; and some centers provide supervised playrooms where small children can be left for several hours while the adults are shopping.

Parking

A very important consideration in shopping center design is parking. Prospective tenants will likely have many questions about parking facilities, and availability of ample customer parking is one of the features a leasing agent can "sell" to them. Sometimes an anchor's build-to-suit negotiations will affect parking lot design, with the number of spaces adjacent to its entrances being optimized for its customers. Generally, however, parking is regulated by local ordinances that may govern the size of the lot or the number of spaces or the angle at which they are set.

Suburban shopping centers and malls automatically include a parking

Parking Lot Design Considerations

- Demand for parking in trade area
- Number of cars that can be accommodated in a given area
- Width of individual stalls
- Access to thoroughfares
- Nature of the shopping center
- Proximity to residential areas
- Availability of public transportation

---

lot as part of their design. Free parking is a convenience that is offered as a matter of course to the consumer. The parking lot is usually intended for exclusive use by shoppers, employees, and office tenants of the center, and both long-term and short-term parking can be accommodated. Conversely, downtown shoppers usually have to park in garages, if parking is available at all, and they pay for the privilege. (The garages may be part of a mixed-use development that includes offices and apartments as well as retail space.) Because space is at a premium in most urban areas, parking fees are generally hourly rates. Designing an appropriate parking lot or garage for a particular center is extremely important (figure 6.1). The demand for parking in the trade area, the number of cars that can be accommodated in the lot, the width of the individual stalls, access to streets or roads, the availability of public transportation, the nature of the retail store or center, and the proximity of residential areas are all important considerations in parking lot design.

The size of a parking lot is related primarily to the GLA of the retail space and secondarily to the needs of the individual businesses. In general, parking lots take up more space than any other part of a shopping center. The relationship between the size of the parking area and the size of the retail building is the *parking area ratio.* At one time it was required that this ratio be three to one (3:1)—three square feet of parking area for each square foot of building area. Put another way, a building might occupy one-fourth of a site while the remaining three-fourths was devoted to parking. In the 1960s, the recommendation was changed to relate parking to the gross leasable area of a center. This relationship, called the *parking index,* was stated as "the number of parking spaces per 1,000 square feet of GLA" and, at that time, was set at 5.5.

In general, the size of the lot must be appropriate for the center it will serve. There is also a difference in parking needs between urban and suburban areas—downtown centers generally have a higher volume of walk-in trade, while most customers of suburban shopping centers drive to their destination. According to standards published by the Urban Land Institute in 1982, centers with a GLA of 25,000 to 400,000 square feet

T A B L E   6.1

Parking Space Requirements

Center Size (GLA in sq ft)	Number of Spaces (per 1,000 sq ft of GLA)
25,000 to 400,000	4
400,000 to 600,000	4 to 5
More than 600,000	5

Recommended standards are subject to adjustment for the presence of offices, cinemas, and food services in shopping centers.

From *Parking Requirements for Shopping Centers: Summary Recommendations and Research Study Report* (Washington, D.C.: ULI—the Urban Land Institute, 1982). Used with permission.

should provide four spaces per 1,000 square feet of GLA; those with a GLA of 400,000 to 600,000 square feet should provide four to five spaces, and centers larger than 600,000 square feet require five spaces per 1,000 square feet of GLA (table 6.1). Some cities still adhere to the earlier standard (5.5 spaces per 1,000 square feet of GLA), and local zoning requirements may be at variance with the ULI parking index recommendations.

Local zoning regulations regarding the size of parking lots must be considered, and they may not always be in the best interests of the property being developed. Off-street parking requirements may not be related to demand. Sometimes an area will be over-zoned for parking, with large unsightly lots that are essentially wasted space. On the other hand, a community that has not zoned adequately for parking will limit customer circulation within the trade area and discourage shoppers. Local governments often attempt to restrict parking in order to encourage people to use public transportation; however, such parking restrictions often lead to traffic jams and generally irritate shoppers. For these reasons, it is usually better to determine parking lot size based on the needs of the individual shopping center.

In addition to the GLA of the center, specific tenants will have an impact on decisions about parking lot design. For example, art galleries and furniture stores encourage browsing. They may have a few customers that stay a long time. On the other hand, health clubs and video rental stores usually have numerous customers arriving and leaving concurrently and staying comparatively short times. Convenience stores such as supermarkets and drugstores require large areas of short-term parking with provision for high turnover and "loading zones" for temporary stops to pick up groceries and other goods. Food service franchises also require parking that accommodates high turnover, and additional parking stalls may be needed. The number will depend on the percentage of the center's GLA that is comprised of food service operations.

A gracious-dining sit-down restaurant where most of the customers arrive at about the same time and stay for fairly long periods will need a great deal of long-term parking. However, this may not be a problem if the mix of stores does not attract large numbers of customers at dinner time. Furthermore, there is usually no need to provide additional parking for movie theaters unless they are very large or the center housing them is comparatively small. If they are only accessible from inside the mall and operate concurrent with mall hours, there may be a greater parking requirement. Theaters that have up to 450 seats in a center with 100,000 to 200,000 square feet of GLA usually will not require additional parking; nor will theaters with up to 750 seats in a center larger than 200,000 square feet of GLA. If additional parking is needed, it can usually be fulfilled by providing three more parking stalls for each 100 seats in the theater. Parking requirements also depend on the hours the center is open. If the stores close early in the evening, the parking lot will be available for movie patrons.

While the varied needs of retail tenants and their particular customers should be a consideration in parking lot design, it is not always practical to plan for specific tenants or uses. Once leases begin to expire and replacement tenants move in, that specificity may be all wrong. Use of the parking index and relating parking to the GLA of the center is the most functional guideline that can be given.

Aside from parking for retail customers, space should also be provided for employees of the center and its tenants. Whenever possible, such long-term parking should be set apart from the regular retail parking area because center employees who have to park for the entire day will occupy space at the expense of retail customers unless there is an alternate parking area for them. If each customer parking space is considered in terms of customer sales, employees who occupy customer stalls do so at a loss to both the store and the center. Large suburban shopping centers and downtown centers with parking garages typically set aside space in areas that will not interfere with customer parking. Strip centers often allocate space behind the stores for employees; this may be combined with a service area or loading dock. Leases for retail space usually include a clause that stipulates where employees may and may not park. Sometimes special identification stickers or cards may also be issued.

If the retail space is in a mixed-use center, there must also be provision for long-term parking for office tenants. If offices take up more than

10 percent of the GLA of a shopping mall, additional parking may be necessary. Centers that lease space to medical professionals (physicians, dentists, podiatrists, etc.) will have added parking requirements. In general, office parking should not be located near retail entrances; that space should be reserved for shoppers. However, the area available for parking will dictate where and how many spaces can be provided for exclusive use of center and tenant employees. Despite lease provisions, rules, fines, etc., good design that provides employees of the center (and offices, if any) a self-service, convenient place to park within the regular parking area will best serve the center, as long as customers are not inconvenienced.

The arrangement of individual parking stalls depends on the shape of the retail site and the location of the buildings on it. Accessibility and security should be major concerns. For a large regional center, the walking distance from the parking lot to the mall ideally should not exceed 400 feet; although in many centers, customers have to walk longer distances than this. Parking designated for handicapped shoppers must be close to mall entrances and have access to a ramp and to doors that are wide enough for wheelchairs to pass through. Parking lots at very large centers can be divided into sections, each containing not more than 800 to 1,000 spaces, and labeled with letters or numbers or both.

In community or neighborhood centers as well as business districts with freestanding stores, parking is often available directly in front of the stores, and specific parking layouts may be dictated by an anchor tenant. Parking spaces parallel to the sidewalk should be at least 10 feet wide and 20 feet long. When a parking lot can be included, parking stalls are arranged in bays, which are driving aisles with stalls on both sides. Aisles or access lanes are at least 24 feet wide to allow for both automobile and pedestrian traffic. Stalls can be aligned perpendicular (90 degrees) or at a 60-degree angle to a curb or a base line. Perpendicular parking requires a standard bay width of 65 feet, which includes two stalls that are 20 feet deep and a center aisle 25 feet wide to accommodate two-way traffic. For angled parking, the center aisle can be slightly narrower because traffic usually flows only one way.

The parking angle affects the area taken up by individual spaces which, in turn, relates to the number of spaces that can be created in a given area. The most commonly used parking angle is 60 degrees because it is easy to turn into and back out of the stall, and the aisle requirement can be reduced. Perpendicular parking (90-degree angle) produces the highest car count in a given area, but it also leads to problems of maneuvering into and out of the stalls. It is recommended for those areas where high turnover is not a consideration—for example, employee parking areas.

Stall widths vary with the amount of turnover in the center and the type of car they are meant to accommodate. Standard stall size is 9–9½ feet wide by 18 feet deep, but the increasing popularity of small cars has led to design of parking lots with "compact" stalls as narrow as 8½ feet wide and only 17 feet deep. However, stores that have high turnover—7-Eleven or White Hen Pantry convenience stores, for example—need the wider stall width because it is easier to drive into and out of a slightly larger space. It is also easier to load a car parked in a wider stall. Employee and office tenant parking usually has a lower turnover rate, and stalls in those designated areas can be reduced to a width of 8 feet to permit a larger area to be devoted to consumer parking. Parking stalls for handicapped shoppers require a width of 13–14 feet. If two such spaces are side by side, their combined width can effect a space savings. In general, parking spaces should be wide enough to allow for clearance of opened doors between two vehicles and deep enough to accommodate station wagons, vans, and large model automobiles.

Parking garages can be constructed for regional malls as well as for downtown centers if space is limited. Garages are advantageous for shoppers because they are usually connected to the shopping center. Direct entrances into the mall on each level of the garage solve two problems for the shopper—long distances to walk and inclement weather. Ramps facilitate movement of cars from one level to another. Individual parking stalls can be smaller because less maneuvering is necessary to drive into and out of spaces. There are disadvantages for customers, however, and these are (1) possible security problems (especially in urban areas) and (2) expense (in the form of hourly charges for such parking).

Food Courts

Placement of a number of self-service booths or stands around a seating area is what has become known as a *food court*. Such courts thrive in high-traffic areas such as entertainment complexes, downtown malls, train stations, and sports arenas. They have become an established feature of enclosed suburban mall design. While food court tenants may be local, regional, or national franchises, they have not often been major operations like McDonald's, Burger King, or Pizza Hut. Major franchises frequently opt to occupy outlying spaces in shopping centers in order to minimize their dependence on access to the mall proper. Use of outlying spaces also means they can offer drive-through service. However, some national fast food operators are beginning to modify their position so that they can "be where the action is"—and in many centers that is the food court.

Local vendors often work well in food courts. When ethnic restaurants in a trade area are invited to set up a fast food service branch, the developer benefits by the diversity of the food court tenant mix, and the vendor has an opportunity to promote the main restaurant and increase its sales overall. For shoppers, the extended variety of the food court affords an opportunity to try different kinds of foods.

Food courts are occasionally leased as blocks of space to a single operator who then sublets the stalls to individual vendors. This saves the leasing agent and developer the time and effort of having to plan for and establish a dozen or so different vendors. Often the professional food court operator will have more knowledge of what kind of food mix will succeed in a given type of center.

Food courts usually are valued highly by other tenants. Tenants in spaces adjacent to these courts benefit from the increase in mall business that this type of food service represents. Developers benefit as well: Stores close to food courts usually command a higher rent because of the increased traffic the food courts generate. Food courts not only cater to the needs of customers, they also help create traffic by attracting shoppers to the mall. This is especially true if the mall is located in an area that has little or no selection of restaurants. Because people tend to spend more time where they can eat as well as shop, a center with a food court usually shows a greater volume of sales overall. Like an outdoor cafe, the food court offers opportunities for socializing as well as eating, reflecting the shopping center's additional role in contemporary society as an entertainment or social center.

Community and neighborhood centers do not usually command sufficient shopper traffic to be able to support a food court, nor are they generally designed to accommodate this type of food service. The food court is an important element in the general scheme of the regional mall, however; and great care must be exercised in designing the court to provide adequate seating, good lighting, and attractive decor. A typical food court occupies a total area of about 25,000 square feet and has twelve to fifteen stalls. Average stall area should be about 850 square feet, and the open seating area should accommodate 350 to 400 people.

If the food court is designed well, it will operate as a single entity. The menu selection and the placement of vendors within the court should enhance the overall effect and increase the profitability of the food court as a whole. Marketing groups recommend that stall arrangement should follow the pattern of a cafeteria, with booths selling ice cream, pies, candy, and other impulse items at either or both ends of the court and booths selling hamburgers, pizza, hot dogs, and similar items in the middle.

However it is designed, development of a food court requires considerable additional investment in infrastructure, and one should proceed with caution and call upon experienced food court designers in order to guarantee the best result. One or even two department stores may not create enough customer traffic to justify a food court from either an owner's or a retailer's perspective. When leasing space in a food court, the agent should be aware of the role of design in directing customer traffic, determining the most appropriate food service tenants, and bringing customers into the shopping center. A food court is one of the best examples of how form and function are integrated into shopping center design.

Mall Configurations

Mall configuration can have a significant effect on the leasing effort. Over the years, shopping center design has progressed from the straight lines of shops fronting on a street to sophisticated, complicated configurations. The shape of a mall depends on several factors including its size, its function, the terrain it is built on, and the image the developer wishes to convey. The number and types of major tenants also play a role.

Most malls are enclosed, and one or more anchor tenants provide a focus for both customers and ancillary retail tenants. Because the anchors are focal points, their placement is crucial to the success of the center as a whole. Their positions should draw customers into the center itself and through the areas occupied by other tenants. Uniformity of widths and depths of stores should be avoided; varied storefronts are more interesting. Also to be avoided are "dead" spaces that limit or prevent pedestrian access.

The configurations discussed in the following sections have been used over and over again and, for the most part, they have proved successful. However, they do not represent the limits of shopping center design, as each site presents unique characteristics to be considered in the development of the retail space that will occupy it.

Strip or Linear Center.   One of the earliest forms of shopping center design, the strip is still used for convenience centers and neighborhood centers located along major streets. Parking is usually provided between the street and the fronts of the stores, and an area behind the stores is used for service, deliveries, and employee parking. Retail "strips" may not always have anchor tenants. When they do, strip "centers" typically have a supermarket or a supermarket-drugstore combination as an anchor. Such anchors are usually positioned at one end, in the middle, or one at each end of the strip. Although this type of center is rarely enclosed, walkways are sometimes covered. Linear centers are usually functional, inexpensive to build, and easy to maintain.

The L Shape.   One of the most widely-used shopping center configurations is the L shape. It is typically used for neighborhood or community centers because this shape provides maximum visibility of all stores when the center is located optimally at the intersection of two major thoroughfares. Anchor tenants can be placed at either end of the L, and visibility of storefronts creates a focus for the customer. Customer parking is usually in front of the shops and employee parking in back.

The U Shape.   Another variation on the linear design, the U-shaped center has two right angles, one at each end of the main strip. This shape allows for anchors at either end and possibly a third anchor in the middle. The major anchor would probably be located in the most visible position—in the center of the main strip.

The Cluster.   Early versions of regional shopping centers used the cluster design, and it is found in some older open (nonenclosed) malls where a loosely formed rectangular shape results from arranging stores on four sides. There is parking near each major tenant, and ancillary tenants are scattered between the anchors. One type of cluster might have a major department store as an anchor in the center, surrounded by a series of small "malls."

The T shape.   A center that has three anchors can be T shaped. One anchor is positioned at each end of the crossbar with the third anchor at the base of the leg of the T. The third anchor usually is not visible from the entrances of the two that form the crossbar, and this third large space may be difficult to lease because anchor tenants may consider the position a disadvantage. From the point of view of ancillary tenants, however, anchors at three "ends" will draw traffic through the entire center when shoppers would otherwise tend to cluster around one corner or at one end. In a T-shaped center, each ancillary tenant is located in the vicinity of an anchor and, theoretically, each ancillary space is equal. T shapes are typically used for regional or super regional centers.

The Triangle.   Another common design for the regional center, the triangle is a more open version of the T. Because the triangle shape allows equivalent visibility for each anchor, its spaces may be easier to lease. If it is possible to construct a triangle on a given site, this shape would be more feasible from the developer's point of view as well. Here again, three anchors are standard, and multiple levels can be accommodated in this configuration.

Dumbbell and Double Dumbbell Shapes.   The dumbbell consists of two strips with storefronts facing each other across a central court or mall. Anchors at both ends draw customers up and down the mall. The double dumbbell has four anchors forming a square around a cross-shaped central mall. This configuration is particularly suitable for large open regional malls.

Other Configurations.   Shopping centers can also be located in reno-vated buildings or historical centers—reconstructed warehouses, wharves, old commercial buildings, former government buildings, old movie the-atres, railroad stations. Some examples include Faneuil Hall Marketplace in Boston, Pier 39 and Ghirardelli Square in San Francisco, the Old Post Office in Washington, D.C., and the South Street Seaport in New York City, all of which are known as *festival centers.* In these situations, design was dependent on the existing structure. The space planner was concerned about integrating the new with the old by defining space for retail stores without disturbing the atmosphere of the original site. These types of cen-ters often include entertainment facilities, so it may be necessary to incor-porate wide-open areas or some kind of stage or platform in the overall design. Space in such centers can usually command high market rents because the tourist trade they attract is essentially a guarantee of high-volume sales—unless the tourist traffic is seasonal and its peaks do not offset the low sales at other times. However, leasing space in festival cen-ters can be more difficult, especially if the retail space is oddly shaped or the site is not easily accessible; buildings that were not designed for retail space originally are likely to present both of these problems.

TENANT PLACEMENT

An important consideration in leasing retail space is the effect the center's design will have on the profitability of the individual store. The developer and architect control the site plan as the center is being developed, and they can change it to accommodate the best possible arrangement of ten-ants once an anchor tenant is secured. Often placement of major tenants affects the general configuration, the overall design, and the size and depth of the other spaces in the center. In a supermarket-anchored center, the size and shape of the adjoining spaces will be determined somewhat by the types of retail businesses that are expected to occupy them initially. A liquor or drug store would have different space and design require-ments than service providers such as beauty parlors, barber shops, tan-ning salons, dry cleaners, and others that are also usually tenants of a supermarket-anchored center. Conversely, a center anchored by an upscale department store would likely incorporate ancillary spaces suitable for boutiques, shoe stores, and jewelry shops. (Retail businesses that comple-ment each other are discussed in detail in chapter 4; see also figure 4.4.)

The configuration of existing spaces in an established shopping cen-ter can affect the sales performance of the retailers that lease them. In order to maximize their sales potential, special care must be taken in plac-ing tenants in an established shopping center. This implies particular attention to the operational requirements of specific types of retailers. There are also special leasing considerations that apply to freestanding space and to spaces in multilevel malls.

Placement of Anchor Tenants

Anchors are usually located in positions that encourage shoppers to walk past other stores in the center in order to reach them. In a two-anchor regional center, the major stores are usually at opposite ends of the center. If there are three or more anchors, these stores are separated as much as possible. In a center with only one anchor, that major tenant is usually at the center of the site to maximize the benefits of proximity to it. When the lone anchor is placed at one end of the site, the retailers at or near the anchorless end generally do not derive as much benefit—in sales volume—as the retailers located closer to the anchor. However, supermarkets and other convenience anchors are generally placed so they can garner the greatest amount of available parking. (They will insist on this arrangement.)

Placement of Ancillary Tenants

Theoretically there should be few if any poor locations in a well-planned shopping center. All tenants should benefit from the center's layout, and as individual sales performances increase, the profitability of the center as a whole should also increase. However, the reality of retail space leasing is that some spaces will be perceived as more valuable than others, and rental rates achieved for individual spaces will reflect differences in location within the center. In order to place tenants to their best advantage, several factors must be taken into consideration.

Each type of retail business will have a particular location that is considered most suitable for selling its merchandise. What will work for one type of retailer will not necessarily work for another. The merchandising principle that supports placement of hosiery and glove departments adjacent to each other in a large department store also holds true for locating a men's shoe store next to a men's clothing store in a shopping mall. On the other hand, some shopping centers group tenants by price, aligning ancillaries and anchors based on comparable pricing of their merchandise. Some retailers want maximum store frontage for displays; others require proximity to another type of store. "Destination" tenants such as tanning salons and beauty shops can often be located in less-visible (often less-expensive) spaces whereas "impulse" tenants such as candy and nut vendors willingly pay premium rents to be located in the most visible spaces. Retailers whose customers need long-term parking have to be separated from other businesses with potentially conflicting parking requirements. For example, a three-screen cinema will have two sets of two-hour parkers that change just before or after a showing. A grocery store adjacent to it would not have adequate shorter-term parking available for its customers. Because of this possible parking conflict, grocers usually will not sign a lease if the proposed space is anywhere near a theater.

As a general rule, the location of the anchor can guide the placement of ancillary tenants. Other positions in a shopping center may be judged by their proximity to the anchor. One of the best locations is *center court,* so called because it is the area midway between two department store anchors. Fashion-oriented retailers are ideally suited to the center court area because they can take advantage of the proximity of the department stores without being overwhelmed by them. Because anchors dominate, positions immediately adjacent to them may be better leased to "destination" retailers. Sometimes "center court" comprises an intersection of malls which creates corner stores. These are a challenge to use most effectively. Normally jewelers are excellent corner tenants, as are some boutiques. However, regular apparel stores that display their merchandise on the walls as well as on floor racks are best placed in in-line stores.

Tenant Placement in Downtown Centers

Developers and leasing agents must be extremely creative when positioning retailers in downtown centers because of the limited amount of space available and the spaces being arranged vertically on multiple levels. In many enclosed downtown malls the anchors are placed at the back of the mall rather than given extensive frontage on the street. That way customers have to walk past the many smaller shops to reach the major department store. Restaurants and services are often grouped on upper floors so their customers are drawn through the entire center. Also important are the placement of washrooms, customer service desks, public telephones, and even gift-wrapping services. Strategic placement of these elements can foster impulse purchases. The same general principles of tenant placement apply in both suburban and downtown shopping malls; the major difference between the two is that the orientation in suburban malls is almost always horizontal while in downtown malls it is usually vertical.

Outlots

An *outlot* (sometimes also referred to as an "out parcel" or a "pad") is a store site that is not attached to the main shopping center structure. It is often located in the parking lot area, at or near the front of the property, and easily visible from the street. Outlots are good locations for *destination retailers* that consumers seek out in order to buy a particular item. Sit-down restaurants in particular are successful in these locations, as are banks, video rental stores, automotive services, optical shops, and photo development booths. These locations are often ideal for franchise fast food operations because of the adjacent parking and the opportunity to offer drive-up service. None of these businesses depends on the proximity of an anchor for its success, yet they benefit from being located in a shopping center because they can capture customers who take care of their service needs while they are shopping. The size of an outlot depends on the tenant occupying it. Fast food operations require 2,500–3,500 square feet of space while sit-down restaurants may need 3,000–5,000 square feet. Banks need 4,000 or more square feet of space. This is exclusive of their parking requirements.

Movie theaters, with their specialized parking requirements, may be located on outlots. However, they should be positioned in a way that will not detract from the stores and their customers' needs. Because movie theaters are destination businesses, they may be effectively placed "behind" the center proper.

Multilevel Shopping Centers

One solution to the problem of long walking distances in tunnel-like malls and in very large shopping centers is the use of multiple levels. It is also a way to conserve space. Although elevators, escalators, and stairways increase construction costs for multilevel malls, these elements can also be distinctive design features of the center. Galleries, cross bridges between two sides of upper stories, and protruding or stepped landings can provide greater visibility for stores in out-of-the-way areas, as well as interrupt the straight-line vertical shaft appearance which can be as monotonous as the tunnel effect of a horizontal linear design. The design should ensure that the different levels will not seem isolated from each other.

Because vertical merchandising arrangements require particular care in the distribution of retail tenants, the owner or developer of a multilevel mall should retain control over tenant location, and this should be stated in each tenant's lease. Tenants can be grouped in various ways—based on type of merchandise or a relationship to stores on other levels. The objective is to keep customers moving through all the different levels: A hosiery store visible from a shoe store on a lower level encourages a visit to the upper level for a related purchase. The relationship between ancillary and anchor tenants is extremely important to the success of a multilevel shopping center. Because of this, department stores frequently access the "mall" area on several levels; these entrances are critical to the success of the ancillary tenants located adjacent to the anchors.

Multilevel malls are chiefly a feature of downtown retail development, although many suburban malls have two or three levels with access to anchor tenants on each of them. Because drive-in convenience and street-front visibility are the main attraction for shoppers at neighborhood or community centers, multiple levels are not viable for these types of centers. Retail stores on the second floor of a neighborhood center usually do not succeed in that location although some types of tenants—beauty shops, photographers, exercise centers, or other services—can do well there. Second-floor space in such a shopping center may be leased as business or professional offices. However, such tenants may have special requirements. They and their clients may occupy parking spaces for long periods of time, or the services they provide may require special electrical wiring or plumbing fixtures that can add to the cost of construction or remodeling. With the possible exception of renovated historical buildings that have been converted into retail space, neighborhood centers usually are built on a single level.

SUMMARY

Understanding both the possibilities and the limitations of a property will facilitate the leasing process. Tenant placement within a center depends largely on the overall design. Different types of retail businesses have different space requirements, and they may operate more profitably in one location than in another. Matching a prospective tenant's needs to the structure of the center is an important part of the leasing agent's job.

The size of a particular space often determines its leasability and the rents that can be achieved from it. Size can also determine the occupant's success: A business that leases too large a space may not be able to generate enough sales per square foot to cover expenses, while one that has too small a space may not be able to maximize its display area. Store frontage and store depth contribute to both display opportunities and customer comfort. Frontage and depth are also related to the type of merchandise being sold.

In an enclosed shopping center, the width and length of the pedestrian mall are crucial factors. If the mall is too wide, stores on either side will not be easily visible; if it is too long, the resulting tunnel effect is monotonous for shoppers. A mall's design should direct pedestrian flow so that customers move past all the stores, preferably in a meandering pattern.

Adequate parking is important for all modern shopping centers. Spaces next to the sidewalk, parking lots, and multilevel garages are among the options to be considered. The size of the parking area is related to the GLA of the center, and the size and orientation of each parking stall can be planned in relation to the type of center.

Food courts have become almost standard in contemporary regional malls that have three or more anchors. Frequently placed so that they benefit the most from overall pedestrian flow, their success depends on visibility, attractive design, and easily accessible cooking, service, and cleaning facilities.

Both shopping center layout and tenant placement within different configurations relate to tenant sales performance. Convenience or neighborhood centers function well with a linear or strip design. Community centers or small regional centers can be built in a U or L shape. T shapes, triangles, and dumbbells are good configurations for regional centers, with anchors located at the ends of pedestrian malls to encourage customer traffic between them.

Placement of ancillary tenants often depends on the anchor locations. A prime location, especially for fashion retailers, is the center of the mall, midway between two anchors. Because stores close to anchors may be overshadowed by them, tenants placed there should be primarily destination retailers that shoppers will seek out. Spaces on outlots or pads are ideal for banks, restaurants, gas stations, and other businesses that prefer excellent visibility and easy accessibility and do not depend on the anchors or the mall atmosphere for their success.

7

The Retail Lease

The lease document is the formal written record of the agreement between the parties to a leasing arrangement. In general, the *retail lease* can be defined as a conveyance of occupancy rights to a piece of property from the owner or landlord to the tenant for a specific use and a specific period of time. A lease is a legally binding contract that outlines each party's obligations and responsibilities to the other party. Its terms should reflect the needs and desires of both parties as well as protect both their interests, especially with regard to payment of rent and other monetary considerations.

Because the leases state conclusively the amount of income to be received in the form of rents, the value of the property is essentially based on them. Lending institutions consider rental income to be security, so signed leases may form the basis for collateral in a loan transaction. Through the lease, the owner seeks protection from loss of income and insurance against undue complications by setting limits on the tenant's usage of the retail space. On the other hand, by defining rental rates and other terms for a specified period of time, the lease also gives the tenant a measure of security.

STANDARD FORM LEASE

No uniform lease document will cover every possible rental agreement between a retailer and a retail space owner because each transaction, each retail center, each tenant, and each owner are different. However, most large leasing organizations have a standard form that they subsequently modify as specific leases are negotiated. Usually the owner or lessor will provide this form, although large retailers (department stores, supermarkets, drugstores) and national chains may have their own lease forms, and these may contain points that do not agree with the clauses in the owner's lease form. Use of a standardized lease form presumes that it has been developed in consultation with an attorney. When such a standard form is used in retail leasing situations, legal counsel is often sought only in regard to specifically negotiated changes.

Basic Lease Information

As part of the standard language incorporated in it, the lease document will always include: the names of the parties involved in the lease (including the broker, if appropriate); a description of the leased premises, including the area of the building or center (square feet of GLA) and the area of the individual tenant's space (square feet of GLA); the term of the lease (commencement and expiration dates) and date of tenant move-in; and the rental rates—including base and percentage rents and a clear definition of gross sales as the basis for percentage rent as well as provisions for rent escalations and pass through of operating costs and other expenses (figure 7.1).

Most leases, especially those for large shopping centers, also include separate clauses covering the use of the space, funding of the merchants' association or marketing fund, subleasing, and other points. There may be information about tenant improvements and allocations of funds for them; statements about options to renew, expand, cancel, or purchase space; and specific concessions such as a period of reduced rent. Provisions for parking, attention to special maintenance problems, and other concerns may also be addressed. Some leases may include statements about exercise of the right of *eminent domain*—the takeover of part of the (private) property for public use, and there may be need to address issues relating to the environment and hazardous substances.

If the lease is long and complex, a table of contents listing exhibits or addenda to the standard form may be necessary. The leasing agent should be familiar with the terminology and descriptions of the components of retail lease documents. The clauses described in this chapter are among those most frequently encountered.

Identification of Parties.   A retail lease begins by identifying the owner or landlord, the tenant, the guarantor, and any other parties involved. The names of persons and companies are stated and addresses may be included. It is important to indicate whether the parties are individuals (or sole pro-

FIGURE   7.1

Basic Lease Components

* Parties to the lease
* Description of the leased space
* Duration
* Specific rent
* Other charges
* Other terms agreed to

prietorships), corporations, or partnerships—as well as their relationship to each other through the lease agreement and their specific authority to sign it. The participation of the broker should also be acknowledged along with a statement of liability for the broker's commission.

Individuals and *sole proprietorships* are one-person businesses, that one individual being personally responsible for paying rents and meeting other financial obligations. Partnerships are a slightly more complicated form of ownership. Partners would be identified individually on the first page of the lease and would also sign their names on the last or signature page. The nature of a partnership should be stated because this has some bearing on the liability of the various partners. In a *general partnership,* all debts and liabilities are shared by all of the general partners. In a *limited partnership,* however, each limited partner is usually financially liable only up to the value of his or her proportionate investment. (Also in a limited partnership, there are usually one or more general partners who carry full liability.) Whether the partnership is general or limited, each of the partners must abide by the contract established through the lease, even though the extent of the individual's liability may vary in case of bankruptcy. If the lease is with a *corporation,* the corporation is the entity that is liable for obligations under a contract, although some personal liability may accrue to its officers or board of directors under certain circumstances. Sometimes when a corporation is a tenant it may be necessary to secure a personal guaranty of the business's financial obligations under the lease.

Lease Term.   The period or duration of the lease should be stated. The date of execution, the dates the *lease term* starts and ends, the date of tenant occupancy, and the commencement of rental payments can all be different and should be clearly noted in the lease. For example, a tenant may sign a lease on April 15, occupy the space on June 1, and not pay rent until August 1. The lease is always in force at the time of tenant occupancy, but rental payments may be delayed through negotiation of a specific starting date.

Description of the Premises.   The lease should include a precise, accurate (legal) description of the tenant's individual leasable area (in terms
of GLA) and of the leasable area of the entire retail center (total GLA). The
street address of the shopping center and of the individual store should
also be given. Typically, a site plan and a floor plan showing the location
and configuration of the individual tenant's space are included with the
lease as appendixes or exhibits.

   The lease usually includes a clause that calls for the tenant to inspect
the property before occupancy to determine any repairs or alterations to
be made and to submit a list of these items to the owner within a specified
time period. A tenant's responsibility for maintenance of its particular
space as well as any requirements to maintain a designated part of a so-
called "common area" should also be clearly defined. This reference to a
common area is not always exclusively to the common area in an enclosed
mall; it can refer to parking lots or other portions of a smaller retail property that does not have the type of coordinated management that a mall
does. Descriptions of the land and the condition of the premises as a
whole are attached to the lease as exhibits.

   Some leases also call for a statement of the tenant's *pro rata share* of
the premises. This is calculated by dividing the GLA of the tenant's space
by the GLA of the entire center and multiplying the answer by one hundred. The resulting percentage is used to compute the tenant's share of
operating expenses, HVAC charges, common area maintenance fees, and
pass-through adjustments for real estate taxes, insurance premiums, and
other items. This straightforward computation is commonly used, but in
some situations a tenant may pay a different pro rata share of different expense items. For example, food court tenants will pay expenses of the
food court area on a pro rata basis, and these expenses would not be prorated among all the other tenants in the mall. The proration should be
reviewed periodically because remodeling of the center could result in
either expansion or reduction of the tenant's pro rata share. It may also be
important to include provision for adjustment of the pro rata share to
avoid having to amend the lease at a later date.

Payment of Rent.   The lease document should clearly state

- the amount of the monthly *base rent*
- when and where it is to be paid
- the amount of the security deposit (if any)
- the first month's base rent (if this will be different)
- the date rent payment commences

If *percentage rent* is to be paid, the percentage rate must be stated along
with how percentage rent relates to the base or minimum rent and how

gross sales are defined for the calculation of percentage rent. These may be set out in the lease in separate clauses. Chapter 3 details how base rent and percentage rent are allocated.

Minimum rent. The minimum or base rent is usually stated in the lease as a monthly amount. However, in some locales it may be necessary to quote the amount for the entire first year along with reference to specific periodic increases "as allowed by the lease." Stating the annual amount of the base rent stresses that the agreement is not based on a monthly rate but rather on a yearly rent that is divided into monthly payments for the tenant's convenience.

The time and method of rent payment is also important. Typically rent is due on or before the first day of each month. If the lease term is scheduled to begin after the first of the month, the tenant's payment for that month should be prorated and all future payments due on the first of the month. The provisions regarding rental rates and structures are among those points subject to specific negotiation.

Percentage rent. Percentage rent is often computed as an *overage.* In other words, the percentage rent due is calculated on the full amount of sales; the amount of percentage rent actually paid is reduced by the amount of the base rent. In this case, the amount of gross sales at which the percentage rent equals the minimum rent—the *breakpoint*—should be stated in the lease as well. (Natural and artificial breakpoints are described in chapter 3.)

Sometimes percentage rent is computed completely separate from the base rent. The specific basis for calculation and payment of percentage rent, along with the time of payment (monthly, quarterly, annually) should be clearly stated. In some instances, percentage rent may be the only rent paid, and owner and tenant may agree on limits to the total amount of sales on which percentage rent is due. However, the retail tenant usually pays both minimum and percentage rent.

Allocation of Operating Expenses. When all maintenance and common area expenses, insurance, taxes, and repairs are passed through to the tenant, the lease is said to be a *net lease.* If these expenses are borne solely by the owner, it is a *gross lease.* Leases for retail space are commonly net, and the types of operating expenses that are prorated among the tenants further define the net lease (figure 7.2).

Methods of calculating pass-through expenses vary with local or regional practices. The standard method is to prorate operating costs on the basis of the tenant's proportionate share of the total GLA of the retail building; however, there may be situations in which it is important to have different prorations for individual pass-through items. The specific method

F I G U R E   7.2

Definitions of Net and Gross Leases

Net Lease.   The tenant pays a prorated share of property taxes.

Net-Net Lease.   The tenant pays a prorated share of both property taxes and insurance costs; the owner still pays for repairs, maintenance, and management fees.

Triple-Net (or Net-Net-Net) Lease.   All operating expenses—taxes, insurance, mainte-nance, repair, utility services, common area fees, etc.—are paid by the tenant on a pro-rated basis. In a *modified triple-net lease* frequently used in shopping centers, the owner is responsible for structural repairs to the building and for payment of management fees.

Gross Lease.   An arrangement whereby the owner pays for taxes, insurance, structural repairs, maintenance, utility services, and other operating expenses. Because the owner pays these costs, the tenant's minimum rent or percentage rent may be higher. (This type of lease is more commonly used for office space.)

for allocating expenses is subject to negotiation and should be stated clearly in the lease document.

Depending on the type of net lease, the tenant may be responsible for taxes, insurance, utilities, property management fees, maintenance costs, roof repairs, and the amortized cost of capital improvements. The lease should specify exactly which of these charges are to be tenant expenses and which are paid by the owner, what percentage of such charges the tenant will owe, and the method of payment. Common practice for an en-closed mall is that major tenants (anchors) are responsible *only* for their pro rata share of parking lot upkeep, although they may occasionally pay a small negotiated amount for the mall upkeep. The greater portion of com-mon area maintenance costs is passed through to the ancillary tenants. In strip centers, where so-called common areas are less extensive, anchors usually contribute their full pro rata share of expenses. (Most net leases also assign responsibility for maintenance of the interior of the leased store space to the tenant.)

Payments for operating expenses are usually made monthly in ad-vance. Typically, expenses for the coming year are estimated and each ten-ant is presented a list of prorated charges. One-twelfth of this annual share is due at the beginning of each month. At the end of the year, the owner prepares an annual statement showing actual expenses compared to the estimate and how much the tenant paid for expenses during the year. Overpayments may be refunded at the end of each year or credited toward the next year's expense proration. Customarily the lease will state that if the settlement statement shows that the tenant has overpaid, the owner will credit the excess amount against the next year's rent payment unless the lease term has ended, in which case the tenant will receive a refund. If the settlement statement shows that the tenant owes money to the owner, this amount will be due within a certain time period, usually thirty days.

On the other hand, some property managers make these adjustments more frequently. It may be practical (or necessary) to adjust maintenance and other operating expenses quarterly; tax and insurance pass throughs may only be adjustable annually. The lease may include a clause stating that the owner retains the right to amend the amount of the estimate if expenses exceed the original estimate at any time during the year and that tenant payments will be revised accordingly. Amendments to the tenant's pro rata share of operating expenses are not common, however, unless an actual bill (such as a real estate tax increase) is received that drastically changes the owner's original estimate. Tenants are permitted to examine the owner's records to verify expenses.

Base Rent Adjustments.   Usually a standard lease will contain a clause that provides for specific periodic rental increases, either fixed or designed to compensate for inflation and the rise in the cost of living. Although these increases in the base monthly rent can be designated in different ways, a commonly used basis is the *Consumer Price Index (CPI)*, in which the cost of goods in different urban areas across the country is compared. Numbers for each year represent percentage increases from the designated base year which has a set value of 100. Through 1987, the CPI base year was 1967. In 1988, a new base year (1982–84) was established, and data for 1988 and subsequent years are currently being reported using both base years. The values based on 1967 = 100 allow comparison with past years up to two decades earlier. A rent increase is computed for succeeding years of the lease term by dividing the most recent CPI by the preceding year's CPI, and multiplying the monthly rent by the result.

$$\frac{\text{CPI January 1989}}{\text{CPI January 1988}} \times 1988 \text{ Monthly Rent} = 1989 \text{ Monthly Rent}$$

$$\frac{362.7}{346.7} \times \$1,000 = \$1,046.15$$

Because actual CPI figures are not published till sometime after the month for which they were collected and therefore not available at the time an increase should be effected, it may be more appropriate to use the CPIs from one year earlier. Using this variation in the preceding calculation, the 1989 monthly rent would be computed from January 1988 and 1987 CPIs. Use of the CPI to compute rent increases was detailed in chapter 3 along with a representative table of CPI values (table 3.4, page 64).

For long lease terms, it is common practice to combine straight CPI increases the first few years with a subsequent adjustment to market rent to provide a new base rent. For example, a store with a ten-year lease might pay regular CPI increases for the first five years; in the sixth year, the rent would be adjusted to the current market rate, and that year would become the new base year for computing CPI adjustments for the seventh through tenth years.

Other methods of increasing rents include specific incremental increases stated in the lease either as specific amounts or as specific percentages, and the time at which increases go into effect may be other than one-year anniversaries. The lease should clearly define the method of calculating rent escalations and when they are to occur (yearly, every other year, etc.) as well as what is meant by "base year," "price index," "lease year," and any other terms to be used in these computations.

Lease Clauses Specific to Shopping Centers

Apart from the general lease terms already stated, leases for space in shopping centers often contain a number of specific additional clauses and articles. A successful shopping center should convey a sense of unity to the customer, and therefore tenants have to work together as a cohesive whole. Leasing negotiations should stress the interdependency of tenants in the shopping center. While many of the issues discussed in the following sections are important considerations in the leasing of retail space generally, as lease clauses they are more common in leases for space in a large, organized center.

Use.   A most important clause, and one that should be in every retail lease, is a use clause. Usually a shopping center is carefully marketed to a certain trade area and a certain population. The use clause in a lease is designed to protect the center from changes in a retailer's merchandise or image that might affect the center's overall sales performance. The owner is primarily interested in maintaining the delicate balance among merchandise, price lines, and tenants—what is referred to as "tenant mix." The quality and reputation of the center are also at stake.

A use clause may require the tenant to stock or sell only items or categories of merchandise listed in the lease. This differs from the continuous operation clause in that a use clause can be much more detailed about types of goods the retailer can market; there is often an emphasis on limiting or prohibiting the selling of certain merchandise. The degree of specificity in the use clause depends on the type of center or store. For strip centers, use clauses generally list only categories of merchandise; for large centers, specific items may be listed because the retailer faces more competition within the center than a retailer in a small center does. For example, an Italian restaurant could be required to provide food service exclusively and to serve only specific foods representative of that ethnic cuisine, or a tobacco store may be required to stock certain brands of cigars. The first is in keeping with a stated type of business operation (food service) and precludes other activities (for example, arranging tours to Italy); the second would maintain a level of quality. Many owners and leasing agents have found that it pays to be as detailed as possible when drawing up the use clause.

At the same time, the tenant should be granted some flexibility. An item or category of merchandise that sells well when the store opens may not be popular throughout the term of a lease. The lease should provide for the tenant to substitute a better-selling item in the same price range and category of merchandise if that becomes desirable. For example, if a tenant leases space to operate a low-priced toy store, a switch to expensive imported toys would be cause for concern; but if a tenant removes stock from the shelves for good business reasons—because it doesn't sell—the practice should not be discouraged. In general, however, tenants should be free to manage their businesses to the best of their ability, and any reasonable changes they make should be considered acceptable.

Another aspect of the use clause, termed *dignified use,* prohibits the use of the retail space for any purpose that would disrupt the peace or otherwise damage the image of the center. Use of the premises for a discount outlet, a second-hand or thrift shop, a disco, a video game arcade, an auction house, or any noisy or offensive activities that are contrary to the center's stated image or policies would be proscribed unless the terms of the lease specifically sanctioned these uses. The tenant usually is not permitted to hold a "fire sale" or a "going out of business sale" without written consent of the owner. Although tenants may be concerned about restrictions on such sales, the lease should clearly distinguish between an occasional markdown sale, which would be permitted, and conversion of a retail business to a discount operation.

A lease may also prohibit vending machines and public telephones in individual retail spaces. However, tenants will often request permission to install telephones and other conveniences for their employees, and the lease should specify which items are permitted and which are not. As another consideration, items that generate income may be subject to percentage rent.

Many national retailers demand and receive more flexibility in use clauses. Their tendency to grow and change merchandise lines requires these large stores to expand their retail concepts as well; many center owners guarantee these important tenants the right to negotiate modifications to their use clauses as they grow.

Exclusive Use. A right granted to the tenant that restricts the owner from leasing space in the same shopping center to other retailers who sell similar merchandise is stated in an *exclusive use* clause. The tenant benefits because this limits specific competition. Generally, the larger the retailer requesting an exclusive use clause and the more comprehensive the coverage of the clause, the more difficult it will be to negotiate. Major tenants are very sophisticated in negotiating exclusive use clauses; their success comes from their strength and product dominance in the market. Although it may be necessary to include an exclusive use clause to satisfy certain tenants, exclusive use is generally not a desirable arrangement. More to the point, antitrust laws enforced by the Federal Trade Commission make certain restrictions illegal.

Competition among tenants is usually healthy for the center; certain retailers thrive on it. For example, shoe stores are often very successful when located next to each other because customers tend to comparison shop, in this case for style, fit, etc., as well as price. If it is absolutely necessary to grant an exclusive in order to secure a lease, an acceptable compromise should be negotiated. Rather than grant a paint store the exclusive right to do business in a particular shopping center, the lease might grant exclusive rights to sell certain brands of paint or a specific price range of paint and related products. Another approach would be to grant an exclusive on the basis of the size or scope of the business. In other words, a competing store with an area less than a certain defined size might be permitted while anything larger would not be. Proximity to the tenant seeking an exclusive is another criterion, and a lease might state a distance from the tenant within which a competitor would not be permitted to open a store. As a means of giving a new tenant a head start, an exclusive may be granted for a certain time period after which the exclusive would be gradually reduced.

Restrictive Covenant.   How the tenant will use a retail space is often a matter for considerable negotiation. Most owners will seek protection by setting limitations on a tenant's operation. Although tenants may not always agree with restrictive covenants, which prohibit use of leased space in any way that might be detrimental to other businesses, they usually realize that restrictions imposed on other retailers will be a protection for them.

Continuous Occupancy.   A clause relating to continuous occupancy calls for the tenant to remain in business in the shopping center location for the duration of the lease term. Although this provision may seem unnecessary, an owner cannot assume that a retailer that signs a lease will always occupy the leased space. For one thing, a tenant could sublet to a business that does not conform to the center's image; or a retailer might decide to change its business from a shoe store to a tobacco shop, and this change could affect the tenant mix at the center. Laws regarding the owner's rights in these situations vary from state to state. In some states, if a tenant moves out before the lease term is over, the owner could not take possession for approximately sixty days. In such a situation, the owner would have a lengthy period of vacancy as well as legal costs to terminate the lease.

There are many reasons a tenant may find it expedient to vacate. Poor sales and high operating costs are just two of them. However, tenants should be discouraged from leaving at will or before the owner has found a replacement. Even if a tenant continues to pay rent, the shopping center will suffer the negative effects of vacant space because shoppers generally are more attracted to a fully leased, active center. A continuous occupancy clause should be worded carefully so that the owner can seek payment for damages if a tenant vacates prematurely.

Continuous Operation.   A shopping center lease may also contain a clause that requires tenants to keep their businesses running smoothly and consistently during occupancy. This means maintaining adequate inventory, keeping shelves stocked and merchandise neatly arranged, hiring and training a large enough staff, and participating in advertising and promotional programs for the center as a whole in addition to their individual promotional efforts. Tenants may also be required to maintain their business or trade names throughout the lease term and to mention the shopping center whenever they advertise. Although the owner cannot ask that the tenant keep a specific brand name or type of goods in stock, the clause should be worded so that the tenant will be required to keep a certain caliber of goods to attract the market being sought. It is possible that if a tenant removed certain merchandise from its shelves, business would not be as brisk for its store or for the center as a whole.

Radius Clause.   A clause that prohibits a tenant from opening a similar store or from developing a chain of similar stores within a certain distance from the shopping center is called a *radius clause*. The typical radius is 3–5 miles. This clause is intended to protect owners from the loss of revenue if a tenant were to direct customers to its other store in order to avoid paying percentage rent in the shopping center. However, a radius clause is difficult to negotiate, and many owners will accept a compromise. (Operation of a nearby [second] store might be permitted if the tenant includes the gross sales or a percentage of the gross sales at the second store in the calculation of percentage rent for the first store.) Radius clauses are also very difficult to enforce legally.

Store Hours.   In neighborhood or strip centers, or in freestanding retail spaces, retailers tend to maximize their own business hours and opportunities regardless of the practices of other nearby businesses as long as local ordinances or the property owner do not set specific limitations. The hours maintained by a supermarket are not practical for most ancillary tenants in the center with it. In large organized shopping centers and enclosed malls, however, the lease may specify opening and closing times each tenant is expected to maintain consistent with the hours of operation designated for the entire center. Regular store hours for all tenants can boost sales performance for the entire center. For example, it would be detrimental to both businesses if a women's clothing store stayed open one or more evenings while the women's shoe store next to it closed every day at five o'clock. The women's shoe store would lose valuable sales, and the clothing store would not be able to benefit from the influx of customers who came to the center primarily to buy shoes.

Today most retail operations have long hours. Shopping in the evening has increased in popularity. Sundays are also prime shopping days. In some areas, it is not unusual for stores to be open seven full days a week or six days plus a half day on Sunday.

It may be inappropriate or uneconomic for some retailers to stay open for extended hours, and an owner should grant some flexibility in terms. A tenant whose business is seasonal—for example, a garden store—may request reduced hours during its off-season. Stores should also be permitted to close if they need extra time to take inventory. A time limit can be specified in the lease, and it may be desirable to determine a schedule in advance so several stores are not closed at the same time. Often retailers have a policy of announcing inventory closures to their customers.

If the store hours of an ancillary tenant are to be tied to the hours of an anchor tenant, the owner should make sure that the anchor's business will also attract customers to the ancillary tenant's business. Otherwise, the ancillary tenant may have to operate at a loss. A fair lease will protect such an ancillary tenant against the negative impact of any "trade wars" between anchor tenants who decide to maintain longer hours to compete with each other.

Some businesses—restaurants, convenience stores, or service centers—tend to stay open later than others (local ordinances permitting), and it may be appropriate to designate a closing time for them as well. This would most likely be required in an enclosed mall. If only one store operator wanted to stay open all night, the owner of the shopping center would have to decide whether the additional operating costs for lighting, heating, security, and other services would be worthwhile for just a single tenant. On the other hand, if one tenant in a strip center stays open late, the problem will not be one of keeping a common area operating but merely the expense of lighting a parking lot. If an exception to mall hours is made, the extra utilities services can be metered separately to the tenant who has later hours. Aside from expenses, the owner should also consider whether nearby residents will be disturbed by an operation with extended hours. Each shopping center should determine the optimum store hours for its particular market, and a clause requiring tenants to abide by these hours should be included in all its leases. The lease should also be carefully worded to limit operating hours for stores whose late hours could pose a problem.

Common Area Charges. The lease document should include a definition of the common area(s) of the mall or shopping center, specifying which fees and expenses for it the tenant will have to pay and itemizing the types of maintenance and repairs these charges will cover. Typically, the common area in an enclosed mall is defined as courts and general landscaping; service areas and loading platforms; elevators, escalators, and stairways not within individual stores; public washrooms, drinking fountains, and telephones; parking lots and access roads; and all utilities—including wiring, drains, sewers, and pipes. In strip centers, parking lots are generally the only "common" areas although sidewalks, service areas, and landscaping may be included. Maintenance and upkeep of common areas in enclosed malls usually include painting and landscaping, window and floor cleaning, snow removal, HVAC maintenance, trash removal, and roof and wall repairs. The charges also reflect labor costs for all of these jobs and include administrative costs and the property manager's fee.

These common area expenses are generally charged to the tenant as pass-through operating expenses along with real estate taxes, etc. In some leases, common area charges and other pass-through expenses are indicated as "additional rent." Each tenant's pro rata share of the common area expenses is based on the GLA of the tenant's space as it relates to the GLA of the entire center. The owner may reserve the right to alter the common area by reducing courtyard size, constructing new retail space, adding parking, or otherwise increasing or decreasing the size of the common area or changing the way it is used.

Temporary tenants may not have any additional costs for common area expenses, or they may simply pay a flat fee. Kiosk tenants generally pay a flat fee that amounts to a rate that may be two to three times higher than an average tenant's pro rata common area charges. This is to compensate for the fact that the kiosk takes advantage of the common areas that are supported for the most part by the permanent tenants. Food court common area expenses may be prorated exclusively among the food court tenants.

If a tenant's GLA is 1,000 square feet in a center with a GLA of 100,000 square feet, its pro rata share would be 1 percent. One percent of a common area cost of $100,000—$1,000—would be $1.00 per square foot. A kiosk, on the other hand, may occupy only 25 square feet of floor space and pay $75 toward the same $100,000 of common area costs—a rate of $3.00 per square foot.

Utilities and Other Services. Tenants are usually responsible for initial deposits or fees for incoming utilities—telephone installation, electricity, gas, water—for their individually leased spaces. In some centers, utilities are metered separately to individual tenants and billed directly to them. Tenants often prefer separate metering because they feel that they are charged more fairly under this system. In other centers, all utilities may be billed to the owner, who then charges the tenants on a pro rata basis through a master-metering program. However, coordination of tenant prorations is more difficult using a master-metering system, and it is not always the most economical method. The lease should clearly state which method of metering is being used and how the bulk charges are to be prorated.

Alterations and Repairs.   The extent to which tenants are allowed to alter or remodel their space over the course of the lease term is another issue for negotiation. These are alterations that are separate from the initial improvements made to the space on tenant move-in. Owners often seek to limit the types of alterations tenants can make by retaining the right to approve them. The owner's lease form will commonly prohibit any unauthorized exterior additions to the property—signs, canopies, billboards, etc. Structural changes to walls, ceilings, and floors are also prohibited. (Anchor tenants with long-term leases may be permitted to make certain structural changes to their buildings, however.) Nonstructural changes may be limited to a certain specified dollar amount each year of the lease term. So-called decorative installations—carpeting, drapes, window blinds, lighting fixtures, air conditioning, fencing, wiring, etc.—may be permitted if the owner approves of these installations in advance. Of concern would be maintenance of a unified image in an organized center, possible damage to finished floor or walls or to the structure itself, and the requirement for a construction permit.

Tenants will usually seek more freedom to make structural changes they consider necessary for the successful operation of their business. An acceptable compromise might be agreement by the tenant to obtain the owner's permission before making any such changes, and the tenant would be required to pay for all labor and materials and to give the owner notice before starting work. Any construction that would detract from the business of other merchants would not be allowed, and the lease would state that all improvements that are not removable become the property of the owner at the expiration of the lease term. (Most leases require the tenant to restore the space to its original condition.)

Over the course of the lease term, the tenant's space may require repairs as a result of ordinary wear and tear or damage. The lease should clearly distinguish between such necessary repairs and true alterations. If the owner undertakes the necessary repairs, the expense may be passed along to the tenant in the form of additional rent or as an operating expense. Some leases require the tenant to be responsible for repairs inside the leased store space. The lease should require the tenant to make a written request for repairs that are the owner's responsibility and to state a time period for the owner to respond. If the owner does not respond within that period, the tenant would have the right to perform the repairs at the owner's expense.

The lease should also include a clause prohibiting the tenant from using the shopping center property as security against unpaid debts for labor and materials which are costs of repairs or alterations. This is a particularly important clause because lenders want to be certain the property is free of encumbrances.

Insurance, Indemnification, and Damages. The owner generally carries insurance for the shopping center as a whole. This usually consists of fire, extended coverage, public liability, and property damage insurance. However, the lease should require the tenant to carry adequate insurance independently—including workers' compensation, business interruption, fire, property damage, merchandise damage, and such other coverages as are necessary for the tenant's particular business—and to name the owner as an additional insured.

Under a net-net or a triple-net lease, the tenant is responsible for a portion of the center's insurance, and the percentage should be specified. However, payment of this expense does not relieve the tenant of the responsibility to carry separate insurance. Large tenants, especially major anchors, may want to purchase all the insurance for their own space rather than participate in the center's policy. In such cases, the owner should verify that the tenant's financial status warrants a completely separate insurance program and that the coverage the tenant arranges is adequate and appropriately documented. For the large tenant, this would be *in addition to* the required business coverages mentioned previously.

The lease should further state how repairs and reconstruction will be handled in the event of damage to the property and who will be responsible for the expenses incurred. If damage to the center will limit or interrupt tenants' operations, the repairs are the owner's responsibility. In such situations, a tenant may also be entitled to a rent abatement, but this usually applies to the monthly base rent only and requires that the damage is *not* caused by the tenant, the tenant's employees, or any visitors to the tenant's premises.

If a certain percentage of the building or common area has been extensively damaged by a cause which is not covered in the standard insurance policies, and if the repairs would take a lengthy period to complete (such as ninety to one hundred eighty days), the tenant may have the right to be released from the remainder of the lease term. This provision is also tied to the number of years remaining in the term of the tenant's lease. In addition to the time factor, the need for a construction permit and any requirements or limitations set by it would be a consideration. The clause must be worded carefully so that it cannot be interpreted that the tenant has the right to terminate the lease automatically in the event of extensive damage. The correct procedure is for the owner to notify the tenant in writing, stating the specific date of release from the lease contract. This procedure should be spelled out in the lease.

If the tenant is responsible for damage to the premises, the lease should require that repairs be done as soon as possible at the tenant's expense (or they will be made by the owner at his or her option and charged back to the tenant). The clause should also state that the tenant will continue to operate during repairs and reconstruction, with or without a rent abatement. This situation re-emphasizes the value of having minimum rents built into a lease: If a tenant paid only percentage rent, the owner could lose money during a period of reduced sales resulting from such reconstruction.

An *indemnification clause* states that the tenant will not hold the owner or the owner's employees liable for any damage to the tenant's property and that any injury or other accident that is *not* a result of the owner's negligence will be the tenant's responsibility. Most insurance companies follow a policy of subrogation whereby they "stand in the shoes" of the insured and exercise the right to take legal action in the name of the insured if they pay for any damage to the insured's property. However, large retailers and owners will usually sign a mutual *waiver of subrogation,* waiving their insurance companies' rights to file claims against each other (with the approval of their insurance carriers).

Parking.   Tenants will be especially interested in their rights regarding parking. Commonly the owner will grant the tenant a nonexclusive parking license. This permits the owner the flexibility to designate employee spaces, to change or remodel parking areas for other uses, and to formulate appropriate rules regarding parking. The lease may include a description of parking ratios.

A lease for a strip center often restricts the times and days for loading and unloading merchandise. A lease for an enclosed mall usually restricts tenant loading docks to a specified area and may limit employee parking spaces. The amount of parking designated for tenants and their employees, the location of this parking, and the length of time they will be permitted to park there should be clearly defined in the lease. The owner usually also has the right to fine a tenant's employees if they violate any parking regulations. Towing rights are granted to the owner.

Advertising, Signs, and Graphics.   Tenant advertising and signage should be carefully controlled. The lease should grant the owner of the shopping center the right to restrict the location, format, design, lettering, and language of all signs used to advertise the tenant's business. In particular, the owner's approval should be required for all permanent exterior signs on the premises and for all methods of illuminating signs and displays. However, the purchase, installation, maintenance, and repair of a tenant's exterior signs should be the tenant's responsibility. The lease might also include a requirement to light the sign until a certain time at night or until the center closes. At the expiration of the lease term, all permanent installations become the owner's property if the owner chooses; otherwise the tenant is required to remove such signs and make the necessary repairs to the building.

Shopping center and mall tenants are often required to spend a specific percentage of their gross sales on advertising and to link their advertising in part to the shopping center. In enclosed malls and large shopping centers, the owner may be granted a right to review the tenant's advertising program before it is initiated because the reputation of the center depends on its ability to convey an appropriate image to the customer, and each tenant's advertising should contribute to this image and not detract from it. The owner will also want to verify that specific promotion has been done and that the specified percentage of gross sales has been spent. This may be done on a quarterly or annual basis.

Merchants' Association and Marketing Fund.   Another important lease clause defines the extent to which the tenant is expected to participate in a shopping center's total promotional efforts. A cohesive marketing program for a shopping center is usually structured one of two ways— as a merchants' association or as a marketing fund. Establishment of a *merchants' association* requires that tenants attend regular meetings and contribute dues that will be used to pay for media and other advertising expenses. Tenants help plan and organize each promotion under the guidance of a marketing director hired by the association, although the property manager may assume the role of marketing director in some situations. A *marketing fund* only requires tenants to make regular monetary contributions, and all marketing decisions are made by the center's staff although there may be an advisory board comprised of tenants' representatives. Marketing funds have become more common in centers developed more recently. Some property managers believe that the marketing fund is more practical, and many older leases that had merchants' association clauses are being converted as the leases renew to require contributions to a marketing fund instead. This conversion requires changes in lease clauses that should be scrutinized by a real estate attorney. Marketing funds are established in some neighborhood centers, with the center owner determining specific expenditures.

Both the merchants' association and the marketing fund have similar methods of financing center promotions. Depending on the size of the center, the owner is usually responsible for up to one quarter of the center's annual advertising budget; the tenants contribute the remainder. Each tenant pays a specified amount based on one or more factors—the amount of space occupied in the center, the amount of store frontage, a percentage of gross sales, the percentage that represents the ratio of the tenant's rent to the total rent paid by all tenants in the center, or some combination of these.

Each tenant is usually responsible for a guaranteed minimum contribution—$500 per year, for example—which is subject to escalation. The formulas apply primarily to ancillary tenants. Major or anchor tenants are often exempted from contributing a prorated amount to the marketing fund or merchants' association because a substantial portion of their expenses is already allocated for advertising and promotion—from which the center as a whole does benefit. Although this concession to an anchor's negotiating power is often granted, the owner will sometimes seek a nominal contribution from an anchor as a means of showing support for the merchants' association because ancillary tenants' leases may require their participation in it.

If a merchants' association is established, the lease should include reference to attendance at regular meetings, if required. Such meetings often begin six or more months before the center opens. In addition, the lease should refer to (1) the association bylaws; (2) the services of personnel such as a promotional manager, a treasurer, and a secretary; and (3) a specific promotional budget for the center. The clause should also grant the owner the right to terminate the lease if the tenant fails to pay the required dues. (The differences between and the advantages and disadvantages of merchants' associations and marketing funds are detailed in appendix E.)

Grand Opening Fund.   Somewhat related to a merchants' association clause is provision for a grand opening fund. This only applies for new unified shopping centers and is in addition to the regular advertising program. The fund requires a one-time payment intended to cover the expenses of promoting the new "mall." The budget is usually equal to one-fourth or one-half of the annual assessment for the marketing fund or merchants' association, and the lease should clearly state the tenant's contribution and the owner's, both of which are usually based on a certain dollar amount per square foot of leasable area. The owner arranges for advance advertising, decorations, and entertainment for the grand opening. The formal opening is usually held between ninety and one hundred eighty days after the first tenant moves in. Even new strip centers and neighborhood and community centers have grand opening ceremonies, and their leases may also contain a grand opening fund reference. Grand opening "dues" in these centers are normally one-fourth of annual dues in the marketing fund.

Default. A default clause is extremely important to both tenant and owner. It states exactly what constitutes default and outlines what is to be done if either party defaults—in other words, the rights and remedies of the parties. During negotiations, the tenant will try to focus the owner's interpretation of what constitutes default and will seek inclusion of a requirement for the owner to notify the tenant of any default by the tenant before the owner takes any action. Most owners will agree to formulate a very specific definition of default, although they will try to retain the right to act without notice or to limit the number of notices they are required to give. In particular, notice periods for monetary and nonmonetary defaults are different.

Basically, default refers to nonperformance of the terms of the lease. If a tenant fails to pay rent for more than a specified period—usually five to ten days after it is due or after the owner has informed the tenant that it is due—the tenant has defaulted. Failure to pay any other charges relating to the property—operating expenses, merchants' association fees, etc.—also constitutes default by the tenant. Owners will want to include a statement that the tenant will not be entitled to a grace period or to any notice if the tenant has failed to pay rent several times during the year. The lease may also provide for payment of a late fee or interest on the amount due.

When a tenant defaults, the owner has certain rights, including the right to terminate the lease, thereby making the space available for a new tenant. The owner may also hold the defaulting tenant responsible for continued payment of rent. The owner's choice to pursue a new tenant or to require the current tenant to continue to pay the rent may depend in part on the manner of default. If a tenant defaults by not paying rent, for example, the problem may simply be one of low cash availability at that time, and the tenant may be able to pay rent in the future. On the other hand, a bankruptcy may preclude recovery of rent because of the tenant's insolvency.

The owner's choice regarding tenant replacement is sometimes based on market conditions as well. If the market is good and a new tenant could pay more rent, the owner would likely terminate the lease. However, if the market is not stable, the owner may prefer to try collecting the outstanding rent owed by the former tenant. The owner must decide which condition would result in the least amount of loss to the center. Once the owner terminates the lease, the right to charge the tenant for the accumulated rent arrearage may be forfeited. However, in some states it may be possible to terminate "possession" of the premises without terminating the lease itself.

Bankruptcy is a specific type of default. Each lease must be carefully worded to protect the owner from the effects a tenant's bankruptcy can have on the owner's financial stability. The Bankruptcy Act prohibits the owner from terminating a tenant's lease after bankruptcy proceedings have begun. The tenant's creditors are entitled to protection, and they can sometimes control the space until it is determined whether the tenant has any leasehold interest of value. This leasehold interest would then belong to the tenant's creditors and not strictly to the center owner, although the center owner would be one of the tenant's creditors. The default clause only allows the owner to assume occupancy of the tenant's space *before* bankruptcy has been declared. If it is obvious that the tenant is going to file for bankruptcy, the owner may want to terminate the lease immediately. Otherwise the owner may not be able to recover possession. If the tenant's creditors decide to assign the lease, the new tenant should be required to provide "adequate assurance" to the owner that (1) the rent will be paid, (2) use clauses will not be violated, (3) the shopping center's tenant mix will remain balanced, and (4) percentage rent will not decline. Additional considerations here are the new tenant's financial situation and experience in the business.

Not all default is monetary in nature although the results of such default may have financial impact. Failure to take possession of the premises on the commencement date of the lease term or abandonment of the premises at any time prior to the expiration of the lease term also constitutes default along with breaches of any of the other terms or conditions of the lease. Vacating the premises—as a temporary interruption of occupancy—should be distinguished in the lease from abandonment, as such, which is vacating without intending to return. Tenants may wish to negotiate a clause regarding vacating the premises such that a specific time period distinguishes vacating from abandonment.

Although the discussion to this point has addressed default by the tenant, a lease may include statements regarding default by the owner. In general, this is boilerplate language relating to performance by the owner of his or her obligations under the lease and efforts to cure the default with relation to specific periods of notice by the tenant.

Notice.   A special clause related to default is the notice clause. It protects and benefits the owner by limiting the number of notices that must be sent to a tenant before action can be taken. Generally, it requires the owner to give the tenant written notice of termination of the lease a certain period beforehand; it does not bind the owner to give notice that the tenant has violated the lease terms or to state the steps the owner plans to take. (Other requirements for notice from tenant to owner or vice versa are stated in the lease in the context of the clauses to which specific notice applies.)

Assignment and Subleasing.   This clause is included to ensure that the owner will have control over how the space is occupied if the tenant leaves before the end of the lease term. *Assignment* is a complete transfer of the lease and contract rights to another party for the remainder of the lease term. It may also occur by a sale of controlling stock or partnership interest in the tenant's business. The new occupant (assignee) assumes the obligations of the tenant for the balance of the lease term. In a *sublease,* the original tenant becomes the new occupant's (subtenant's) landlord. The lease may prohibit outright any assignment or subleasing, or it may require the tenant to obtain written consent of the owner before either assignment or subleasing can occur.

It is the tenant's responsibility to find a financially stable replacement as an assignee. The owner is usually granted the right to withhold consent to a lease assignment or subleasing if the replacement tenant is not credit-worthy or if the change would be detrimental to the tenant mix of the center; however, the owner cannot unreasonably withhold consent to sub-leasing or assignment, and what constitutes a "reasonable" objection is usually carefully outlined in the lease clause. The owner judges the sub-lessee on the basis of use of the space, financial strength, and experience.

In the case of default by the new tenant, the original tenant can still be liable under an assignment or sublease agreement, and the original lease should protect this right for the owner. The owner retains some rights in the negotiation process for a sublease or assignment, and during negotia-tions, the owner's rights to a space that is being subleased may be ques-tioned only partially. Often this will depend on the size of the space and the bargaining power of the tenant seeking to sublease it. An owner may also be entitled to receive a portion of the tenant's financial gain in any subleasing or assignment transaction—in other words, if the sublease is at a higher rental rate, the owner should benefit as well. This usually de-pends on whether the lease has a percentage rent clause; if it doesn't, the owner may have the right to negotiate for compensation. Automatic mini-mum rent escalations can be built into the lease to assure that the owner will not lose money as a result of loss of percentage rent if the original tenant subleases the space.

Take Back.   Also related to subleasing is a *take back* or recapture clause, which is commonly included in leases for large tenants when a broad use clause has been negotiated. Instead of accepting a sublease, the owner has the right to terminate the current tenant's lease, take back the space, and lease it to a new tenant—possibly at a higher rent. However, the owner can only exercise this privilege under certain conditions. The owner can-not recapture the space until or unless the current tenant provides either (1) written notice of the terms of the sublease or assignment agreement or (2) an actual agreement signed by the proposed new tenant. This protects the tenant from being evicted or otherwise losing the space before the final decision to sublease has been made.

The owner benefits from the take back clause because an executed sublease agreement will include complete information about the prospec-tive tenant along with the rental rate and other sublease terms. This provides the owner with definite information about the amount of rent the space can command on the open market, and the owner will be able to make a more informed decision than if the original tenant simply announced a tentative decision to sublease.

An owner's decision to take back the space will depend in part on market conditions. If the market is high—that is, if the current tenant's rent is below market rates—the owner will usually choose to re-lease to another tenant. If market rates are the same as the current rental rates, the decision to recapture may depend on the prospects for the space: Another tenant may want to expand, or a retailer that would be more valuable to the center might be interested in leasing. If the market is low—in other words, if the current rent is above market rates—the owner may not be able to find a replacement tenant. In this situation, the owner probably would not try to re-lease the space unless the current tenant was doing very poorly. The leasing agent should understand what is involved in take back as it relates to the lease document and negotiations with some (usually major) prospects. However, the leasing agent is rarely involved in the decision to take back the space, which may occur during the term of the lease.

Holdover.   A tenant may occupy the premises beyond the expiration of the lease term. If there is no option to extend the lease, neither the tenant nor the owner may assume automatic renewal, and the owner has the right to evict the tenant in this situation. However, if the owner continues to accept rent, this right is conditioned on the owner giving the tenant certain additional notice. In some situations, the right may be forfeited. To discourage tenant occupancy without a valid lease, the lease document should state that holdover is on a month-to-month basis. It may also state that holdover without the owner's consent results in an increase in rent—to at least twice the amount paid in the last term of the lease—and that all the rules and regulations set forth in the original lease remain in force.

Subordination.   Subordination refers to the condition whereby the tenant's lease is transferred to the mortgagee in the event of a foreclosure on the owner's mortgage. If the owner declares bankruptcy or transfers ownership of the property in a foreclosure, tenants will be understandably concerned about being evicted or having to completely renegotiate the terms of their leases, and they will want to be assured of their rights and status under these circumstances. Tenants depend heavily on site identity for their business and losing a location can mean losing customers. Although most lease forms will treat subordination as mandatory, and tenants will have no choice but to accept it, the question of whether a tenant will be allowed to remain in occupancy with the same rights and privileges as under the previous lease becomes open to negotiation. Major or anchor tenants usually will have more bargaining power in this situation than ancillary tenants. Owners and tenants can usually negotiate a compromise by adding a nondisturbance and attornment agreement to the subordination clause. This gives additional protection to the tenant without impairing the rights of the mortgagee.

Nondisturbance and Attornment Agreement. Under this agreement, the tenant is guaranteed continued occupancy until the expiration of the lease term. The tenant will also seek to retain the right to all reimbursements—for improvements and rent abatements—to which it is entitled under the original lease. Typically a new owner will grant nondisturbance agreements only under the condition that he or she is not liable for any of the original owner's unfulfilled promises; a new owner does not want construction responsibilities, for example. A compromise clause would specify which owner-tenant agreements would be honored under subordination and which would not. Also, lenders will want to be reassured that the lease has not been modified beforehand without their consent. They will also want tenants to provide an appraisal certifying that the rent they are currently paying is a fair value for the space; otherwise the lenders may retain the right to raise the rent or to find a new tenant at market rates.

Tenant Improvement Allowance. The amount of money tenants are granted by the owner to spend on improvements to their space before they open for business is called a *tenant improvement allowance.* The standard allowance for a given center is set by the owner—separate and apart from any other concessions—and is based on a dollar amount per square foot. This amount varies with the geographic location of the center and the type of center. For shell space in a new building in a strip center, an allowance of $10–14 per square foot of GLA might be appropriate in an average market. Tenants may negotiate a larger allowance, however. (See the discussion of negotiating tenant improvement allowances in chapter 8.)

The lease should have attached to it an exhibit that outlines exactly what the tenant will receive as the bare shell space and how the costs for the improvements to the space will be divided between tenant and owner. (A description of standard landlord and tenant work is included as appendix F.) If a new tenant accepts a space "as is"—that is, the bare shell and the standard improvement allowance—then the expense of any improvements beyond the amount of the allowance is the tenant's responsibility. Before construction on the space is started, the tenant must give the owner a detailed list of the changes to be made, along with the costs of these changes and the names and addresses of contractors and laborers who will do the work.

In addition, a workletter should be agreed to by both parties. Such a letter states that the tenant agrees to pay all construction costs above the allowance and that the owner has the right to approve all materials and methods of construction. The letter should also state the hours during which work is allowed. The tenant is required to agree not to hold the owner responsible for any damages to the property or for any debts owed to the contractors, laborers, suppliers, or others. In addition, the tenant's contractors are prohibited from interfering with any other contractors who may be working on the property at the same time. The workletter is discussed in more detail later in this chapter in the section on Exhibits.

Security Deposit.   Security deposits are common in retail lease arrangements. However, creditworthy retailers may be exempted from this requirement, or they may be asked to pay a security deposit only if their sales volume falls below an established level or if they become delinquent in their rent payments. The amount of the deposit is negotiable. Market conditions, the tenant's credit, and the owner's investment in space improvements all make a difference when computing the amount of the security deposit. If an owner pays an above-standard amount for improvements, the owner may ask for a larger deposit.

The deposit is held by the owner until the tenant's lease term expires. In the event the tenant defaults in payment of monthly base rent, operating expenses, additional or percentage rent, or any other financial obligations required by the lease, the security deposit may be used to compensate the owner. In such a situation, the tenant is obligated to repay the security deposit within a certain period. If the tenant has fulfilled every article of the lease and there has been no significant damage to the property, the full amount of the security deposit will be returned to the tenant, usually within sixty days after the lease terminates. Some states have laws that require payment of interest on security deposit funds. The amount of the deposit, the condition of its return to the tenant, and any details regarding interest on the deposit should all be stated clearly in the lease.

ADDENDA TO THE STANDARD FORM LEASE

Most standard retail lease forms require incorporation of supplemental information to cover the various legal issues that arise during negotiation of the individual lease agreement. As negotiations progress, the lease will undergo many changes, and these can be referred to easily if they are handled as addenda. Two of the most common types of attachments to the standard retail lease are statements of options and specific exhibits.

Options

Options are sometimes negotiated for renewal, expansion, or cancellation of the retail lease. The *option to renew* may allow the tenant to renew its

FIGURE   7.3

**Exhibits Attached to a Retail Lease
Commonly Include:**

- Rules and regulations
- Signage criteria and limitations
- Detailed floor plan of individual space
- Relation of leased space to entire center
- Legal forms (workletter, guaranty, etc.)

lease—on the same terms or on some other terms as specified in the original lease. The *option to expand* provides the tenant that has long-range growth plans the opportunity to expand into additional (possibly adjacent) space after the expiration of (or during) the original lease term. Frequently linked to this option is an *option to cancel,* which grants the tenant the right to terminate the lease before the expiration date if the owner cannot make additional space available as promised. The tenant may seek an option to cancel if a more suitable space becomes available in a different center at the same time the expansion space becomes available—thus foregoing its option to expand—or if its sales have not reached a certain dollar amount.

Negotiating options can be a complex procedure. Options are more commonly granted in soft markets or when dealing with very strong prospects. Chapter 8 discusses this aspect of negotiation in more detail.

Exhibits

Exhibits or schedules clarify and illustrate specific points that have been negotiated as variants from the standard form lease. They can also be used to record renegotiation of certain items. If there is a conflict between the lease and an exhibit, the exhibit will usually take precedence over the lease form itself in a legal resolution, and the lease document should include a statement to that effect. Exhibits (figure 7.3) may include rules and regulations, descriptions of signage criteria, a detailed floor plan of the leased space, and any legal forms that may be necessary. Exhibits should be as complete as possible. They are usually assigned letters or numbers and referred to specifically at appropriate points in the lease document. Specific exhibits may vary from lease to lease because what applies to one tenant may not apply to another. The advantage of exhibits is that they can be updated and amended—both during the process of negotiations and over the course of the lease term. Although the exhibits are cited in the body of the lease, they are placed after the signatures of the various parties for convenience because the exhibits are usually long digressions that

F I G U R E   7.4

Shopping Center Rules Commonly Cover

- Use of common or mall areas
- Maintenance of sidewalks
- Protruding signs or awnings
- Defacement of exterior
- Proper use of plumbing
- Harmful substances
- Offensive noise and odors
- Trash and garbage disposal
- Maintenance of alarms
- Locks and keys
- Employee parking

would interrupt the specific lease terms and make the document itself difficult to understand.

Rules and Regulations.   For the general good of the shopping center's operations as well as to assure compliance with applicable federal, state, and local laws, the owner often attaches to each lease a list of rules and regulations that the tenant must follow. These rules are intended to protect the owner's rights in the investment as well as the rights of the tenant who expects to do business in a safe and secure environment. The rules and regulations for a given retail center will depend on its needs and characteristics. However, most retail centers will have some rules in common (figure 7.4).

For example, typical rules prohibit use of the common area or mall for any purpose other than walking into and out of the shopping center. Tenants in a strip center may be required to keep sidewalks and curbs in front of their store space reasonably clean and free of snow and ice. No awnings, shades, or other types of protruding objects are permitted to be placed on the tenant's storefront without the owner's permission. The tenant is not allowed to drill holes, apply paint, or otherwise deface the exterior of the premises, and inside plumbing fixtures such as toilets and sinks are to be used only for the purposes for which they are intended.

Tenants are prohibited from using flammable or other hazardous substances, causing objectionable odors, keeping animals or bicycles on the premises, and playing loud or disruptive music. They are also prohibited from placing trash anywhere but in a neat and adequate receptacle which must be maintained in an area specifically designated for trash removal. Rules may also specify that recyclable items must be separated for disposal or that food and related wastes must be handled in a special way. Tenants will be required to maintain in good working condition the smoke and burglar alarms that the owner has installed and to lock all entrances to the premises each evening. (All keys must be returned to the owner when the tenant vacates the premises.) Tenants' employees may park in designated areas only. The owner is responsible for sending the tenant copies of all amendments to the rules and regulations.

Workletter.   Sometimes called a construction rider, the *workletter* describes the exact construction to be done in the tenant's shell space, what amenities the owner will provide, what improvements are the tenant's responsibility, and any prerequisites for reimbursement if an allowance is negotiated. It also establishes a schedule for construction and sets a date for commencement and completion of the work. Exact costs are usually not described. Depending on the size of the tenant's space or the size of the site, the workletter can become long and complex. Most workletters consist of two parts: one describing the supervision of construction, preparation of plans, and actual delivery of the work; the other detailing the process of construction, materials to be used, percentage of costs to be spent on each phase of the project, and how the costs are to be divided between the tenant and the owner.

The workletter is an extremely important exhibit; it is a necessary addendum to the tenant improvement allowance clause. Tenant move-in dates, the term of the lease, and the commencement of rent payment will all be affected by the terms of the workletter because occupancy is dependent on the construction schedule. Both tenant and owner should be in total agreement on the terms of the workletter before a final draft is completed.

Guaranty.   If a prospective tenant does not have sufficient credit, a *guaranty* may be required. A guaranty calls for the *guarantor* to pay all of the tenant's obligations to the owner in case the tenant defaults. This includes attorneys' fees for any action taken by the owner against the tenant. The guarantor is not relieved of liability to the owner regardless of any modifications in the terms of the lease or any other agreements between the owner and the tenant. If the tenant declares bankruptcy, the guarantor is still legally responsible for the lease. Nor is the owner obliged to inform the guarantor of any changes in his or her relationship with the tenant, any changes in the lease, or any other arrangements that may affect the payment of rent.

Lending institutions often require a guarantor for the small retailer whose financial stability is questionable. Sometimes a lease with a corporation may require an individual to sign the lease, in effect as a personal guarantor of the corporation. If necessary, there can be several guarantors. The guaranty document usually includes a page for the signature of the guarantor or guarantors and for witnesses to the agreement. This page is dated and may be stamped with the guarantor's seal if required by state law.

OTHER LEASE COMPONENTS

The preceding discussions have covered specific clauses that are among the more commonly negotiated points in the development of retail leases for spaces in organized shopping centers. There are numerous other clauses that may or can be incorporated in a retail lease. Often they are part of what is referred to as "boilerplate"—standardized language for certain lease terms that generally apply to all tenants and all leases on the property. Other elements may vary with the size or complexity of the retail site or with the part of the country in which it is located. There are discrete differences between tenancies in enclosed malls and other types of shopping centers, and these differ from tenancies in store spaces in downtown business districts. Among the constituents that are common to all retail leases are estoppel certificates and the signatures of the parties to the lease.

Estoppel Certificate

An *estoppel certificate* is a statement declaring the rental rate the tenant is paying, the amount of the security deposit (if any), and the term of the lease. It may also include information regarding the condition of the premises; adjustments, supplements, and amendments of the terms of the lease, if any; the existence of any condition of default on the tenant's part (delinquent rent, for example); and whether the owner has completed the promised improvements and repairs on the property.

The form and content of an estoppel certificate will depend on the specific situation for which it is requested. Estoppel certificates are generally required at the initial (construction) financing and subsequent refinancing of a property at the time of a sale. These certifications assure the lender or potential purchaser that the owner is receiving nothing more for the property than the rent that is stated in the lease and that there are no outstanding claims on the property or uncompleted work that would indicate the owner had not used the construction loan for the purpose for which it was intended.

The lease usually includes a statement that confirms the reliability of the estoppel certificate for the use of all mortgagees, purchasers, and beneficiaries. The lease may also state that the lender has the right to request this certificate at any time. If the lender requests it, the owner submits a written request to the tenant who is then required to deliver the document to the owner within ten days. A new owner will also require the tenant to submit an estoppel certificate to make sure the lease the seller gave him or her is complete. The actual certificate may be inserted with the exhibits at the back of the lease.

Signatures

The last formal action with regard to the lease document is the signing of the lease by all the parties to it. The last page of the lease document is typically a signature page requiring the authorized signatures of the lessor, the lessee, and the guarantor or notary if necessary. Some states may require that the parties to the lease also initial each page of the document.

Authority to sign a lease often depends on the form of ownership. A corporation can act through an agent who is authorized to sign contracts, or the president or another officer may have sole authority. However, if a corporation does not have a strong track record, the tenant may be required to sign the lease both as the corporation and as an individual. For a general partnership, each of the partners should sign the lease, even though the signature of one general partner is legally binding. For a limited partnership, the signature of one of the general partners is required because a limited partner would not have authority to sign contracts. If a signature is questioned, the leasing agent should ask to see articles of incorporation or a partnership agreement to confirm that person's authority to execute a lease. Individual business owners will sign for themselves. The date the lease is being signed should also be included at this point. When all parties have signed the lease, the transaction is considered concluded. Who signs the lease first and other details regarding completion of the legal transaction are covered in chapter 8.

SUMMARY

A signed lease is the agent's goal. Usually the owner's standard lease form is the starting point for discussion, although major and anchor tenant prospects such as department stores and supermarkets may present their own lease forms to the owner. Either the owner's or the tenant's real estate attorney can draft the lease and the supporting documents.

All retail leases contain certain basic information: the names of the parties to the lease, a description of the leased premises, the length of the lease term, rental rates, and how operating expenses are allocated. If expenses are passed through to the tenant, the lease should specify the manner and time of payment and how the tenant's pro rata share is calculated. Occupancy and move-in dates are crucial elements, and the lease should also clearly define how base rent adjustments or rent escalations will be computed.

Leases for spaces in large shopping centers include several additional clauses. The same may apply for retail space in mixed-use developments, office buildings, or other locations where retail activity is only part of the use of the premises. Various types of use clauses prohibit tenants from selling anything other than what is specified in their leases or from opening competitive stores within a certain distance from the shopping center, and some tenants may request an exclusive use clause which would give them a competitive edge. Some clauses relate to tenant operations—hours of business, continuity of business and occupancy, sufficiency of inventory and staff. Others relate to common area charges, insurance, utilities, repairs and alterations, and other services, defining these aspects of the lease and assigning financial or other responsibility for them. Funds to promote the shopping center and advertising by the tenant may also be addressed, as well as any tenant improvement allowance.

The relationship between the tenant and the owner and their obligations to each other are covered in still other clauses. These protect the owner in case the tenant should default or misuse the space. Tenant default should be carefully defined; usually it means failure to pay rent or to achieve a certain level of sales. Separate clauses guarantee the tenant continued occupancy if the lease is transferred to the mortgagee. Limitations on assignment and subleasing are also stated separately.

Addenda to the retail lease include documents pertaining to options—to renew the lease after the term has expired, to expand the space, or to cancel the lease (under certain circumstances)—and specific exhibits such as rules and regulations for the center or building, floor plans, workletters, etc. The leasing process concludes when all parties to the lease have signed it.

Because most clauses in a retail lease are subject to negotiation, it is likely that the original document will be amended and expanded considerably as negotiations proceed. Legal guidance should be sought throughout the negotiation process to assure accurate expression and understanding of agreed-upon terms and compliance of the lease with applicable laws.

Negotiating the Retail Lease

All of the specific clauses defined in the previous chapter are negotiable, and drafting a lease that both owner and prospective tenant will agree to necessitates considerable negotiation. *Negotiation* is the process whereby tenant-to-be and owner discuss their individual wants and preferences and agree on terms that are mutually acceptable. The owner rarely participates directly in negotiations, which are the domain of the leasing agent, and the prospective tenant may be represented by an "agent" as well.

For new retail space or shopping centers, some of the lengthiest discussions relate to concessions or reductions in minimum rents, above-standard tenant improvement allowances, and tenant options. The agent must be cautious when negotiating concessions and options because they can have a long-term influence on the property's value. A skillful negotiator will be able to design concessions that will provide an attractive package for the prospect without reducing the owner's income significantly. For established centers and those that are being rehabilitated, many of the same negotiating issues and techniques apply. In these cases, however, reduction of spaces that are too large by creating two stores out of one or replacing old tenants with new ones who can pay market rates may require negotiation of different kinds of terms.

No prewritten, standard lease form will satisfy every owner-tenant transaction, and no established set of rules can guarantee that every negotiation will be successful. Some leases can be negotiated in two days; others may take two years. The length of time required will depend on such factors as the size and importance of the prospect, the size of the retail space, lender requirements with respect to financing the property, and the difficulty and complexity of the issues being negotiated. In most situations the leasing agent, representing the owner, initially presents a lease to the prospect for acceptance; the prospective tenant is usually the one who brings up points to be negotiated.

THE LEASING AGENT'S ROLE

The agent's role in the formal negotiation of a retail lease is to maintain an atmosphere of professionalism in which the parties can discuss their needs and expectations calmly and intelligently. The agent usually represents the principal in the transaction—the owner—but may suggest compromises to meet the expectations of both parties. It is the agent's responsibility to organize and administer the negotiation sessions and to help rank the various issues in order of their importance.

The leasing agent is in the best position to see both sides of every issue. From all the work that has been done in advance of the negotiations, the agent will know the prospective tenant's priorities and method of conducting business. This insight is invaluable in expediting the negotiation process. There can be no commission without a signed lease; therefore, it is to the agent's advantage if both prospect and owner conclude their negotiations as quickly as possible. However, considerable harm can result from rushing a leasing transaction. Often it is better to move slowly than to risk antagonizing prospective tenants by pressuring them for a decision before they are ready.

If the shopping center is already established, introducing prospects to satisfied established tenants in the center will show them how the shopping center operates as well as demonstrate the owner's desire to be open and aboveboard in lease negotiations. This affords the prospect an opportunity to see first hand that each tenant is required to follow the same rules and regulations and to inquire about whether and how policies on common area maintenance and other aspects of a retail lease apply to all the tenants in the center. As various issues are discussed during negotiations, emphasis should be on the success of the shopping center and its operation—rather than on the needs of the owner. The prospect should be shown that the individual tenant benefits when the center as a whole prospers.

Structuring the Negotiation Process

Negotiation of a retail lease can be simple and straightforward. The leasing agent tells the prospect the owner's lease terms regarding base rent (per square foot of GLA), percentage rent (payable as overage), pass-through proration of specific expenses (taxes, insurance, CAM charges, etc.), use limitations on the space, and other specific considerations. For a defined space in an established shopping center, this information might be presented in a telephone conversation or as a "summation" at the end of the prospect's tour of the site. If the prospect agrees, the lease showing the terms in detail is prepared and sent to the prospect for acceptance and signature. If the prospect signs the lease as presented, there is no real "negotiation."

However, everything may proceed identically through preparation of the lease and submission to the prospect only to have the prospect not sign the lease "as is." In reviewing the formal document, the prospect may find some details regarding the lease terms, more than likely about financial issues (base and percentage rent and pass-through expenses) or use limitations, that are not acceptable to the prospect as written. In this case, the prospect may opt to "negotiate" by writing in (and initialing) minor changes on the lease and signing the modified version. If these changes are acceptable to the owner, he or she can signal agreement by also initialing the prospect's changes and signing the lease. For any substantial changes, however, the prospect's attorney (and the owner's attorney as well) may be asked to review the changes to assure that the lease contract is correctly prepared and will be legally binding as amended. In fact, a fully revised lease document may be prepared for both parties' signatures.

Leases for large spaces (major or anchor tenants) can be complex and necessitate face-to-face negotiations. The longer duration of anchor leases and the various concessions that may be offered to or required by major retailers generally demand careful consideration. Participants in these negotiation sessions should be limited initially to the leasing agent representing the owner and the prospective tenant's representative, with attorneys or others called upon if they are needed.

Before the negotiators meet, the leasing agent should prepare a list of the points that are to be discussed. This list should also indicate any clauses that are deviations from the owner's standard lease provisions. For complicated negotiations, it may be necessary or appropriate to prepare a more detailed lease review form that includes a summary of the objectives of each clause, with references to specific sections in the actual lease document, and ranks them in order of importance. Items such as minimum and percentage rent, escalation rates, operating expenses, and lease commencement dates are listed at the beginning, with the remaining items categorized according to function:

- *Marketing considerations*—including parking and signage
- *Architectural considerations*—including site plan review and instructions for completion of tenant improvement work

FIGURE   8.1

Lease Review Checklist

Clause	Section in Lease	Matter for Consideration
Legal description	____	To be verified
Term of lease	____	Includes option to renew
	____	Does *not* include option to renew
	____	Option to renew to be added
Rent	____	Minimum rent stated
	____	Percentage rent stated
	____	Provides for deduction of disputed amounts
	____	*No* provision for deduction of disputed amounts
	____	Rent escalation included
Late charge	____	None stated
	____	Exceeds ____% of rent
Operating expenses	____	Tenant share prorated
	____	Verify fairness of formula
	____	Includes provision to revise formula
Insurance	____	Cost is acceptable
	____	Requirement is excessive
	____	Check compatibility with current coverages
Signage	____	Specifications stated
	____	Landlord consent required

- *Legal considerations*—including default and assignment and sub-leasing agreements

If the negotiations will require more than one meeting, structuring individual negotiating sessions around these categories will allow the owner and prospective tenant to discuss all the legal considerations as one block, architectural considerations as another, and so on, making the negotiation process more manageable. An example of a lease negotiation checklist is provided in appendix G.

On the other hand, the negotiation process may be better served by a simple list of all the possible questions that could be raised during the discussions. An abbreviated lease review checklist is shown in figure 8.1; this example lists some of the types of items that should be covered and specific considerations related to them. An actual form will account for each clause in the lease that is being reviewed and include ample space to add details about specific changes and variations. These checklists are primarily for the leasing agent's (and owner's) reference with respect to a specific lease and usually are not shared with the prospect.

Because the largest number of store spaces are smaller sized and, in shopping centers, leased to ancillary tenants, negotiation sessions need not involve attorneys for the parties. However, attorneys for both owner and prospective tenant should review the negotiated lease to assure that all legal issues have been resolved satisfactorily.

Some deals may require more sophisticated prenegotiations. In such situations, the leasing agent will prepare a *letter of intent* which may contain information about the location of the property, the term of the lease and its commencement date, the amount of rent, the use of the retail space, the allocation of property taxes and insurance, and other terms the parties expect the lease to include. The length and complexity of such a letter of intent will depend on the magnitude of the deal being negotiated. A copy is sent to the prospective tenant before formal negotiations begin.

The setting for the negotiations helps to create an overall mood and tone for the discussions. Lease negotiations can be conducted in the prospect's store or the broker's office or possibly in the office of the property manager (on the retail site). The choice of location usually depends on the prospect's influence or the size of the deal. If the prospective tenant is a large department store or a supermarket chain, the negotiations may be conducted at the prospect's headquarters; negotiations for smaller spaces are often conducted in the agent's office.

Handling Concessions

Knowing when and how to offer *concessions* to the prospective tenant is one of the agent's most important negotiating skills. Almost all retail leasing transactions involve some concessions. What is conceded to a particular prospect will depend on the bargaining strength of that prospect as well as on market conditions, lender restrictions, and other factors. Negotiators for anchor tenants and national chains are generally more sophisticated, and these operations are capable of demanding more concessions from the owner because of their strong position. Small businesses are not always able to negotiate as many different terms of a lease, and they will likely be satisfied if their requests related to base rent, improvement allowances, and the length of the lease term have been settled reasonably.

When considering what and how much to concede, fiscal impact becomes significant. In a slow market, concessions are granted as incentives for the prospect to lease a particular space, and they usually involve an offer from the owner to pay some tenant expenses. *The objective of concessions is to avoid lowering the dollar amount of the rental rate,* which lowers the value of the shopping center. A rent-free period or partial or full payment for tenant improvements may be offered instead. Granting concessions can fill a vacancy faster or close a deal more quickly, both of which can benefit the owner. However, leasing expenses can affect profitability, especially in a new shopping center. Therefore, concessions should be offered prudently.

Financing arrangements also have an effect on concession offerings. Prior to and during the construction of a new site, *construction or interim financing* is in effect. Because tenant improvements to individual spaces are often the last phase of construction, their financing is often included in the construction loan. *Permanent financing,* on the other hand, is usually negotiated before construction is started and scheduled to commence when the site has a certain percentage of occupancy. The property's income is always less in the initial months or years of operation because of leasing and occupancy variables, and it is desirable to stabilize income as quickly as possible. The actual amount of income will determine to some extent how much permanent financing is required. Because concessions that delay or reduce rental payments will reduce initial cash flow, the owner will expect the leasing agent to negotiate leases that bring the center or the individual stores to full revenue production as quickly as possible given the market circumstances. Thus the agent's role includes working with the owner to design a concession program that will maintain high occupancy and avoid long-term financial pitfalls.

It is important to deal with each prospective tenant on an individual basis. What may be appropriate for one retailer may not work for another. Different approaches may also be necessary. Clauses that grant large concessions to a prospective tenant but could damage the center as a whole should be avoided. An example would be exemption from the requirement to contribute to the center's marketing fund; such an exemption could reduce advertising and promotional efforts for the center and create hard feelings among other tenants. However, it is common practice for anchor tenants to contribute *less* to such funds because they advertise heavily on their own, and the center benefits from that advertising when shoppers drawn to the anchor store stay in the center to shop at other stores.

Agent and owner should agree in advance on the concessions that may and may not be considered. The agent's priority, then, is to learn what a particular prospect considers important and to adjust the allowable concessions accordingly. The list of allowable concessions should not be revealed to the prospective tenant during discussions, otherwise the prospect may sense that certain points are, in fact, being given away.

Technique is extremely important. The agent should develop a sense for which points can be conceded to the prospect without loss to the owner and which ones cannot. Concessions can also be traded. For example, to secure an escalation clause in a restaurant lease, the agent might be able to trade an offer to pay for its initial investment in linens, tableware, or other furnishings. Usually traded concessions should be comparable in dollar value. A willingness to be flexible about concessions will demonstrate the good faith with which the owner is participating in the transaction, and consequently the prospect will be more willing to concede some issues to the owner. When concessions are handled wisely, both the prospect and the owner benefit.

NEGOTIATING SPECIFIC POINTS

There are some issues in shopping center leases that constantly recur in negotiating sessions. Although the exact nature of these discussions may differ depending on the type of shopping center, the basic premises and negotiating techniques remain the same. Commonly negotiated points include (1) minimum rents and rent concessions, (2) above-standard tenant improvement allowances, and (3) options to renew, expand, and cancel. The number of negotiated points will depend on whether the market favors the owner or the tenant. Some prospects will seek more concessions, and different types of transactions may require different approaches to the lease negotiations.

Negotiating Rents

Rent is one of the most important points that will be discussed during lease negotiations. Owners and prospective tenants frequently have different ideas about what constitutes an appropriate rent for a particular space; in order to offer the prospect an attractive space without jeopardizing the center's income, some creative negotiating may be required.

Changes in the base rate will change the fundamental rent structure in each lease and will have ongoing effects on owner income for many years. The smallest deviation from the market rate can have a significant effect on both income and property value. No matter how slow market conditions are, *the agent should always resist lowering the base rent.* Conceding rent reductions may not even be allowed by the lender that is financing the project. When the established rent is lower than the market rate, occupancy levels may be high but the income will be low, and the property value will be reduced. For example, if the rent for a 1,000-square-foot space is only five cents per square foot lower than the standard market rate, collected rent is reduced by $600 a year. Over the course of a ten-year lease, that rent loss will be $6,000. The loss is compounded if the inflation rate increases over that same period. In some cases, if a lowered base rent is also combined with a short-term lease, the rent can be increased when the lease expires—if market conditions have improved. Although lower rent may be an acceptable concession with a short-term lease, it can be detrimental to the owner who accepts a long-term lease.

Even though the base rent may not be lowered, the *effective rent*—the amount actually paid by the tenant—may be substantially reduced. The distinction between effective rent and quoted rent is an important one for the tenant to understand. While the tenant may be paying $9.00 per square foot in rent as quoted, extra improvement allowances or a month's free rent can reduce the amount per square foot to an effective rent of $6.00, and the savings over a period of time can be considerable. While the tenant may pay a lower effective rent and reduced charges over the term of the lease, the owner will be able to maintain the quoted rent and avoid jeopardizing the value of the property. Other concessions relating to rent have also proved successful. A few months' free rent is one alternative to consider; this does not reduce the economic value of the property, and renewals start at the highest possible rent. Revenue increases rapidly thereafter because the shortfall occurs up front instead of being spread over the entire lease term. Although a period of free rent may be preferable to a vacancy, an agent should proceed with caution when offering this concession. Both owners and lending institutions generally view the payment of rent as sacred, and therefore almost any other concession is preferable. However, market conditions often require an offer of free rent. In many markets, it has become something that prospective tenants expect and owners must concede in order for them to do business.

A second alternative—not usually comparable in dollar amounts—is an offer to pay the prospective tenant's moving expenses. This usually includes moving of all merchandise and furniture from the tenant's previous location and may also include installation of telephones. Instead of or in addition to moving expenses, the owner may pay for a tenant's sign or contribute to the tenant's initial advertising at the new location.

If the challenge is to persuade a particularly desirable retailer to move from one location to another, negotiations might result in an offer to buy out the prospect's current lease by paying the former landlord a lump sum to terminate it. The prospect then moves to the new site and pays rent only to the new landlord. A variation of this would be to allow the old lease to remain in effect after the tenant is relocated, with the space at the new site being occupied rent-free until the former lease expires or is cancelled. A rent "exchange" may also be considered. In this type of arrangement, if the new rent of $2,400 a month is twice the amount paid previously, a 50-percent rent concession at the new location—just until the old obligation is paid—would reduce the hardship for the tenant. The tenant would still be paying double the former rent ($1,200 plus $1,200) but not the triple rate ($1,200 plus $2,400) it would pay without the concession. The problem with this arrangement is that there is always the risk of the tenant defaulting and the owner of the new location being responsible for that tenant's old and new leases.

A lease exchange can be structured in different ways. The leasing agent should be aware of the owner's financial situation when negotiating such concessions so that the owner's cash flow can be maximized while still creating a deal that will be favorable for the prospect's situation. The leasing agent should give all parties in this type of situation—prospective tenant, new landlord, and former landlord—the utmost consideration because it can lead to an opportunity to list the vacated space and, ultimately, to earn two commissions.

Negotiating Improvement Allowances

Although tenant improvement allowances are not available for every leased retail space, they are commonly offered in new shopping centers where interior finishing of ancillary spaces can be expedited as part of the overall construction. The owner's standard tenant improvement allowance can be expressed as either a maximum rate (amount per square foot of GLA) or a maximum dollar amount. Some prospects will negotiate for a larger improvement allowance than the standard.

In many retail leasing situations, especially for repeatedly leased spaces that are not in unified major shopping centers, there may be no provision for a tenant improvement allowance. However, the agent must know if the owner will permit negotiation of an allowance if it is necessary as a means to secure a particular retailer as tenant and what limits the owner wishes to set. When there is no specific provision for an improvement allowance, a prospect may ask for it outright. On the other hand, the agent may discover during negotiations that the prospect is concerned about construction and financing of improvements to the leased space. The agent who knows in advance what the owner is willing to do can offer either of these prospects a tenant improvement allowance, which may be a concession because it is an exception to the lease practice for the property under consideration. In either situation, the negotiations should lead to adjustment of the rent if the original rental rate did not include any consideration of a tenant improvement allowance. The leasing agent can then hold firm against other concessions, especially those that might lower the base rent.

Negotiating Options

Options always benefit the tenant rather than the owner, because they grant the tenant rights and privileges that exceed the terms of the standard lease agreement. Options can affect both the owner's immediate cash flow and the long-term value of the property. Because long-term options tend to hold rents to a certain rate over a number of years, buyers and investors are less likely to pay a premium price for a property burdened with them.

The advantages and disadvantages of options as a means to obtain a signed lease must be carefully considered by both owners and leasing agents. Leasing agents may be tempted to grant options to hasten the decision-making process for the prospect and because they may be entitled to an extra commission on certain types of options, particularly renewals.

The decision to build options into a lease often depends on the market conditions at the time. In a slow market, the owner may be more willing to grant a prospective tenant greater privileges regarding renewal and expansion options. Owner and prospect will have to reach a compromise about the types of options to be granted and the period for which they are granted.

Options should not be granted unconditionally. In fairness to the owner, the lease statement granting options should require for their exercise that (1) the tenant must not be in default of the lease, (2) the tenant must give the owner written notice a specific period in advance, and (3) only the original tenant can exercise the option. As a further consideration, the tenant may be required to maintain a certain volume of sales in order to be eligible to exercise the option.

Option to Renew.   Prospects often seek an option to renew their leases at expiration on the same terms as the original lease. This gives tenants not only a greater sense of security but also an opportunity to take advantage of terms of the original lease that may have been particularly favorable to them.

When granted, this option may allow for renewal of the lease at the same base rental rate with the same provisions for regular increases. Although periodic increases will give the owner some relief, they are usually not large enough to bring the rent up to market rates by the time the original lease would expire. For this reason, an option to renew should state that rental rates are to be negotiated when the option is exercised. For example, if a mall tenant were to pay $30 per square foot plus an escalation increase of $1 per square foot each year over a three-year term, the rent would be $33 per square foot at the end of the lease term. If the market rent remained stable at the rate the tenant was paying at the beginning of the term—that is, at about $30 per square foot—the owner would be at an advantage if the tenant chose to renew at the new rate. However, it is more likely that the market rent would have increased more than $3 per square foot over the three-year period. If the tenant had been granted such an option to renew, the rent under the new lease would start at $33 despite the increase in the market rent. An escalation clause requiring use of the CPI as the basis for rent increases is a way to avoid this type of problem.

Owners generally prefer short-term leases. It may not always be possible to arrange a short-term lease if a prospective tenant in a strong negotiating position wants the assurance of continued occupancy. Market conditions also contribute to the duration of a lease because the owners have to compete against the rental rates others are offering. In a soft market, prospects may insist on longer-term leases, and owners may be obliged to agree so that they can avoid vacancies. Otherwise a prospect might choose to lease at another location where the terms are more favorable. Sometimes an owner will negotiate a renewal option that gives the tenant the right to continue leasing the space but permits renegotiation of the lease terms so that the owner can increase the rent to market rates.

The renewal option should always require the tenant to give the owner advance written notice of its intent to renew and clearly state that failure to give adequate notice will lead to a forfeiture of the tenant's privileges. In some situations, especially for leases exceeding a five-year term, up to one year's advance notice may be required. It may also be wise to include as a requirement for renewal that the tenant redecorate or remodel the space periodically so that the store's displays do not lose their impact. Neither the tenant nor the owner should assume that the lease will be renewed automatically. A written statement of intent is always required.

Option to Expand.   Expansion of retail stores is not very common. Most retailers, particularly chain stores, have standard store size requirements, although efforts to reposition a retail operation in the market could alter that standard at any time. However, some prospects with long-range growth plans may ask specifically for an option to expand their space during the original lease term or when it expires. Expansion into adjacent space is quite common in office buildings, but it is not necessarily practical in a shopping center where the actual area to be used for expansion is open to negotiation. If the lease option were to identify a specific space, the owner would be required to restrict the use of that space—at least for a certain period—so that it would be available for the tenant that wished to move into it. Either the requested space would have to remain vacant, or it would have to be rented to a temporary tenant (on a month-to-month basis) or to a permanent tenant with a lease expiration date identical with that of the growing tenant. An option to expand can pose several problems for the owner. An owner does not want to have valuable space off the market for any length of time. Prospects being shown space that is held for expansion must be told that the space is under option, a fact that will likely discourage them.

To overcome the potential negative impact of this option on the owner, several compromises may be sought. One is for the owner to grant the negotiating prospect the right of first refusal on the expansion space. In other words, if and when additional space became available, the tenant would have the option to match any other offer made for the space within a specified time. Another compromise would be for the prospect to be granted an expansion option for one year at a time—for example, during the third and seventh year of a seven-year lease. During those years, the owner would have to make the space available to the tenant. For the owner, this usually means the specified space could only be rented on a short-term basis during the years that the option can be exercised, with that lease possibly requiring relocation of the occupant when or if the option were exercised. If the negotiating tenant did not act upon the expansion option within that year, the option on the space would be lost. A third possible compromise would be for the prospective tenant to agree to make a decision about expansion at a very specific time—for example, two years after the lease term begins—and, depending on the amount of space involved, to give the owner a certain amount of notice regarding the decision.

Other compromises may be negotiated relative to the amount of rent to be charged for the expansion space. The rent for such space may be the market rate that exists at the time the expansion option is to begin, or it may be the rental rate the tenant is paying for its original space with an added escalation charge. Another possibility is to state a higher rent in the lease agreement for the original space reasoning that the owner should be compensated for granting the option to expand.

The agent's responsibility in the negotiation of an expansion option is to protect the owner's interests as much as possible, since the owner is the one who will most likely be inconvenienced by having to create rental programs to suit such expansion. One of the biggest problems with space that is already filled is replacing the old tenant. This may involve both construction costs and legal fees. If the tenant occupying the potential expansion space is as viable as the expanding tenant, the owner risks alienating one of them. The owner must be sure that accommodating an expansion is worthwhile. However, there are ways that owners can protect their interests. In particular, the tenant can be required to lease the expansion space initially and sublease or assign the extra space. In this way, the expansion space is included in the original lease term; it becomes the tenant's responsibility, and the owner is assured of receiving rent for it on a monthly basis. Throughout these negotiations, the agent should strive to avoid granting a prospect the right to hold onto an optioned space indefinitely.

Option to Cancel.   Occasionally an option to expand may be linked to a specific option to cancel that grants the tenant the right to terminate the lease before the expiration date if the owner cannot make additional space available as promised. Owners rarely grant such an option to cancel because of the risk of having vacant space in an uncertain future market. Cancellation options tied to expansion options are almost nonexistent in strip centers. The cancellation provision usually requires the tenant to give the owner advance notice and sometimes requires the tenant to compensate the owner financially. The notice requirement protects the owner who, knowing in advance when space will be vacated, can begin early to make arrangements to re-lease it. If exercise of a cancellation option requires a penalty, this may take the form of forfeiture of part or all of a security deposit or return of extra improvement costs paid by the owner, or it may require a separate specific payment to the owner. Penalties and notice requirement clauses should be negotiated at the same time as the option to cancel.

Another type of option to cancel relates strictly to the retailer's sales. This option, usually negotiated so it can be exercised by either party, requires that the tenant achieve a preset sales volume.

THE TENANT'S PERSPECTIVE

A retailer in a new shopping center stands to lose quite a bit of money if the center is not successful. Inventory, improvements to the space, overhead, and other expenses associated with retailing usually represent a substantial investment for the average retailer. As a result, most prospective tenants will focus on different aspects of a leasable space than the owner or developer would. Rather than concentrating on land costs, financing, zoning regulations, and design problems, the prospect will be interested in whether the center will be profitable and whether it will be an appropriate location to do business. While owners are trying to achieve the greatest amount of rent from every space in the center, retailers consider whether they can afford to pay those rents. They are also calculating the minimum gross sales per square foot they must achieve in order to make a profit and asking whether locating in the center will allow them to maintain that sales figure. They will judge each unit a leasing agent shows them within a center on the basis of its

- Location
- Frontage (visibility)
- Amount and regularity of traffic
- Type of service areas, storage space, and loading docks available

Prospects will also be interested in the nature of the adjacent space as it relates to possibilities for expansion. Also important are the center's and the prospect's target markets.

Common Issues for Negotiation

Every clause in a retail lease is potentially negotiable. Some issues that are extremely important to the owner—for example, the amount of rent—are equally important to the prospect but for different reasons. An abbrevi-

FIGURE   8.2

Commonly Negotiated Points in a Retail Space Lease

Term
  Actual duration of the lease
  Starting and ending dates
  Date of occupancy
  Date of rent commencement
Rent
  Base or minimum rental rate
  Percentage rent
    Definition of gross sales
    Breakpoint
  Adjustments (reduction) for construction delays
  Basis for escalation of rent
Tenant improvement allowance
Operating expenses
  Specific expenses passed through
  Proration basis for pass through
  Gross occupied space versus gross leasable area as basis
  Other charges and fees
    Common area maintenance (CAM)
    Utilities
    Promotional expenses (marketing funds)
Audits of tenant operations
Use restrictions
Continuous operation
Cancellation and Condemnation provisions
Options
  Renewal
  Expansion
  Cancellation

ated list of commonly negotiated items is shown in figure 8.2. The following discussions cover points that prospective tenants are most likely to focus on during negotiations.

Term.   The lease term is often a matter for considerable negotiation between an owner and a prospective tenant. The owner's preference will usually be for a shorter lease term that includes provisions for the owner to raise the rent or replace the tenant at will. The prospective tenant's preference will be for a longer lease term with an option to renew at a fixed rate. A longer lease term can benefit both parties as it provides the tenant a measure of security and guarantees the owner a steady income with which to service debts and accumulate capital. On the other hand, options to renew at a fixed rate are granted only rarely and then usually only to major or anchor tenants. Lease terms depend on the owner's and the prospect's perceptions of future market rates, the desirability of the space, and the retailer's potential for expansion or relocation after a certain period of time.

Prospects will want to delay the date when rent falls due. Retailers often need thirty to ninety days to "customize" a new space—install fixtures, construct displays—and generally prepare to open for business; restaurants may require even more time. Depending on the condition of the space and the changes that must be made, the owner will sometimes grant the prospect's request for a rent-free period. The length of time allowed before rental payments start largely depends on the type of retail business, and the tenant may be required to pay for utilities—and sometimes CAM charges—during the rent-free construction period.

Rent Reductions.   Prospects will often seek a provision for a reduction in rent if there are events or circumstances beyond their control. Occasionally construction of a new or renovated center is not completed on schedule. On rare occasions, an anchor tenant will default or cancel a lease before move-in. In such situations, ancillary tenants may be able to occupy their spaces before the center would open officially with its anchor or anchors ready for business. Because such conditions are not ideal for business, the prospect may ask that the lease provide for adjustments to rents and other tenant payments. In response, the owner may allow the tenant to pay less rent (or percentage rent only) until the anchor tenants are open for business or until a certain percentage of the center is leased. The assumption is that the opening of anchor stores or the leasing of a large percentage of the space (usually 75–80 percent) guarantees expected normal or near-normal business throughout the center. In enclosed malls, where the success of ancillary tenants is heavily dependent on the success of the anchor tenants, such initial rent reduction is common. Whether rent is reduced or eliminated during construction and whether the unpaid amount is to be paid later or waived are subject to negotiation. The owner may agree to a stated lease-up requirement with a time limit—for example, one year after opening—after which the tenant pays full rent. However, everyone's objective should be to maximize lease-up and store openings so that the tenants and the center as a whole will have the greatest chance to succeed.

Tenant Improvement Allowances.   Depending on the market and the prospect's bargaining power, the owner may agree to pay more than the standard allowance for improvements. Prospects will sometimes accept additional financing instead of a rent abatement; this financing arrangement is useful to owners when lender restrictions prohibit concessions that affect immediate cash flow. The lease document should clearly state the responsibility of the parties with respect to finishing the tenant's interior space. (See also appendix F.)

Occasionally a prospect will try to negotiate for a *turnkey operation,* whereby the owner agrees to provide a completely finished store that is ready for business. While the owner will finance the improvements, supervision of a turnkey arrangement can be handled in several ways. Usually a prospect will want the freedom to completely plan and oversee the construction. Sometimes, however, the owner may prefer to retain more control and supervise the construction. When this is the case, the prospect will seek the right to have the construction adhere to the prospect's specifications. Both parties should have copies of cost estimates, a list of all contractors and laborers, and other pertinent documents related to the construction. If construction or installation costs exceed what the owner is willing to pay, prospects are usually agreeable to a loan for the extra improvements, which is repaid over the course of the lease term as additional rent.

Operating Expenses.   Most retailers pay a pro rata share of the center's common area maintenance expenses, utility costs, taxes, and insurance. Their share is figured by dividing the total expenses by the GLA of the center to arrive at a per square foot cost that is allocated to each individual tenant, usually based on the GLA of the individual store. However, prospects will want the clause to specify that only the *gross leasable area* and not the *gross occupied space* of the center will be used as the denominator in this fraction. Otherwise, the costs for the vacant space in the center would be absorbed by the tenant. For example, in a center with a GLA of 200,000 square feet, a tenant with a store size of 2,000 square feet would have a pro rata share of 1 percent. If the center were not fully leased and the occupied spaces totaled only 160,000 square feet, the same tenant with a 2,000-square-foot store would have a pro rata share of 1.25 percent.

Defining Gross Sales.   Percentage rents are directly related to gross sales. However, many retailers receive income from sources that are not strictly part of their own business and from which they do not always profit. As a result, prospects will naturally want to exclude from the total as many of these sources of income as possible, and many owners are willing to compromise on the definition of gross sales that is incorporated in the lease. Generally, retailers will want to exclude some or all of the following:

- Sales taxes
- Unpaid balances on layaway purchases
- Finance charges to credit customers
- Service charges

- Discounted sales to employees
- Gift certificates
- Vending machine revenue
- Lottery ticket sales

Some of these are not true "sales income." Sales taxes are collected for and paid to government agencies, and they should be deducted from gross sales for purposes of computing percentage rent because they are not income. Likewise, outstanding layaway balances represent uncollected funds, although interest collected on layaway balances could be considered income. Income from such interest and from finance charges for credit may not offset the costs of repeated billings or the actual costs of financing, so they are often excluded. (For purposes of cash flow, the business may have to borrow money in order to replace the uncollected sales income.) In addition, discounts paid to credit card companies may be deducted because they reduce the amount of the recorded sale.

Service charges, especially those for apparel alterations, can be good revenue generators, so an owner may not want to exclude them. Discounted sales to employees, including meals (in tenant-operated restaurants), can be an area for concern by both parties. Their exclusion depends largely on how they are computed; an owner may allow deduction of "the amount of the discount" on sales to employees, but it may be appropriate to set limits on the portion of gross sales that can be deducted for this reason. Gift certificates may not constitute sales until they are redeemed. However, they can be very profitable for retailers, particularly if they are not used to the full amount of the gift, so an owner may not be willing to exclude them. Both vending machine revenue and lottery ticket sales generate income for retailers, otherwise there would be no reason to offer them. Even though retailers may not invest in "inventory" for such sales, they do receive some financial consideration for offering these services.

Common practice in the area served may determine to what extent different items may be deducted or excluded from gross sales. *Deductions* should reflect collected sales income the retailer does not keep (for example, sales taxes and refunds for returned merchandise), while true *exclusions* represent amounts that should not be part of gross sales in the first place. Examples of the latter are merchandise returned to manufacturers and goods given in exchange for trading stamps.

Audits.   Periodically owners audit tenant's records to make sure the tenants are reporting all their sales. Prospects will seek to limit audits to once a year and will request sufficient notice before an audit. Otherwise, their business could be disrupted. The cost of such audits is borne by the owner unless a tenant's sales have been found to be underreported. The lease clause usually states the percentage of underreported sales that makes the audit a tenant expense.

Use.   The use clause is often a point of contention between owner and prospect. The owner will want to protect the balance of the tenant mix and the overall image of the center by restricting the use of the tenant's space to selling the merchandise it was selling when it signed the lease. Sometimes the owner becomes very specific about types of merchandise (see the discussion of use clauses in general in chapter 7). Prospects, on the other hand, will want a use clause that is as broad as possible, allowing expansion into different merchandise lines or a change of merchandise altogether.

Negotiating use clauses can be difficult. Rather than extend negotiations needlessly, it is better to be prepared to compromise. For example, the owner may allow the prospect to stock a new type of merchandise as long as the retailer agrees not to introduce price lines that are substantially higher or lower than those that customers have come to expect from the store, provided the change does not infringe another tenant's use clause.

Continuous Operation.   Another area where prospect and owner may encounter difficulty is the requirement for continuous operation. Most owners regard vacant space as anathema, especially when that vacant space is currently under lease. They understandably seek to protect themselves from tenants that for one reason or another abandon the premises they have leased, effectively taking valuable business away from the center and creating a gap in the center's design. (See the discussion of continuous operation clauses in chapter 7.) Prospects, on the other hand, will want protection against the owner's failure to keep the center competitive and profitable. The prospect may want to include a statement in the clause that in order for the store to remain open for business, all anchor and major tenants and not less than 75 percent of the other tenants must also be open. The prospect may also want to negotiate exemption from the continuous operation agreement in the event of fires, strikes, or weather disasters. This is a very sensitive area of negotiation. The owner naturally will want as few exemptions for the tenant as possible, and it is rare that a concession or exception to the continuous operation clause is granted, especially with regard to occupancy levels.

Cancellation and Condemnation.   Some prospects will negotiate for the right to cancel their leases if the anchor tenant defaults on its lease before (or after) construction of the center is completed. The owner may try to avert this situation by writing ancillary tenants' leases to refer to anchor tenants by size—in other words, any occupant of the 60,000-square-foot space in the center—and not by name, and none of the tenants of smaller spaces would be exempt from their lease terms as long as this large space is occupied. Occasionally, a prospect or the owner may be granted an option to terminate the lease after a certain number of months if gross accumulated sales dollars up to that point do not reach a specified amount.

Acts of God and nature are not under the control of the parties to a lease. If the shopping center is damaged to a certain extent, the owner often has the exclusive right to cancel a tenant's lease (1) if that damage occurs in the last three years of a lease term, (2) if the damage is not covered by the owner's insurance, or (3) if the insurance is not sufficient to cover the cost of repairs. The owner may also have the right to cancel a tenant's lease if the whole or a significant portion of the property is condemned. Both of these situations can be detrimental to a tenant. A prospect will want assurance that the lease will not be cancelled unless the leases of other tenants are also cancelled or that they will be offered another lease at equivalent terms if the center is rebuilt within a certain time period. If the owner does not require a tenant to cancel in the event of damages, the tenant will often be at a disadvantage because of decreased customer traffic. To avert this, the prospect may negotiate to include a requirement for (1) a rent abatement for at least sixty days after repairs have been made and (2) the right to cancel the lease if the owner does not undertake repairs within a certain time period. The prospect will want to be assured that if the property is condemned, the cost of fixtures and other improvements made to the property at its expense will be reimbursed.

Miscellaneous Charges.   Many clauses in a retail lease require the tenant to pay a number of separate fees or charges in addition to the basic rent and a share of the overall operating expenses. These include merchants' association dues, costs of additional centerwide promotions, and extra utility or maintenance charges, among others. The prospective tenant will want to limit the extent of its obligations by qualifying these clauses in various ways. Usually the prospect will negotiate to avoid paying above-average maintenance and other operating costs and to be allowed to monitor electricity consumption. The prospect may also seek to be excused from general promotions if they conflict with its own promotional activities, and to be exempt from merchants' association participation and dues unless a certain percentage of all the tenants are also members.

NEGOTIATING WITH TENANTS IN AN ESTABLISHED CENTER

Leasing in an established center can be as simple as renewing a tenant's lease or as difficult as creating an entirely new tenant mix. Some shopping centers that are several years old may only have a few vacancies to fill;

others may need to reposition themselves in the market. As prime locations become harder to find, rehabilitation of old centers rather than construction of completely new ones is becoming quite common. The leasing agent should be familiar with negotiating procedures in different scenarios.

The success of a shopping center depends largely on its ability to respond to changes in customer needs, to appear modern in both merchandise presentation and physical design, and to remain competitive with neighboring centers. While a shopping center may be viable for several decades, one that has not been renovated or rehabilitated in any way will begin to decline in sales performance over time. To remain economically viable, shopping centers have to be evaluated on a regular basis. Leasing should be regarded as an ongoing activity. Shopping centers are renovated in order to improve tenant mix, use of the leased space, and the financial terms of their leases. Renewal and replacement leasing are the two most common means of achieving these goals.

When deciding if a tenant's lease should be renewed, the leasing agent should look at the tenant's contribution to the center's performance as a whole. In general, a tenant's sales performance should relate to a trade area's expenditure profile for identical categories of merchandise. Leasing agents should ask whether a particular tenant has experienced relative growth or has not been performing as expected. The tenant's sales performance should be monitored consistently, along with sales performance data from comparable centers, if available. These figures can be checked against industry data reported periodically by the Urban Land Institute in *Dollars and Cents of Shopping Centers.* Leasing agents should also evaluate the relationship of a specific tenant to all the other tenants in the shopping center. If there are two card shops, for example, the agent should question whether they increase each other's business or merely split the sales. If the latter is true, the GLA of one of the card shops might serve the center better if it were leased to a different kind of retailer. Leasing agents might also ask if certain types of retailers are not sufficiently represented in the center, or if the merchandise mix of the center is heavily weighted toward certain types of stores. There may be a disparity if there are six women's shoe stores and only two dress shops. Perhaps an ice cream parlor would serve the center better than the fast food chain currently operating there, or perhaps an established ice cream parlor should be replaced with a yogurt vendor. The tenant's participation in the merchants' association or marketing fund is another consideration.

If renewing a tenant's lease is not feasible, replacing that tenant may offer the opportunity to respond to changing demographic or economic conditions in the trade area. It may be advisable to re-lease the space to a tenant whose merchandise is more suited to the current market. Rather than simply replace one tenant with another, owners sometimes choose to split a large store space into two or more units or to open up a small space for an adjacent tenant that needs to expand. Negotiating replacements and store splits is not easy. It may be necessary to buy out an old tenant's lease in order to compensate for the inconvenience that tenant will experience by moving.

Renewing Leases

One of the first things an agent should be aware of is how much of the gross leasable space in the center is represented by leases that will expire within a certain period of time and which of those leases are expiring with a fixed-rate option or with no option at all. In addition, the agent should inquire whether lease expirations in a particular center represent contiguous spaces and how many spaces will be vacant at the same time. Fixed-rate options are relatively rare. When they do occur, they are usually holdovers from long-term leases that were written during more economically stable periods. A tenant without a fixed-rate option must renegotiate the lease, usually with a rent increase based on an escalation index or on market rates. An owner interested in increasing the rental income of a property will be more concerned with tenants that do *not* have a fixed-rate renewal option. Other points to keep in mind are the tenant's contributions to the general shopping center expenses. The agent should find out how much the tenant currently pays in minimum rent per square foot, if percentage rent is paid, and whether or to what extent common area maintenance fees, taxes, insurance, or other charges are the tenant's responsibility—in other words, whether the existing lease is gross or net. The agent should also keep track of when lease terms expire, making it possible to change leases.

Replacing Tenants

The leasing agent should also be familiar with the process of *replacement leasing.* It may be necessary to replace a tenant for several reasons. Poor sales performance or failure to pay rent and other expenses are grounds for replacing an individual tenant. Changing demographics in a trade area may necessitate a "face lift" for the center in order to reposition it in the current marketplace. Centers that are being rehabilitated sometimes extend their land, acquiring properties that were formerly used for purposes other than retailing. Changes in ownership of the retail property or of an individual business may be causes—or offer opportunities—to replace existing tenants. On the other hand, a tenant might decide to vacate voluntarily and not seek to renew its lease. (The tenant may wish to expand its operations or relocate to a more upscale location.) Occasionally a tenant may want to sell its business altogether.

Store Splits.   One way to change the face of a shopping center is to reorganize its space to create new opportunities for leasing. Dividing a single large space into two or more smaller ones is called a *store split.* Many older centers were built with larger ancillary spaces than are necessary or leasable in today's market. Retailers have been able to reduce the amount of stock they carry because computers have made it easier to reorder and maintain an adequate inventory; they no longer have to rely on overstock to avoid running out of merchandise. In addition, advances in store fixture design permit the use of more compact displays in stores, and these innovations enable retailers to operate more efficiently in less space. A space that is too large for a retailer's business will yield meager sales per square foot, and the retailer's overhead expenses can be exorbitant. Assuming the tenant wishes to remain at the location, dividing the oversized store can work to both parties' advantage. A reduction in square footage can reduce the retailer's operating costs. Sales per square foot may increase as a result, perhaps sufficiently to make regular payments of percentage rent possible. In addition, new space will be available for the owner to rent at market rates to another retailer, thus attracting more business to the center.

Store splits have to be considered carefully, however. Construction costs not only include a new dividing wall but also modifications of electrical wiring, additional plumbing lines and fixtures if washrooms are part of the store spaces, and changes to the storefront, including new doors. These expenses plus added leasing commissions have to be offset by increased rental income in order for the split to be justified.

Expansion.   Adding space is another way to make a center more profitable as well as increase its value. If the expansion is to create a larger space for a single tenant, it may be appropriate to charge different rental rates for the "old" and the "new" space.

The cost of the new construction may be paid in part by the new tenant. To compensate for the new tenant's upfront investment, the base rent for the new space may be set lower than the rate set for the existing space, although that rate should account for improvements to the "old" space if they were made. Having varied rental rates can allow the new tenant to operate profitably while sharing part of the cost of the conversion, and the shopping center owner will benefit both immediately (from the increased rental income on the larger total GLA) and long term (from the substantial increase to the value of the center).

Buy Out.   When a tenant's presence no longer contributes to the overall success of an established center—and another retailer is eager to rent that space—the most beneficial negotiation alternative may be a *buy out.* A buy out involves paying the tenant a sum of money or offering favorable terms to break its lease. When the rent an owner could receive for a given space is considerably greater than the rent a current tenant is paying, a buy out can be very effective.

How well tenants have been performing in their current space is a good indication of the probability of their continued success. As mentioned previously, industry data on sales per square foot in particular retail categories can be useful in evaluating tenants, especially if percentage rents are involved. Sometimes a particular tenant would be better off in a smaller or larger space or in a more- or less-visible location. Sales records and the tenant's ability to draw customer traffic into the center have to be evaluated, and the tenant's present rent has to be compared with the market rate to decide whether the space could be used more profitably if it were leased to a new tenant. Other important considerations are (1) whether the tenant is still a valuable component of the tenant mix of the shopping center—and, if so, how the tenant's sales performance could be improved by either relocation or a reduction of its GLA—and (2) what it will cost the center to relocate that tenant.

THE CLOSE

There are many different ways of bringing negotiations to a conclusion. Each tenant-owner relationship will require a different approach. A prospect may still have concerns about some clauses in the final version of the lease, and this may lead to reluctance to sign. The leasing agent must know how to respond to a prospect's hesitation. Strong objections may necessitate further negotiations.

A good technique for testing the prospect's intentions is the interim or "trial" close, in which the agent assumes that the transaction will be completed and asks the prospect questions that presuppose the signing of the lease. An indecisive prospect may be spurred to action by the question, "What merchandise do you plan to promote for our grand opening?" The prospect with valid concerns about the lease may answer that same question by bringing the issues into the open.

The agent may respond by trying to convince the prospect that the reasons in favor of leasing the space are stronger than those against it. This can be done as a comparison of the retail space under consideration to spaces in similar centers or buildings, emphasizing whatever feature is most attractive in the subject property (location, rents, market demographic profile, etc.). In making such comparisons, the agent should never speak disparagingly of the competition; such a technique will damage the agent's reputation. It is more important to emphasize the features of the space under consideration and reiterate the ways the retailer will benefit from that particular location. The agent may try to persuade the prospective tenant that its business will be in good company by mentioning the

FIGURE   8.3

Retail Lease Summation Record

Date of Lease _____   Occupancy Date _____
Date Prepared _____   Prepared By _____

Site _____   Owner _____
Address _____

Type of Lease _____   Name of Store _____
Principal Product Lines _____
Address _____
Local Contact _____   Position _____
Phone _____

	Sq Ft	Unit No.	Base Rent	% Rent	Term	Beginning	Ending
Original Lease							
New Lease							
Totals							

Security Deposit $ _____Rec'd By _____Date _____

Changes to Lease Paragraphs _____
_____
_____

Renewal Option _____   Notification Date _____
Expansion Option _____   Area _____
Other Option(s) _____
Cancellation _____   Penalty _____
Escalation Terms _____Base Year _____ CPI _____%
Parking Assignment _____

names of other tenants that have already signed leases. The goal is to make the prospect believe the owner considers this retailer to be the best possible tenant despite the fact that others were interested in the space and given serious consideration. Reopening negotiations is usually out of the question at this late stage, but the owner may be willing to make further minor adjustments or compromises, especially if such adjustments do not require extensive changes in the lease document or specific dollar commitments.

F I G U R E   8.3   (continued)

Proration of Operating Expenses
HVAC _____ Utilities _____
Common Area Charges (per sq ft) _____
Property Taxes (per sq ft) _____
Insurance (per sq ft) _____
Trash Removal _____ Security _____
Other(s) _____
Merchants' Association/Marketing Fund Dues _____
Grand Opening Fund _____

Leased By (Co.) _____   Agent _____
Commission (Co.) $_____   Agent $_____
Credit Report _____   Reference _____
Approved _____
Legal Review by _____

Estimated Construction Costs
Total $_____   Cost Per Sq Ft $_____
Allowance $_____   Per Sq Ft $_____
Difference $_____   Per Sq Ft $_____
Tenant Improvement   Extra Allowance
Allowance (standard) $_____   for Lessee $_____
Amortization $_____   Interest Rate _____%
Approved _____

Move-in Information
Rent Commencement Date _____   Termination Date _____
Unit Occupied _____   Unit Inspected _____
Information Packet Issued _____   Keys Issued _____ Key No. _____
Signs Installed _____ Parking Permits _____ Directory Listing _____

Move-in Charges to Lessee
Keys $_____
Directory $_____
Construction $_____
Other $_____
   Total $_____

Rent Effective Letter Received _____
Approved (Site Mgr.) _____
Comments _____
_____
_____

Negotiations are considered completed and the deal *closed* once the lease document has been signed by both tenant and owner and they have their respective copies of it. The steps leading up to the close are as follows:

1. After negotiations have been completed and the owner and the owner's attorney have drafted a final version of the lease, at least two originals are prepared, one for each party, with permanent file copies for the management company and brokerage firm made after the document is signed. In some situations, additional originals may be prepared—an extra for the owner and one for the lender. The final lease should include a floor plan with the tenant's space clearly marked (by a method that will reproduce during photocopying), a list of the center's rules and regulations, a copy of the workletter or construction rider, and all other exhibits or addendums agreed upon in the negotiations. The final lease should be delivered to the prospect in person whenever possible. (In some situations, the lease may be accompanied by a transmittal letter that summarizes the contents and states a deadline for response. The prospective tenant is expected to sign this lease transmittal letter as proof that the lease has been received.) In most cases (except for anchor tenants), the prospect is required to sign the lease first. At this point the prospect should be advised that the owner still retains the right not to sign.

2. When the signed lease documents have been received from the prospect, the agent should check them carefully to make sure nothing has been omitted or changed and that it is properly signed— and initialed, if required. All attachments to the lease should be accounted for. At this point, the agent should also ascertain whether the commission statement is in order. When everything has been accounted for, the agent transmits the lease to the owner.

3. The lease is reviewed once more by the owner or developer, the property manager, and the agent. It may also undergo a legal review, and a formal meeting may be arranged. The agent is responsible for carefully checking the lease document to be sure that the agreed-upon terms are stated as both parties have understood them. At this final all-important meeting there should be no surprises. Once the owner signs the lease, it is considered fully executed.

4. The agent will then transfer the final, fully executed lease to the tenant. This may be done in person with an acknowledgment receipt to be signed by the tenant, or the lease may be mailed with a return receipt requested. Once the fully signed lease is mailed or delivered, the last of the requirements for the document to be legally binding is considered to have been met. Photocopies of the

final lease are made for the property manager in order to facilitate move-in arrangements. At occupancy, the agent or property manager will usually ask the tenant to sign a final acceptance form, stating that the space, as delivered, meets the terms of the agreement. Copies may also be sent to lenders. The agent should set up a leasing file with copies of the fully executed lease.

Careful records must be kept of who has the lease at any given time. To do this, the agent should maintain a log that is used solely to record this information. It may also be helpful to prepare a lease summation record containing information about the tenant, the date of the lease and period of occupancy, the nature of the store or shopping center, and construction costs (figure 8.3, pages 200–201). Owners can use this record to monitor specific expenses and payments for the individual space as well as changes in lease terms. Another option for recording specific data about a lease as well as its movement among the various parties is to use a computer.

SUMMARY

While the leasing agent's role during negotiations is to represent the owner, he or she should listen carefully to prospective tenants' suggestions and not pressure them to make decisions before they are ready. In the negotiation of a retail lease, many factors must be weighed. The agent has to know the condition of the market, the owner's cash flow requirements, any lender restrictions that may apply, and the tenant's specifications. Knowledge of the fiscal impact of concessions is extremely important; the long-term negative effects on cash flow and property value usually discourage the use of rent concessions as incentives. In general, all terms of a lease should be negotiated in consideration of the future value of the retail property and its position in a competitive marketplace.

There are some clauses that both owners and prospects will perceive differently. Most prospects will want broader use clauses than owners are willing to give, and they may ask to pay less rent during the first few months of occupancy in a new shopping center. Their goal is to protect their own interests if the shopping center as a whole is doing poorly.

Specific points to be negotiated will vary with the tenant, the property, and the space being leased. For a new shopping center, minimum rents, renewal and other options, tenant improvement allowances, use clauses, rental concessions, and continuous operation requirements are some of the most commonly discussed issues. For a center that is being renovated or rehabilitated, an important consideration is the effect of space changes on both the owner's and the tenants' profits. In order to maximize the

204 Leasing Retail Space

sales potential of all the tenants in a center that is undergoing rehabilitation, it may be necessary to change a tenant's space (reduction, expansion) or to change the tenant mix (outright replacement or relocation of tenants) to maintain the best balance among rental rates, GLA, and profits.

Once both parties have agreed on the terms of the lease, a document stating the agreed-upon terms and conditions is prepared for the parties' signatures, and any significant changes to that document should always be reviewed by appropriate legal counsel. After the final document has been signed by both tenant and owner (and their respective copies returned to them), the lease transaction is considered closed.

During all stages of the negotiation process, the agent acts as liaison between prospective tenant and owner. Whether the agent is involved in physical preparation of the lease or not, it is the agent's responsibility to transmit the lease to the tenant for signatures, to review the document signed by the tenant, then to send it to the owner to be signed, and, finally, to return a copy of the fully executed lease to the tenant. The agent is also responsible for setting up a leasing file containing copies of the final document and any other information pertinent to the transaction. (Steps in leasing a new shopping center are outlined in appendix H.)

CHAPTER

9

Leasing Downtown
Retail Space

The rebirth of the city as a place to work and live has turned the attention of retail site developers to downtowns. Major cities support renovation of historic buildings or districts to create or revitalize downtown areas, and downtown revitalization in both large and small cities has generated a new energy in retailing. Rehabilitation of existing buildings—converting nonretail space to retail uses—is becoming an important issue in retail development as well. Faneuil Hall Marketplace in Boston and Trappers Alley in Detroit—festival centers developed in rehabilitation projects— are examples of other primarily urban forms of retail space that have become extensions of so-called downtown shopping areas through adaptive reuse. Mixed-use developments that include retail space in office buildings, hotel lobbies, and transportation depots, as well as in organized areas devoted to retailing, are becoming common in large cities as well as in the suburbs. In the past, enclosed shopping centers on the scale of suburban regional malls were not often built downtown, but this, too, has been changing.

The term "downtown" refers not only to the central business district of a major metropolis but also to the main shopping street in any town or small city. A large city often has more than one shopping district. In Chicago, for example, both North Michigan Avenue and the Loop can be considered "downtown"; both have department stores and other retail space located close to office buildings. In addition, major cities have numerous neighborhood business districts that include offices and retail activities.

Suburban development of business centers has been growing, too, and the costs of having offices there has increased as well. As these costs approach parity with the costs of downtown office space, businesses can justify locating downtown, which is where they often prefer to be.

Often a property is developed by out-of-town owners who do not fully understand the characteristics of a particular site. In general, retail space is scarcer downtown, and both construction and occupancy costs are higher than in the suburbs. Individual store spaces in downtown locations tend to be smaller than corresponding suburban stores, and rents are generally higher. Perhaps the most visible difference, however, is the emphasis on vertical space rather than horizontal spread, as in the suburbs.

A downtown district has a different image than its suburban counterpart, and this has to be taken into account when marketing downtown retail space. Many cities have to fight a negative image because shoppers tend to associate crime, crowds, and dirty streets with urban areas. On the other hand, cities can be cultural havens with centers for musical and theatrical performances, libraries, sculpture, art museums, etc., that cater to a wide range of interests. These add measurably to the attraction of downtown shopping areas, because most suburbs cannot support such diverse cultural activities.

Downtown customers differ as well. People who shop at suburban centers usually live in the surrounding area. They use the mall or shopping center on a fairly regular basis throughout the week, especially evenings and weekends. Conversely, downtown shoppers are more transient. They may be tourists or office workers, but they usually do not live in the area—except in those cities that have substantial residential space downtown in the form of condominiums and rental apartments. People who travel downtown to work seldom shop there on weekends; they shop most often on their lunch hours or immediately after work. However, where transportation between downtown and suburbs or outlying city neighborhoods is available on weekends, people will travel downtown to shop.

Merchandise offered in downtown developments tends to be tailored more to the type of employment that exists nearby than to income level, which is a common denominator for suburban developments. Restaurants of all kinds can do well downtown, although they may depend on the lunch trade for the largest part of their receipts.

Competition with suburban shopping centers is one of the major issues the agent has to face when leasing downtown retail space. Suburban malls generally are designed for shopper comfort and convenience. They have been developed exclusively for retailing, and consequently they present a uniformity of design, management, and purpose that is not always present in downtown developments. Suburban centers provide seating in common areas and spacious pedestrian walkways. They are well-lighted and temperature-controlled. Being under a single management, a suburban center can coordinate its operating hours for shopper convenience. In order to be able to lease downtown retail space success-fully, the leasing agent has to be knowledgeable not only about the space being leased but also about comparable suburban space. Higher down-town rents and operating costs are offset by potentially greater sales vol-ume, and the pedestrian traffic in the area of the downtown site means a large part of the potential market does not have to travel in order to shop.

Because the leasing of downtown retail space takes place in a different environment than the leasing of suburban properties, it requires different approaches to marketing, prospecting, and rent pricing. In some regions, leasing of downtown retail space is considered a specialized field by itself.

THE CHALLENGE OF DOWNTOWN RETAIL SPACE LEASING

Downtown retail space is limited. Even with the large amount of new de-velopment begun in the early 1980s, downtown areas overall showed a net loss in the number of retail stores between 1977 and 1982 (table 9.1). However, as the decade of the 1980s came to an end, this trend appeared to be reversing in many cities.

There is a tendency today to seek downtown tenancies from the same chain stores that are wooed by suburban malls. While it is true that in order to succeed downtown the retailer must sell more per square foot of GLA than in a comparable suburban store, it is also evident that stores that once located only in suburban malls are appearing in downtown retail spaces. Often chain operations will open stores within a couple of blocks of each other downtown because shoppers on foot are less likely to walk long distances, and sister stores—even in the next block—are not viewed as specific competition.

Economic factors that contribute to high rents for downtown retail space include development costs and their financing. The configuration of downtown retail space differs from that in the suburbs, mostly in having more varied sizes, shapes, and locations, and this makes it difficult to com-pare individual spaces as well as retail properties. Last but not least, the characteristics of downtown as an entity add to the leasing challenge.

Economic Considerations

Many of the factors that contribute to the challenge of downtown retail leasing have specific economic impact. Limited available land—which is therefore expensive—and the high costs of building and operating a downtown site result in higher occupancy costs for the tenant; financing is another consideration. Operating costs, in turn, affect various terms of the retail lease. The times shoppers are present determine business hours,

T A B L E   9.1

Net Decline in the Number of Downtown Retail Stores between 1977 and 1982

City	1977	1982	Stores Lost	Percent Loss
Atlanta	426	346	80	18.7
Boston*	1,175	985	190	16.2
Chicago†	1,633	1,251	382	23.4
Dallas	388	273	115	29.6
Denver	421	314	107	25.4
New Orleans	786	618	168	21.4
New York	4,989	4,152	837	16.8
Philadelphia	1,887	1,445	442	23.4
Saint Louis	388	277	111	28.6
San Francisco	1,926	1,330	596	30.9
Washington, D.C.	896	726	170	19.0

*Figures for Boston include Back Bay.

†Figures for Chicago include North Michigan Avenue.

Of the 39 cities reported in the *1982 Census of Retail Trade,* data on store numbers were available for 38 cities only. All 38 reporting cities showed a net loss of retail stores between 1977 and 1982: The total declined from 26,187 to 20,515 stores over the 5-year period, a loss of 5,672 stores (or nearly 22%).

Compiled from *Downtown Retail Markets* (Chicago: Downtown Research Corporation, 1986). Reproduced with permission.

which in turn influence a retailer's success. The goals of ownership also have an effect.

Development Costs.   To accommodate to smaller land areas, buildings and parking lots are built vertically downtown. This places constraints on design and engineering that are not required for suburban developments where large plots of vacant land are available. Downtown building codes differ and are usually stricter, and materials and labor may be more expensive. Permits, fees, and site assembly and preparation add to the complexity. As a result, construction costs are often much higher downtown than in the suburbs.

Data for a variety of retail projects developed in the early and mid-1980s have been published by the Urban Land Institute in a series of individual *Project Reference Files,* which provide representative dollar amounts for comparison of development costs. In general, large tracts of land in metropolitan suburbs were acquired for a fraction of the cost of land downtown. A parcel of land for a community center in Los Angeles, California, consisted of less than ten acres and cost nearly $2 million—or about $4.60 per square foot, while nearly ten times as much land for a super regional center in Dallas, Texas, cost nearly $3 million—or only about 75 cents per square foot. Construction costs for the gross building area (GBA) of different properties varied similarly: $30 or less per square foot of GBA built new in the suburbs compared to $60–70 per square foot downtown. Renovation or rehab costs might be more or less than new construction, depending on the region and the extent of the work. For example, Harborplace in Baltimore was said to have development costs that exceeded costs in the suburbs by 150 percent.

Because of these differences in development costs, the suburban centers in these reports could succeed with low minimum rents (average $15 or less per square foot of GLA) while the downtown centers had to achieve average rents in the area of $15–50 or higher. The reported range for tenants in a downtown center might be from $10 to $100 per square foot of GLA. Both suburban and downtown centers required percentage rents in the range of less than 2 percent up to 12 percent of gross sales, with smaller percentages typical of suburban centers (as low as 1.5 percent for some tenants) and larger percentages more common downtown. Tenants in *smaller* spaces almost always paid *higher* minimum and percentage rents than tenants in large spaces. Common area charges typically were *additional* as well. However, downtown tenants recorded average sales of $200–500 or more per square foot of GLA while suburban tenants typically averaged less than $200 per square foot ($140–175).

Financing. Downtown projects are expensive to build. The expense of acquiring land that is usually scarce and costly, construction on sites that may be inefficient, and provision for parking in multilevel structures makes these projects cost more than developers can readily finance through one conventional channel. As a result, funding for downtown retail developments usually comes from a variety of sources, both private and public. Whether the project calls for new construction or rehabilitation and reuse of existing structures, *downtown sites are more likely candidates for public funding,* especially as development is part of revitalization of a commercial area.

All borrowed money comes with strings attached. Private sources receive interest on the money loaned in addition to collateral in the form of lease contracts and other considerations, and they may require periodic accounting for or reporting on expenditure of the loaned funds. Public funding may be in the form of grants or loans, low-cost leases of city-owned lands or buildings, or tax abatements. While projects built on public lands sometimes have no direct land acquisition costs, construction costs for new or upgraded site improvements may offset that benefit. In addition to interest payments and accounting requirements, public funds may come with political "strings" and other considerations. Governmental agencies may require minority participation in construction contracts, or there may be contingencies regarding tenant mix or use of space because of city ownership or zoning requirements. Usually the most workable strategy involves establishing a quasi-public development corporation that is empowered to operate in a way that effectively balances the private and public sectors' needs. The cost of this borrowed money is what contributes to the higher rents at downtown sites. (See appendix B for a detailed discussion of development financing.)

Operating Costs.   Downtown rental rates reflect higher costs for such items as security, trash removal, and lighting, although organized retail centers charge separate fees for common area expenses as they do in suburban malls. (The cost of operating a downtown retail center is two to three times that of suburban centers.) A retailer's occupancy costs determine to some extent its merchandise price lines, and a downtown retailer generally must price merchandise higher in order to meet its rent obligations, although chain stores usually sell the same item for the same price throughout their various locations in a metropolitan area.

One of the greatest challenges for leasing agents is finding tenants that can afford to pay the rental rates dictated by the downtown market. Prospects will be legitimately concerned about (1) whether they can sell enough volume per square foot to survive in the downtown space, (2) what percentage of their overall revenues will be taken up by occupancy costs, and (3) whether the benefits of leasing downtown will outweigh the expense.

East 57th Street in New York City is the most expensive street in the world; rents there averaged $425 per square foot in the late 1980s. Rents on Rodeo Drive in Beverly Hills averaged $200 per square foot; on North Michigan Avenue in Chicago, they averaged $150 per square foot. The prices of merchandise sold in stores in these locations reflected these high occupancy costs. Considering that ancillary spaces in a typical regional shopping center were renting for as little as $25.00 per square foot or less at the end of the 1980s, the rental advantage of suburban retail space is great. Retailers can succeed with lower sales volumes in the suburbs and, therefore, the number of prospects is greater. However, the larger potential sales volume downtown (two to three times that in the suburbs as noted earlier) should encourage retailers. Often they can operate successfully in smaller spaces for fewer business hours per week and sell more per square foot than their suburban counterparts. Thus volume alone can permit them to compete effectively without too great an increase in prices. The rewards of higher sales achieved in fewer store hours extend as well to employee expenses, which are reduced. Being open shorter hours, downtown stores do not have to pay salaries for the hours they are not open in the evenings or on Sundays, as stores in suburban centers do although this, too, is changing as downtown retailers explore evening and Sunday shopping hours to increase their sales. In truth, the prospective tenant with an established identity and unique product can succeed anywhere, including downtown.

Lease Terms. In addition to their impact on rental rates, high operating costs also affect the terms of downtown retail leases. The type of project and the parties involved will determine whether net or gross leases are used. In heavily trafficked areas or in popular projects, developers can require that tenants share in the expenses of insurance, taxes, security, HVAC, and general maintenance via net leases. On the other hand, developers in areas where retail activity is just gaining a foothold may be compelled to offer gross leases to attract potential tenants. Office or apartment buildings may use gross leases for their retail space because the stores provide needed services to people who work or live there or because they project the type of image the owner wants. However, gross leases are less desirable overall. Operating expenses of all retail centers are subject to change—usually increasing—and downtowns are no exception. It is preferable by far to have tenants share these costs via pass-throughs in a net lease.

Downtown retailers often ask for and receive rent concessions. It may take three months to build custom-designed shelves for a jeweler, for example; it can take two to three months for a restaurant to obtain a liquor license. In a large city, it can take three to five months *after* a lease has been signed just to obtain a construction permit. For special situations, an owner may offer several months' free rent rather than lower the rental rate. This may be done by extending the term of the lease, adding the period of free rent onto the beginning of the lease and writing it so the tenant pays full rent for the remainder. In other words, an effective three-year lease could be written for a term of thirty-eight months, providing two months' free rent initially and a full thirty-six months' lease term at the agreed-upon rent. The result would extend the period of the lease but not jeopardize its contribution to the value of the property. The duration of the lease actually depends on many factors, including the nature of the retailer's business and the market conditions in the area to be served. A strong downtown economy will encourage longer-term leases. Conversely, short-term leases are more feasible for both retailers and owners in an economically volatile business district.

Operating Hours. Another factor that has economic impact is operating hours. Suburban centers are commonly open seven days a week, with evening hours at least Monday through Friday. In many downtown districts, however, retailers are limited to a five-day business week. They must operate in an environment that is transient. Most potential customers of downtown stores work eight hours a day in an office building, and shopping is not their top priority; once workers go home for the evening, many downtowns are virtually deserted. Downtown retailers must capitalize on the available shopping hours: They commonly do their best business during lunchtime—from about 11:00 A.M. to 2:00 P.M.—and during the hours immediately after work—4:00–6:00 P.M. If a store's merchandise is not likely to sell during these hours, it probably will not succeed. In cities where workers' hours reflect inflexible commuter train schedules, business districts may empty out even earlier. To compensate for the loss of evening business, some apparel stores have started opening as early as 7:00 A.M. in an effort to capture morning trade. Generally, however, the most successful downtown retail operations are restaurants.

There are exceptions to the limited operating hours for downtown shopping districts. Shops along major shopping streets enjoy a longer period of activity. Some regularly stay open till seven o'clock—and occasionally later—on weekday evenings. Stores on Union Square in San Francisco and along North Michigan Avenue in Chicago are open seven days a week. An abundance of movie theaters in an area can contribute to customer traffic, as does proximity to a city's nightlife. These can create an eighteen-hour business environment that is especially conducive to a flourishing restaurant trade. Usually areas that attract large numbers of tourists or have a high concentration of entertainment facilities such as cinemas, theaters, and discotheques will be able to support retail businesses that stay open later than the normal business hours. When targeting prospects, the leasing agent has to have analyzed an area's customer traffic carefully and know its source.

Out-of-Town and Corporate Owners.   Ownership and management of downtown space are important considerations in leasing. As indicated earlier, private and public partnership is common. The motivation of downtown investors may be completely different from that of suburban investors. The leasing agent will have to ascertain what the goals of these different types of owners are and how best to achieve them through the leasing plan.

Out-of-town ownership of downtown properties is common today, and some of these owners do extensive research so that they may know the market even better than local owners do. However, out-of-town owners often have ideas about retail leasing and operations that are at variance with what the agent who has daily business in the trade area knows to be true. The interests of owners who are not familiar with the idiosyncrasies of a particular downtown district can make it more difficult for the agent to lease space to a prospective tenant.

Ownership of retail businesses themselves changes hands rather frequently. Many large freestanding department stores are no longer independent operations but rather are owned by large corporations whose business is not solely or even primarily retailing. Being profit-driven, the corporations are more concerned with maximizing the amount of money to be gotten out of a given space, and they may not always understand the finer points of downtown retailing or the types of consumers in the area.

Competition with Suburban Shopping Centers. For many downtown retail developments, the perceived competition is the suburban shopping center. In order to meet that competition, the tenant mix and merchandise offering at a downtown development may be likened to a regional mall. In fact, there are many *similarities* between them.

- Space designed exclusively for retail businesses
- Centralized management
- Provision of customer "comforts" (seating, restrooms, etc.)
- Spacious, well-lighted, enclosed walkways or malls
- Common areas and prorated fees for their upkeep
- Accessibility (suburban automobile traffic, downtown foot traffic)

However, the *differences* between downtown and suburban retail space are also important. Traditionally downtown shopping areas were built near a center of industry or commerce. Retail stores were developed secondarily and, with the exception of downtown department stores, were not necessarily designed with the shopper in mind. The inclusion of retail stores in office buildings adds another dimension to downtown leasing—the dominance of offices in a particular area commonly limits retailing hours in that area to those of the office business day, five days a week.

Often there is no one management organization coordinating the leasing or tenant development of these kinds of downtown retail spaces. However, downtowns with strong retailing areas may see the development of voluntary associations that represent the interests of the various downtown businesses and coordinate advertising programs that promote the business district as a whole.

Single freestanding stores other than department stores have to use all their available space (GLA) for merchandising and cannot offer restrooms, waiting areas, or other customer comforts. Because they front directly on downtown streets, they have no control over the condition of nearby walkways; nor are they obliged to pay common area charges when there are no common areas.

Although suburban shopping centers are often accessible via public transportation, and developers of major downtown properties may be able to influence routing of buses to serve their centers, the more tradi-

T A B L E   9.2

Examples of Downtown Retail Projects in the United States

Name	Type	City	GLA* (Sq Ft)	Number of Tenants	Tenant Mix
Charleston Place	Mixed-use†	Charleston, SC	52,600	27	No anchor. Predominantly apparel, gifts, upscale boutiques, candy.
Faneuil Hall Marketplace	Festival (historic)	Boston, MA	219,000	160	No anchor. Specialty, food courts, pushcarts in converted buildings.
The Grand Avenue	Festival (historic)	Milwaukee, WI	895,000	125	27,000 sq ft food court (3d flr); Approx 60% local merchants.
Greenway Plaza	Neighborhood	Yonkers, NY	70,000	8	Supermarket anchor. Food service, personal service, liquors (2d flr).
Harborplace	Specialty/Festival	Baltimore, MD	140,000	140	No anchor. Restaurants/cafes (41%), fast food (14%), market produce (7%).
Horton Plaza	Regional/Festival	San Diego, CA	885,000	140	Anchored by 4 dept stores. Restaurants, apparel, specialty.
The Pavilion (Old Post Office)	Festival (historic)	Washington, DC	53,000	45	No anchor. 73% food service, 27% specialty.
Water Tower Place	Regional/Mixed-use	Chicago, IL	613,000	136	Anchored by 2 dept stores. Fashion, specialty, novelty stores dominate.

*GLA = retail space (excluding office, hotel, residential space).

†Hotel/retail/parking complex.

Information used with permission of ULI—the Urban Land Institute.

tional downtown areas may be less readily accessible for the shopper who drives in from the suburbs and cannot easily find a place to park. On the other hand, the concentration of downtown workers who pass by these stores walking between their jobs and commuter train stations or bus stops twice a day, as well as the numbers of workers who leave their workplaces at lunchtime, provide a captive market that suburban centers cannot approach.

Configuration of Downtown Retail Space

Many new downtown developments in major cities are configured to provide a tenant and merchandise mix that would rival a regional or super regional mall in the suburbs (table 9.2). Others make shopping a form of entertainment by providing small, interesting, "specialty" shops in unique, "festival" environments. Downtown retail space also includes department store spinoffs as well as licensed or leased space within department stores, ground-floor and second-floor spaces in office buildings and transportation centers, and shops in older buildings originally designed as retail "arcades." The variety of forms adds to the challenge of leasing the right space to the right retail tenant to secure the highest rental rate possible.

Malls and Shopping Centers.   Conventional shopping centers with a tenant mix comparable to suburban regional malls have sometimes been developed in downtown areas, often as part of mixed-use developments (Trump Tower in New York City, Water Tower Place in Chicago). Like outlying regional shopping centers, these downtown centers are freestanding structures with at least one department store as an anchor tenant, and they are usually located in a central business district. The scarcity of downtown land demands a vertical design, so new urban retail centers are typically many-storied with multilevel parking garages—attached to or incorporated within the building—taking the place of the extensive surface-level parking lots at suburban centers.

Other examples of regional-type "malls" in a downtown location are The Gallery at Market East in Philadelphia and The Grand Avenue in Milwaukee, both designed to regenerate retailing in their respective locations by incorporating existing retail space in the form of department stores into a larger, more diversified structural complex. Crossroads Plaza in Salt Lake City offers four floors of varied shops and boutiques along with movie theaters, a sports complex, offices, and eight floors of parking. Still other examples are cited in figure 9.1.

A comparatively recent development in downtown retailing is the so-called "festival center." These centers are designed to create a unique shopping environment through the use of imaginative architecture, creative renovation of an historic structure, or location near a prominent sce-

FIGURE 9.1

Examples of Downtown Shopping Centers

Copley Place has two levels of shopping and restaurants plus a Nieman-Marcus store incorporated in a large mixed-use complex that includes two hotels, offices, and residences.

Faneuil Hall Marketplace occupies 219,000 square feet of GLA in three converted industrial and market buildings. Some 160 stores, including a variety of food vendors, comprise the tenant mix of this festival center.

The Gallery at Market East is 191,000 square feet of GLA in a 1.3 million square foot of GLA regional shopping center developed in the old downtown area of Philadelphia. Its tenant mix includes a relocated Gimbels stores and a renovated Strawbridge and Clothier store. Expansion added more than 100 stores and restaurants (including a J. C. Penney department store).

The Grand Avenue is a four-block long multilevel arcade constructed between two major department stores—Gimbels and the Boston Store. This regional center has 245,000 square feet of GLA on two levels of the arcade occupied by 125 specialty shops; a third-level food court has 18 food vendor tenants in 27,000 square feet of GLA.

Horton Plaza incorporates a three-level shopping center and four major department stores in a mixed-use development in downtown San Diego. The 150 shops and restaurants were chosen to position the retail component with Nordstrom's, Robinson's, Mervyn's, and The Broadway department stores as a regional-festival center to compete effectively against surrounding suburban shopping areas.

The Pavilion in the Old Post Office in Washington, D.C., is a festival-specialty center with 52,939 square feet of GLA that occupies the lower three levels. It features 45 specialty shops and restaurants; upper floors in the building house offices of several federal agencies.

St. Louis Centre is the result of development of a major portion of the downtown retail core of the city of St. Louis. A four-level mall with 330,000 square feet of GLA was constructed to link the Famous-Barr and Stix, Baer & Fuller stores. The two department stores and the 175 retail tenants in the mall are linked by pedestrian bridges to a nearby parking garage. The tenant configuration is similar to a high-end regional mall.

Tabor Center created 117,000 square feet of retail GLA on two and three levels in a mixed-use development in the Skyline Urban Renewal Area of downtown Denver. Built along the 16th Street pedestrian and transit mall, it places 67 additional stores in the area of the large May D&F department store. Except for direct outside access, the only access to the office building in the project is through the retail area.

Trappers Alley is the result of redevelopment of the Greektown area on the edge of Detroit's downtown. Established restaurants and shops that had storefront spaces upgraded their stores which were connected to the five-level enclosed area. Some 70 tenants have been recruited to sell a variety of goods in the approximately 73,500 square feet of redeveloped GLA.

Water Tower Place in Chicago is part of a larger mixed-use development. It consists of an eight-level regional mall with 136 specialty shops "anchored" by Marshall Field's and Lord & Taylor stores in 613,000 square feet of GLA. This is one of the few downtown projects financed totally by private funds.

nic natural resource such as a river or lake. Faneuil Hall Marketplace in Boston was created by renovating three industrial and public market buildings in the city's deteriorating downtown district; Ghirardelli Square and The Cannery in San Francisco converted a chocolate manufactory and a fruit canning plant, respectively, into retail shops. On the other hand, Harborplace in Baltimore consists of two new glass-enclosed towers built as part of the revitalization of the city's Inner Harbor area. The ability of these centers to draw on both downtown office workers and a large tourist population has resulted in extremely high annual sales per square foot. The festival-type specialty center has become the most successful and the most visible form of downtown shopping center development. Other festival centers are also named in figure 9.1.

Festival centers generally are unique to downtown areas. They usually have more restaurants, food retailers, and on-site food vendors than traditional malls; emphasis is on regional cuisine, specialty foods, and unique local goods such as arts and crafts and souvenirs. Unique location, the presence of entertainment activities in addition to shops, and the prevalence of gift and impulse items all tend to attract shoppers whose primary purpose is sightseeing rather than shopping. Although festival malls rely primarily on sales to tourists—approximately 44 percent of their retail sales in some cities—they only succeed in areas that have both a significant tourist trade and a large enough trade area population to support the specialty retail merchants. In other words, they have to attract the local shopper as well.

Retail Space in Nonretail Properties. Retail spaces are leased in a variety of downtown properties, including those with functions that are primarily nonretail. Mixed-use developments often have a significant retail component; office buildings and some residential properties include a few retail stores, and transportation centers have a variety of retail activities under their roofs. Sometimes street-level shopping is set off as a "center" by creating a so-called pedestrian mall.

Mixed-use developments are large multifunctional projects, with hotels, private housing, offices, and recreation facilities among their most common components in addition to retail space. They usually include at least three such components and, by definition, exhibit a highly intensive use of land. Each major function is architecturally integrated with the others. The size of the retail component varies. Some developments feature only convenience retailers that cater primarily to the shopping needs of the other tenants of the site. High-rise apartment buildings may lease to health clubs, convenience grocery stores, hair salons, restaurants, travel agents, and other service-oriented stores. The Riverplace in Portland, Oregon, for example, is basically an urban residential development with a 47,000-square-foot health club and 23,220 square feet of waterfront retail out of a total GLA of 420,000 square feet. Other mixed-use developments contain full-fledged regional shopping centers as a major component. Like freestanding downtown shopping centers, these large centers have at least one major department store anchor and a relatively traditional tenant mix. Examples (figure 9.1) include Canal Place in New Orleans—a 32-story office building with 50,000 square feet of retail space on the first three floors, a 440-room luxury hotel, and a separate three-level Fashion Center with another 210,000 square feet of retail space; Copley Place in Boston—anchored by Neiman-Marcus and including 100 ancillary stores and restaurants, two hotels, four office buildings, and 100 residential units; and very large developments such as Horton Plaza in San Diego and Water Tower Place in Chicago, which include two or more major department stores. Water Tower Place also contains 200,000 square feet of office space, luxury condominiums, and the Ritz-Carlton Hotel. Horton Plaza houses an entertainment center called the Lyceum Theatre, a seven-screen movie theater, and numerous restaurants and cafes. Retail spaces in these properties may be leased by the building management or by individual brokers.

Another re-emerging form of traditional retail space is the independent, specialized store located on the ground floor of a commercial building. These small, single-line retail shops offering shoes, books, apparel, and other types of merchandise once formed the backbone of most downtown shopping districts. Like flagship department stores, however, ground-floor retailers suffered dramatic losses in sales and in their customer bases when the population shifted from the city to the suburbs in the late 1940s and early 1950s. Another factor was that they alone could not generate enough traffic to compete with sites that served multiple needs, which was one reason why remodeling, store splits, and changes from one tenant to multiple tenants occurred. Traffic building became crucial to the leasing agent's plans. These small stores also lost display area to attract customers as new and remodeled buildings were constructed without street-level storefronts. Without such display, passersby would not be aware that these stores existed. In recent years, however, these retailers have started to rebound as downtown business districts have begun to redevelop economically.

Retail space generally represents only a small percentage of the rental income in an office building—the ground floor of a twenty-story building will comprise 5 percent or less of its leasable space—yet retail stores are a convenience for employees of tenants and provide a focus for the lobbies of these buildings. Ground-floor retail space not only attracts customers from among office workers in the building itself but also from commuter traffic passing the building and from residents in nearby downtown apartments. A general increase in the number of downtown office buildings has not only increased the number of potential customers but also added retail space. Some cities, aware of the impact of retail sales on the economic revitalization of the central business district, have begun to insist that new office buildings include retail space in their lobbies. If one new commercial building leases retail space, another will generally follow suit, although developers may prefer to rent to stores with a "business" image rather than to a fashion merchandiser. Food service operations are also desirable tenants, and restaurants in office buildings tend toward the extremes—either they are sit-down, white table cloth operations or self-service fast food stalls. Other successful food operations are single-item businesses such as cookie stores or fancy candy shops.

Some retailers are also establishing stores on the second floors of well-located, highly visible office buildings. While second-floor space is generally ill-suited for retailers that rely on off-the-street impulse shopping for a significant portion of their sales (for example, bookstores), merchants whose clientele usually make a special trip to buy their goods—furriers, fashion retailers, art galleries—are often successful on a second floor. Restaurants are beginning to seek second-floor locations as well, and many service vendors such as tailors or shoemakers are also going upstairs in neighborhoods that are being "gentrified" because these spaces usually rent at lower rates. A retail business can succeed more readily in a second-floor location if a small street-level area is provided for "storefront" display and customer access.

Second-floor and basement space in older buildings—nonyield space that was formerly not rentable—is being converted to retail use in downtown areas. New centers may locate restaurants and cinemas in lower level (basement) space. Rehabbed retail sites may include other types of businesses in newly created basement space if high visibility is not an absolute necessity for their success. The Underground in Atlanta and Atlantic Richfield (ARCO) Plaza in Los Angeles are examples of subterranean "malls" that have successfully revitalized a downtown area by making use of two or more levels below ground. Superimposing glass-fronted "atriums" on renovated structures opens up retail leasing opportunities on two and even three levels of formerly nonyield space. Modernization programs that include careful attention to entrances and visibility increase the chances for success of retailers that lease such rehabbed space.

The general popularity of revitalizing retail sites has led to the renovation of storefronts and existing retail corridors in the downtown sections of smaller cities. Competition from nearby regional shopping centers has made this overall facelift of downtown retail areas almost a necessity in order to draw shoppers back into town. In some cities, scattered stores have been unified into integrated retail corridors through the redesign of storefronts, coordination of signage, and the selective conversion of downtown streets into pedestrian malls. Although there is no strict definition of what constitutes a "pedestrian mall," it is usually an area that is closed to vehicular traffic along one or more blocks on a single street (for example, Nicollet Mall in Minneapolis). Like a suburban shopping mall, many urban pedestrian malls are managed by a central organization that helps maintain the property, sets rules and regulations, requires tenants to keep standard operating hours, and plans mall promotions. Regular community involvement makes the malls a vital and exciting place both to do business and to shop.

Pedestrian malls have been successful in several cities: The 16th Street Mall built on a half-mile long street in downtown Denver is one example. The mall is anchored at the south end by May D & F, a full-service department store, and at the north end by Tabor Center, a 117,000-square-foot festival-type center; 16th Street is blocked to all traffic except free shuttle buses that take shoppers from one end of the mall to the other. Daytime downtown workers are the mall's largest customer base; it is closed in the evenings, and weekends tend to be quiet because most of its customers are suburban residents.

The disadvantages of pedestrian malls should not be overlooked, however. Although people theoretically should be able to shop comfortably without having to worry about excessive vehicular traffic, such malls have often proved inconvenient. Limited availability or absence of nearby parking lots discourages customers from shopping at downtown pedestrian malls. Automobile traffic may be rerouted, usually along one-way streets, making it difficult to drive around or through the downtown area to access the mall. Retailers also lose visibility to vehicular traffic. Because the pedestrian mall areas span what were once a street and its adjacent sidewalks, there is the added distraction of apparent extra distance between shops. Fumes from the buses that are permitted on the mall add to customers' discomforts. Being set apart from mainstream traffic flow and having many benches and fountains, pedestrian malls can also be subject to loitering and increased crime.

Airports, commuter train stations, rapid transit (subway) stops, and bus depots cater to thousands of passengers daily, making them an excellent location for convenience and service stores. Airport retail space, in fact, has evolved to include shops selling perfume, jewelry, tobacco, and clothing in addition to the usual magazine and candy stores. Florists and newsstands are well adapted to the atmosphere of train stations where they are able to capture both morning and evening commuter trade. Underground arcades have been developed in cities where the climate necessitated building enclosed passageways between buildings or from train stops to major commercial or government buildings. Businesses that cater to the needs and whims of people in a hurry are likely to succeed in such a retail environment. Although some transportation centers—Northwestern Atrium Center in Chicago; Union Station in Washington, D.C.—have been extensively refurbished and have shopping center-like atmospheres and tenancies, others offer mostly kiosks or less-than-permanent space configurations. Much of the available retail space may be leased as a block to one retailer as a "concession" to operate multiple food services, newsstands, or gift shops in the center.

Freestanding Retail Space. The characteristic form of freestanding retail space is the traditional full-line department store although towns and cities do have numerous freestanding specialty shops. Despite overwhelming competition from outlets in suburban shopping centers, department store owners are reluctant to abandon the downtown area entirely because the presence of a "flagship" store is a reflection of the company's prestige. Many downtown department stores also have fixed-term leases, and this long-term downtown tenancy translates into both low rents and low overhead costs.

Renovation of downtown shopping districts, incorporation into larger retail projects, and the benefits of renewed consumer interest in the central city have led to a resurgence of the traditional, freestanding department store in some areas. The gains made by other forms of downtown retail space have been greater, however; and department store executives are less optimistic about the future of downtown sites than are chain store operators and retail center developers.

In addition to participation in downtown shopping center projects, department stores have turned to other uses of downtown space to maintain their positions in the downtown market and respond to new consumer trends. Some department stores have created new boutiques within the store to cater to a very particular segment of their market. Other stores have leased space in commercial office buildings, opening small specialty shops to sell ladies' accessories and fashion items. These spin-off stores are independent of the larger store and usually sell a single line of merchandise using the name and image of the original department in the parent store.

A department store may license part of its space to an independent retailer, usually an outlet of a national chain. The chain retailer then operates its business at that location in a manner reflecting the image of the department store. The store and the independent retailer sign an agreement whereby the department store receives a minimum rental or license fee plus a specified commission from the retailer's sales in exchange for use of the store's space for a given period of time. Such leased departments are usually service merchants (optometrists, income tax consultants, insurance agencies) or specialty merchandise retailers offering consumer electronics, recreational equipment, cosmetics, health care products, and gourmet foods. In the case of cosmetics, the "retailer" may be the brand-name manufacturer.

Although the department store usually sets up such licenses directly, agents should observe how such specialty subtenants merchandise their products as a key to evaluating the success potential of their prospects. Also, placement of these subtenants in the store—their juxtaposition to specific departments or types of merchandise in the department store— can be a guideline for locating retail tenants and creating tenant mix in a downtown center. Knowledge of leased department activity in the agent's area can be very useful. The agent preparing to lease space in a downtown "regional" mall to a financial services chain might change that decision if a nearby department store has just signed a leased department arrangement with another financial services company. The agent who is unaware of such leasing activity could add redundant and unprofitable retail activity to the trade area and strain the center's credibility among retailers and property owners.

Department stores themselves can be a source of information and ideas about product merchandising and tenant mix. They originated many of the ways to promote merchandise that are used by large shopping centers. Having women's shoe salons adjacent to where dresses are sold or offering gloves at counters next to those where handbags or hosiery are sold were ways to encourage additional purchases by a shopper willing to accessorize a new outfit on the spot. The same principle is applied in shopping centers that position shoe stores next to apparel shops, etc.

Characteristics of Downtown Areas

In downtown business districts, there is often little continuity among retail sites. There may be shops at opposite ends of a block with warehouses and other nonretail businesses between them. Such isolated stores tend to deteriorate because fewer people come there to shop and sales volumes diminish. Such locations can be particularly difficult to lease.

Also, the ideal store size for most retailers is about 1,000 square feet, and frontage on a street with heavy pedestrian traffic is much sought after—some downtown retailers require a minimum frontage of fifteen feet. However, frontage may be limited in office buildings, and the lack of visibility can be a handicap for retail tenants in them.

Retailers will be interested in the number of people who shop in the area during the day, the mix of businesses and their employees (clerical, executive, professional) and the levels of their salaries, as well as whether the buildings are well maintained, the streets are adequately lighted at night, and transportation is safe and accessible. The success of many stores depends on the accessibility of public transportation or the availability of parking.

When a space is less than ideal for a prospect's purposes, build-outs and tenant improvement allowances become extremely important. When leasing lobby space to retailers, many office building owners will offer to pay for build-outs in order to attract tenants for whom that expense might be prohibitive. Jewelry stores and restaurants are examples of tenants whose build-out expenses can be extremely high.

Influence of Nonretail Facilities on Retail Tenant Mix.   Tenant selection is closely linked to nearby businesses and the characteristics of their employees. An apparel store featuring high-quality business clothing can be expected to succeed if there are law firms in the vicinity. So can a nice restaurant that caters to the business lunch trade. On the other hand, students, faculty, and staff at a city college might be more likely to shop at stores that feature casual clothes, inexpensive fast food, music and recording equipment, and books.

An example of how retail businesses downtown depend on the nonretail facilities nearby is the story of two different restaurants that successively occupied the same 3,000-square-foot corner site in the warehouse district of a busy city. One restaurant failed; the other succeeded. The first occupant, a moderate-priced steakhouse offering table service exclusively, did only a fair lunch trade despite excellent street exposure. Most workers in the district had neither the time nor the money—nor the inclination—to sit down for a leisurely lunch, and the neighborhood did not customarily attract evening trade. The out-of-town developer of this restaurant did not understand the neighborhood or its worker population, and the business failed. The site remained empty for most of the restaurant's lease term. Subsequently a new tenant opened a delicatessen that offered both carryouts and table service at economical prices. Patrons could pick up breakfast in the morning and eat in or carry out sandwiches and salads for lunch. Within a few months of its start-up date, the delicatessen was considered a success, doing twice the business that the steakhouse had done. The reason for the success of the second restaurant is apparent. It served affordable meals and snacks over a time period that optimized its potential business: It responded to the existing customer base.

Importance of Parking and Public Transportation.   Free on-street parking is virtually nonexistent downtown; if there is parking, it is usually metered. The alternatives—parking lots and garages—are expensive both to construct and to use. Vertical parking space downtown costs eight to ten times as much to build as single-level parking lots in the suburbs. Parking charges may be by the quarter or half hour unless there is special provision for shoppers; and whether it costs $3.00 or $10.00 to park for the day, that cost will be a consideration for the shopper. In some areas, retailers and other businesses arrange to use parking facilities in other nearby properties. Sometimes arrangements are made for discounted rates for shoppers whose parking "tickets" have been validated by the store where they shopped. These and other creative approaches can be used to reduce if not eliminate the "impediment" of parking expenses for shoppers.

F I G U R E   9.2

Representative Size of Worker Population within Walking Distance of Downtown Shopping (St. Louis, Missouri)

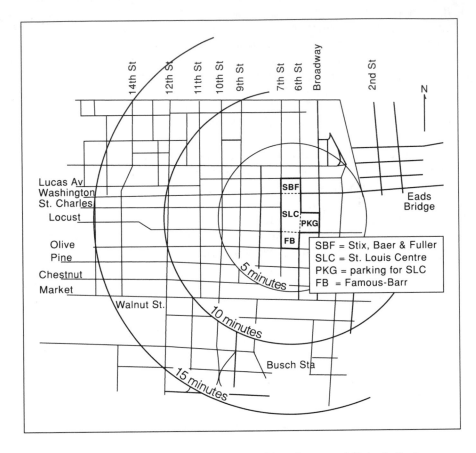

Circles show numbers of workers within various walking distances of St. Louis Centre:
5 minutes = 33,000; 10 minutes = 61,100; 15 minutes = 73,000.
These walking distances represent approximately 3-, 6-, and 9-block
radiuses from the site.

Reproduced with permission from *Downtown Retail Development* (Washington,
D.C.: ULI—the Urban Land Institute, 1983).

Downtown parking has to be arranged physically so that it will be as convenient to enter and leave as it is at suburban malls. The ratio of parking spaces to GLA is also important although fewer spaces are required than in a suburban project of comparable size because office workers and other pedestrians can be expected to comprise a large part of the downtown consumer population (figure 9.2). Downtown parking facilities require extra security, however, which adds to their operating costs; and if it is necessary to offer discount rates for the first few hours of parking in order to compete effectively with the free parking at suburban centers, such discounts will reduce the income from parking.

While some cities have succeeded in attracting customers to downtown shopping areas by offering affordable public transportation, parking is an absolute necessity for retail areas that depend on tourists or suburban shoppers or for areas where there are no nearby residential properties. Availability of parking definitely affects the leasing of downtown retail space. It can be an excellent selling tool when prospecting for tenants that might otherwise locate only in suburban malls. Retailers generally will be more likely to consider leasing at a site where parking is available; however, rental rates for downtown retail space will vary with the type and amount of parking available and its proximity, and this must be taken into account in the leasing process.

Whether parking is available or not, many downtown retailers depend on public transportation systems to bring the customers that will make their businesses succeed, and location along popular pedestrian routes to and from commuter train stations or on streets or corners where buses stop or there is access to rapid transit (subway) lines should be a particularly good selling point. Frequency of transit services and safety of waiting areas and carriers are considerations not only for those who travel downtown to shop but also for those workers who stay downtown after office hours, either to shop or to take advantage of other amenities of the big city. Without convenient and inexpensive access to downtown, shoppers would not take their trade to these stores and sales volumes would be reduced.

Both developers of new properties and prospective retail tenants will question the reliability of a particular area's public transportation system. They will want to know whether specific bus or train routes will still be operating in the near future, whether the frequency of service is sufficient for their purposes, and whether there is the possibility that any proposed changes to the transportation service might seriously affect the customers' access to the site.

Overall Image.   The image of downtowns as crowded, dirty, and crime-infested is an ever-present obstacle to the leasing of retail space there. Suburban shoppers are often reluctant to venture downtown for this very reason. A positive image can be created and fostered by the cities themselves, however. In addition, chambers of commerce, local merchants' groups, and managers of retail developments, working together or independently, can undertake and encourage numerous activities that will draw people downtown. Among them are various seasonal, theme-related festivals. Some other ideas that have been successful include:

- Increasing security and sidewalk lighting, putting up new signs, replacing old trash cans, improving street cleaning
- Working with the metropolitan (public) transportation board or other governing bodies to improve public transportation service as well as to encourage changes in routes to provide direct service to newly developed sites
- Putting up street banners with logos of local businesses to decorate retail areas
- Using sidewalk vendors and pushcarts to sell food
- Offering tickets for discounted parking to be validated by local retailers and restaurants or providing free or reduced-rate parking during off-hours
- Publishing a guide to city activities or using an electronic information system to guide consumers to various retailers
- Offering slide shows or short video presentations highlighting some of the city's events
- Selling tickets to plays, concerts, sporting events, and other entertainments in the city from a centrally located kiosk
- Sponsoring contests and awards
- Encouraging volunteer groups to get involved in downtown by organizing festivals and other civic activities

Although many of these activities may be considered primarily promotional, knowledge about what is being done in his or her city can be a selling tool for the leasing agent. A list of such activities might be used in conjunction with the leasing plan as additional selling points—in other words, to show that there are established traffic builders in the area. The retailer that can anticipate increased sales because of focused activities will be encouraged to lease downtown.

EVALUATING THE DOWNTOWN MARKET

Market research for downtown retail businesses focuses on the economic status of the city and the purchasing power of the consumers who visit downtown shopping districts. As with suburban shopping centers, the economic picture of the downtown "market" is made up of many parts. Retailers considering a downtown site will be interested in a number of different factors that influence sales potential. A good market survey of the downtown retail area should incorporate the following types of information.

- *Consumer Profile*—including demographic information about the present and projected size of the population from which the downtown shopping area as a whole draws most of its business (income levels, types of employment, and location of residential areas within the city and overall metropolitan area)
- *Downtown Area Profile*—including cultural and recreational amenities, transportation, and a ratio of retail to business to personal services
- *Economic Feasibility*—including information about growth prospects for the city and the city's role in the regional economy, statistics about construction and publicly sponsored renovation programs, historic and current trends in retail sales, shifts in types of stores and sales figures within the city, sales projections and a capture rate analysis for the particular site
- *Site Evaluation*—including traffic counts, pedestrian counts, numbers of office workers (or other types of workers) in the immediate area, dollars spent on specific types of merchandise in adjacent or nearby retail establishments, market rents, and operating costs
- *Analysis of Competition*—including the location and drawing power of both suburban centers and competing retail stores within the city

The types of information being sought should be accessible from a variety of sources, including redevelopment agencies, government statistical reports, and special issues of publications such as *Sales and Marketing Management* (July and October). Other possible resources are brokers, appraisers, and other real estate professionals in the area. (Agent networking and cooperation are beneficial to all.)

One of the best ways to assess the market is to conduct consumer surveys. These can be used to measure both the percentage of consumers who live in the metropolitan area and the percentage who are out-of-town visitors. In general, a random telephone survey of 500 households will produce a fairly accurate picture of the metropolitan market; however, on-site interviews or surveys conducted at properties near the subject site—office buildings, restaurants, and transportation terminals such as bus stations, train stations, or subway stops—will generate more relevant data. The results of the market survey will indicate how much of the market is being penetrated by established retailers and what portion of the market incoming retailers will be able to capture. The sales potential and economic feasibility of the new site can also be determined.

Consumer Profile

One of the primary aims of any market research effort is to find out who is shopping, where these shoppers come from, and how much they typically spend. However, the focus of a downtown consumer profile is different

F I G U R E   9.3

Representative Consumer Profile

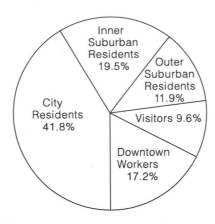

Mix of prospective customers shown is a profile of downtown St. Louis
shoppers identified in a 1982 survey.

Reproduced with permission from *Downtown Retail Development*
(Washington, D.C.: ULI—the Urban Land Institute, 1983).

from that of a suburban consumer profile. For one thing, trade areas cannot be defined as easily as they are for suburban retail sites. It is nearly impossible to use driving time as a criterion or to subdivide the area into primary, secondary, and tertiary zones by other measures of distance from the site. Instead, the market "area" is subdivided into smaller sectors based on such determinants as zip codes, employee income levels, proximity to the business district, etc. These sectors can be marked on a map for easy reference.

Basically, there are four categories of downtown shoppers: those who live in the city, those who work in the city, those who live in the greater metropolitan area (including the suburbs), and tourists and other transients. Data available for St. Louis, Missouri, are an example for comparison of the percentages of different types of customers in a downtown market (figure 9.3). Actually, the identified groups frequently overlap because people who work downtown may also live downtown, and people who travel from the suburbs to shop downtown may work downtown as well.

City Residents.   People living within the city limits normally comprise the largest percentage of downtown consumers. Their proximity to the

F I G U R E   9.4

Population within Two Miles of Downtown (1980)

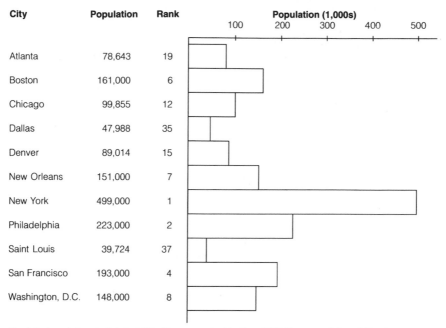

City	Population	Rank
Atlanta	78,643	19
Boston	161,000	6
Chicago	99,855	12
Dallas	47,988	35
Denver	89,014	15
New Orleans	151,000	7
New York	499,000	1
Philadelphia	223,000	2
Saint Louis	39,724	37
San Francisco	193,000	4
Washington, D.C.	148,000	8

Rank is in relation to total of 39 cities reported in the *1982 Census of Retail Trade*.

Compiled from *Downtown Retail Markets* (Chicago: Downtown Research Corporation, 1986). Reproduced with permission.

central business district makes it most convenient for them to shop there. Most of the people who live within two miles of the downtown areas of major cities (figure 9.4) have lower incomes generally, and therefore their purchasing power is limited. In recent years, however, there has been a resurgence of downtown residential development, and the numbers of middle- and upper-income residents in the cities have been growing. Downtown retailers rely on this "built-in" residential base for their economic survival. Cities whose dominant population is urban will attract discount stores, drugstores, personal service providers, and retailers that sell convenience items.

Metropolitan (Suburban) Residents. This group includes people who live in the suburbs surrounding a city. The size and per capita income of this suburban population have been increasing over the years. Many of them prefer to shop in suburban malls, but the amount of money they spend downtown is considerable. They visit the city primarily for its vari-

FIGURE   9.5

**Square Footage of Downtown Office Space
Constructed Between 1950 and 1980 (Millions of
Square Feet)**

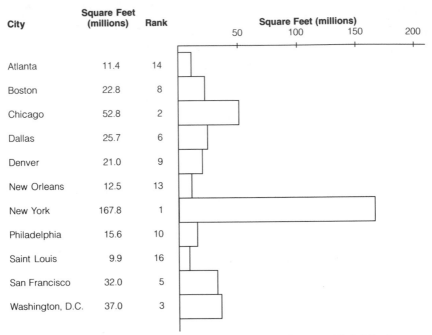

City	Square Feet (millions)	Rank
Atlanta	11.4	14
Boston	22.8	8
Chicago	52.8	2
Dallas	25.7	6
Denver	21.0	9
New Orleans	12.5	13
New York	167.8	1
Philadelphia	15.6	10
Saint Louis	9.9	16
San Francisco	32.0	5
Washington, D.C.	37.0	3

Rank is in relation to total of 39 cities reported in the *1982 Census of Retail Trade*.

Compiled from *Downtown Retail Markets* (Chicago: Downtown Research Corporation, 1986). Reproduced with permission.

ous entertainment and cultural amenities—theater, concerts, museums, restaurants, festivals, and sporting events; retail businesses located near these attractions will usually do well. Location is often the key to capturing the metropolitan portion of the consumer market.

Downtown Workers.   As the amount of office space in cities (figure 9.5) and the number of downtown workers in cities (table 9.3) has continued to increase, the downtown market continues to provide strong support for retailers. Downtown office workers, in particular, are a growing source of potential sales for downtown retailers. Also, when there is a clear choice between alternative office locations, businesses tend to lease less-expensive space in the suburbs for strictly clerical functions, investing in downtown space so their office professionals can be where their clients are. The

T A B L E   9.3

Change in Number of Downtown Employees
Between 1970 and 1980 (in Thousands)

City	1970	1980	Change	Rank
Atlanta	56.5	73.6	17.1	8
Boston*	94.0	91.0	(3.0)	35
Chicago†	230.0	306.4	76.4	1
Dallas	71.0	86.2	15.2	10
Denver	44.8	59.2	14.4	11
New Orleans	69.6	78.9	9.3	22
New York	NA	NA	NA	——
Philadelphia	121.3	185.7	64.4	2
Saint Louis	34.4	71.8	37.4	4
San Francisco	144.9	181.0	36.1	5
Washington, D.C.	141.7	135.9	(5.8)	38

Rank is in relation to total of 39 cities reported.

Figures in parentheses are losses.

NA = information not available.

*Figure for Boston does not include Back Bay.

†Figure for Chicago does not include North Michigan Avenue.

Compiled from *Downtown Retail Markets* (Chicago: Downtown Research Corporation, 1986). Reproduced with permission.

effect is not only one of increasing numbers of office workers downtown but also of larger numbers of higher-paid office workers.

The results of an Urban Land Institute study correlating 1977 central business district retail sales for fifteen cities showed a definite relationship between the number of office workers and the volume of retail sales. On average, an increase of 1,000 office workers is accompanied by a $3.32 million increase in retail sales. Two-worker households have contributed to this increase, too. Career apparel stores, restaurants, and other retail businesses located on the ground floors of office buildings serve this segment of the market well. It is apparent, however, that restaurants of all types have the greatest proportionate share of sales. Some 50–60 percent of the money spent annually by downtown workers goes to eating and drinking establishments (figure 9.6).

In general, the number of downtown workers who shop at any given retail site depends on how far the site is from their work. On the average, people will walk ten minutes from their job, twenty minutes at most. Local planning agencies and chambers of commerce often have statistics on the number of employees within a certain walking time from a retail site. Another way of estimating the number of downtown workers is to assume

FIGURE   9.6

Eating and Drinking Place Sales Per Downtown Worker*

City	Sales in Dollars	Rank	Dollars

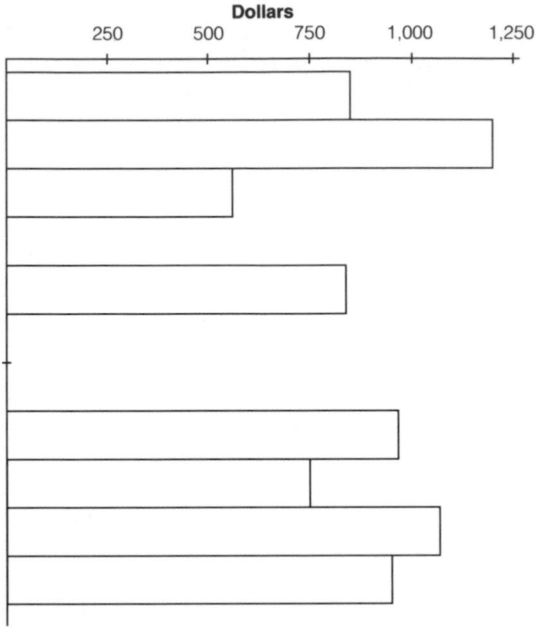

Rank is in relation to total of 39 cities reported in the *1982 Census of Retail Trade*.

NA = information not available

*Exclusive of hotel restaurants and bars.

†Figure for Boston includes Back Bay.

‡Figure for Chicago includes North Michigan Avenue.

Compiled from *Downtown Retail Markets* (Chicago: Downtown Research Corporation, 1986). Reproduced with permission.

that each employee will use 150 to 200 square feet of office space. This area can be divided into the total square footage of occupied available office space to determine the number of workers within a given area such as a block or within a radius from an intersection of two streets.

Tourists and Business Travelers.   Accurate counts of transients may be difficult to obtain. Some local chambers of commerce keep records of the numbers of tourists and business travelers passing through their cities each year, and the number of downtown hotel rooms can be a good in-

F I G U R E   9.7

Number of Downtown Hotel Rooms (1985)

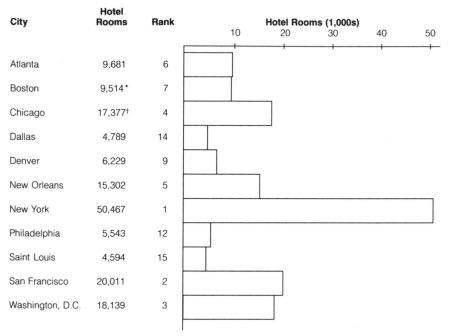

City	Hotel Rooms	Rank
Atlanta	9,681	6
Boston	9,514*	7
Chicago	17,377†	4
Dallas	4,789	14
Denver	6,229	9
New Orleans	15,302	5
New York	50,467	1
Philadelphia	5,543	12
Saint Louis	4,594	15
San Francisco	20,011	2
Washington, D.C.	18,139	3

Rank is in relation to total of 39 cities reported in the *1982 Census of Retail Trade.*

NA = information not available

*Figure for Boston includes Back Bay.

†Figure for Chicago includes North Michigan Avenue.

Compiled from *Downtown Retail Markets* (Chicago: Downtown Research Corporation, 1986). Reproduced with permission.

dication (figure 9.7). Some cities also have concentrations of hotel rooms near airports, and if these are counted as in-city rooms, they could misrepresent the real potential. State and local convention and visitor bureaus, local and national associations of hotel and motel operators, and the American Automobile Association (headquartered in Falls Church, Virginia) may have statistics on travelers in different areas of the United States as well.

Dot maps can be prepared showing the proximity of shopping areas to hotels and convention centers. Retail stores in hotel lobbies and restaurants located nearby should do good business in a city with a large tourist population. Specialty and festival centers also do well in such areas. With the exception of a few major cities—notably New York, Boston, Washington D.C., New Orleans, and San Francisco—urban retail businesses cannot rely solely on tourist and visitor trade as a consistent source of revenue. However, the tourist trade is undeniably an important submarket. Most tourists spend more money in festival marketplaces than ordinary shoppers do, and conventioneers and business travelers spend more money than ordinary tourists. The success of some festival centers indicates just how much these visitors spend: Harborplace in Baltimore has average annual retail sales in excess of $400 per square foot of GLA, and Faneuil Hall Marketplace in Boston, around $350. By comparison, median sales per square foot in comparable-sized "regular" shopping centers are much lower—community shopping center sales in the Southeast, including Baltimore, were around $75–225 per square foot and in the Northeast, including Boston, around $100–200 per square foot, as reported in *Dollars and Cents of Shopping Centers: 1987.* (Community centers average 100,000–300,000 square feet of GLA; many festival centers are within that size range, around 150,000–225,000 square feet of GLA.)

Area and Site Profiles

One of the best ways to create interest in a downtown area is to encourage residents to take advantage of the various cultural and entertainment amenities there. Museums, theaters, libraries, etc., offer programs year-round. Festivals and sporting events provide seasonal or intermittent attractions. A good marketing and public relations program will exploit the city's natural role as a center of activity. Linking retail business with events sponsored by the city and its cultural institutions is a way of tapping the city's resources.

Another important consideration for retailers is the nature of the downtown area itself and how the retail site fits into it. Prospects will want to know what the downtown's "drawing power" is compared to regional malls and other types of suburban retail space, whether and how much parking is available, if there is public transportation, and whether the system is efficient and well-used. Market research can project what share of business will be walk-in trade, the percentage of customers that will require parking and the percentage that will likely use public transportation. The availability of and access to these amenities is vital to downtown retail businesses. While large independent retail projects may have parking garages of their own, people who shop away from those projects will be obliged to park elsewhere. If captive or public parking is not immediately available, it may be possible for retail customers to use parking facilities belonging to nearby hotels or office complexes. Pedestrian traffic counts for a particular block or a busy street corner will indicate how many potential customers are in an area at peak shopping hours. Cham-

T A B L E   9.4

Change in Downtown Sales Volume between 1972 and 1982 (Millions of Dollars)

City	1972–77	1977–82	Difference	Rank
Atlanta	(49.9)	(34.2)	15.7	18
Boston*	75.8	227.0	151.0	2
Chicago†	212.0	361.3	149.3	3
Dallas	68.8	36.6	(32.2)	31
Denver	NA	44.2	NA	——
New Orleans	62.4	56.7	(5.7)	24
New York	(29.3)	1,583.1	1,612.4	1
Philadelphia	188.8	172.5	(16.3)	28
Saint Louis	26.1	(7.9)	(34.0)	33
San Francisco	280.9	158.2	(122.7)	37
Washington, D.C.	6.1	74.8	68.7	4

Rank is in relation to total of 39 cities reported.

Figures in parentheses are losses.

NA = information not available.

*Figure for Boston includes Back Bay.

†Figure for Chicago includes North Michigan Avenue.

Compiled from *Downtown Retail Markets* (Chicago: Downtown Research Corporation, 1986). Reproduced with permission.

bers of commerce or merchants' associations localized to the shopping district should be able to provide data on pedestrian traffic as well as on numbers and types of businesses (and their employees) for the locale of a specific site. Numbers of commuters (depot surveys) and favored pedestrian routes from depots to workplaces should also be available. These types of data will provide the most accurate measure of potential "customers." (While data from local chambers of commerce can be useful, the agent is cautioned not to rely *solely* on such statistics because, in their efforts to "sell" their city, these bodies may paint a rosier picture than actually exists.)

Economic Feasibility and Sales Potential

Prospective retail tenants will be interested in the economic status of the downtown area. This type of information includes who the major employers are, the relationship between office space and retail space, what real estate developers and city planning officials are doing to improve the city's image and strengthen its economic base, and projections of future growth. They are also concerned about how much money is being spent on renovations and the kinds of funding available to finance retail development. The role of the city in the regional or national economic scene is a good predictor of future patterns of development; in addition, employment data will indicate whether the downtown still plays a viable role in the general metropolitan area. Growth can be measured by comparing historic retail sales data with current sales figures, as has been done for two five-year periods in table 9.4 (page 235). Information about local businesses and industries and future building projects is, for the most part, obtainable from local planning agencies and chambers of commerce. As a rule, retail businesses will have a greater chance to succeed in a city that is concentrating on overall renewal and revitalization. Attempts to improve residential neighborhoods also lead to increased retail activity.

Retailers use current sales figures and the total sales contributions from the various market sectors defined in the consumer profile to determine the overall sales potential for the retail site. Sales tax receipts of a state or city also reflect the volume of retail sales, and they are another good determinant of the area's economic status. The various sales figures can be used to determine the number of square feet of retail space necessary to achieve a targeted sales volume. Although different types of stores will have different space requirements, an enclosed downtown mall generally must have at least 600,000 square feet of retail space in order to compete successfully with suburban centers. However, the "mall" may not have to be so large if there are department stores or small shops nearby, because it and the adjacent retailers will jointly attract more people to the area.

Analysis of Competition

For downtown retail businesses, competition comes from both nearby businesses and shopping areas and outlying suburban shopping centers. The location of specific competitors as well as their drawing power will be important considerations. Accessibility, availability of parking and public transportation, store hours, and similar factors should be taken into account in making comparisons. Such facts as the GLA of individual spaces and general information about the facilities; minimum and percentage rents, pass-through expenses, tenant improvement allowances, and other lease terms; sales volumes, parking ratios, etc., will also be of interest. In general, the leasing agent should be prepared to conduct such a comparison in the same manner as was discussed in chapter 2 although there may be additional data to be compared to properly assess a downtown site. As with any assessment of comparable sites, it is important to have many individual facts of the same type. In order to sell a retailer on the idea of leasing downtown, the agent must know and understand all the elements that comprise that retailer's competition.

LEASING DOWNTOWN RETAIL SPACE

Leasing retail space downtown requires many of the same skills employed in leasing retail space in suburban centers. Armed with information from the market survey, the agent forms a leasing plan which pinpoints an ideal tenant mix and outlines a rental schedule for the various spaces. Prospecting and canvassing for retailers is followed by qualifying of prospects. As with suburban projects, the leasing campaign will culminate in negotiations and, hopefully, a signed lease.

The basics of downtown retail leasing may be similar to suburban leasing, but the nature of downtown space requires a different approach. For one thing, the retail space may not be in a property devoted exclusively to retailing. Often it is part of a larger mixed-use development or located on the ground floor of office buildings. When prospecting, the agent has to consider how the potential tenant will be affected by the presence of nonretail facilities and whether those facilities will enhance the retailer's business. The agent may be able to use the property's location as a selling point, especially if the building has a prestigious name. In seeking certain types of business support tenants (office supplies, computer sales and service), the agent may refer to other tenants of the building or complex that are likely to need their products or services.

The agent leasing downtown space likely will be dealing less with new space and more with revitalized or redesigned space in already existing buildings. He or she will have to sell prospects on different-sized spaces than may be found in the suburbs—the GLAs of individual spaces are generally smaller downtown, and more economy of space is evident. Desirability of individual store spaces is always a consideration, and corner locations that offer greater on-street visibility usually are more desirable and therefore command higher rents.

While common area fees are not a factor for freestanding retail space, the retailer in an enclosed downtown mall will usually be required to pay for parking, extra security, and lighting in addition to the usual common area charges. Rents per square foot of GLA are usually considerably higher downtown due to higher construction and operating costs as discussed earlier. Also contributing to high rents is the fact that there is less retail space available downtown. Because available space is limited, the competition for that space is generally greater, or it should be—especially for first-rate sites.

Retail leasing for a new project in the city's business district begins early in the development process, especially if retail space is the only component of the project or a major portion of it, and such preleasing is often tied in with design. It is more economical to design for a tenant whose space and operational needs are a known factor; fewer changes will have to be made, and consequently less time and less money will have to be spent on the project. In fact, developers prefer to prelease large blocks of space before construction begins. Another reason for substantial pre-leasing has to do with lender requirements. Most financing institutions will expect a certain percentage of a downtown site to be preleased in order for the project to receive maximum financing: Unleased space necessitates higher financing costs in general. For this reason, most developers try to have leases signed for a large part of a project's space well before it is ready for occupancy. On the other hand, retail space that is a minor component of a mixed-use project or a small part of a new office building will not necessarily be preleased. The major users will be the focus of any preleasing from both design and financing perspectives. Economy and lending requirements are strong motivations to lease-up early in the development process. An agent who understands the special problems and pitfalls of downtown leasing will be better equipped to handle such a project.

Prospecting

A major challenge of prospecting for downtown tenants is identifying the types of retailers best suited to the particular retail site. One of the best ways of doing this is to examine the type of employees located near the retail site. Office workers with a preponderance of professionals among them will be likely to patronize an apparel store featuring high quality career clothes. A fairly expensive restaurant suitable for business lunches on expense accounts will need a similar customer base. On the other hand, if the office worker base is mostly clerical, fast food services or a cafeteria might be more likely to succeed. All types of restaurants and food services should be welcome tenants if the major portion of customers is expected to be tourists or business travelers. Tenant selection is closely linked to nearby business and employee characteristics as well as to the consumers profiled in the market survey.

Networking and cold calling are even more important for the agent leasing downtown retail space. Prospecting resources include financial institutions, tenants in other malls, accounting or law firms in the area which may do business with retailers, restaurant equipment suppliers, city planning departments in the local government, the city chamber of commerce and local business district merchants' associations, retail trade journals, and retail-related trade shows or conventions that take place in the city. Retailers in other downtown locations and in competing suburban malls may be interested in relocating themselves or able to provide information about others who are. Cooperation with other brokers in the downtown community is also important.

The presence of a department store or other type of major tenant can be a powerful selling tool in promoting a downtown center to prospective tenants for small spaces. This is especially true because the business risks in a downtown market are greater. Despite these risks, many retail chains will lease spaces that are geographically closer together because downtown customers generally walk to shopping and restaurants, and the distance they will walk is fairly short. Chains like Naturalizer shoes and McDonald's restaurants can locate stores within two blocks of each other and not be too concerned about competing against themselves. Other points to promote include the location and the surrounding area, especially if the space is located in a prominent office building or the retail project is on an attractive street or near businesses that are likely to increase the retailer's trade. Nearby parking garages, public amenities, and food outlets are other selling points. If the project is new and is government-funded, the agent might want to point out the advantages of leasing in a project being sponsored by the city and the community. Government support of projects usually goes beyond financing to include promotion of the site and possible tax incentives that can trickle down to the tenants. Retailers that are established in an area may view rehabs or new construction in their area as an opportunity to improve their stores without much physical relocation.

The Downtown Retail Lease

The downtown retail lease closely resembles any other retail lease. It defines the size and use of the leased premises, the names of the lessor and lessee, the length of the lease term, the base rental rate and any adjustments such as percentage rent, escalation clauses, and common area maintenance (CAM) charges. Special provisions pertaining to the site should also be mentioned. Examples of these would be store hours and participation in a validated parking program for customers. Downtown leases should also specify whether they are for whole floors or partial floors and how these areas will be measured.

Most downtown leases are net, passing through taxes, insurance, and other operating expenses to the tenant. Percentage rents are particularly useful downtown, where there is greater financial risk for the retailer. Low base rents will attract retailers that might otherwise be reluctant to lease downtown space. Base rent, which may be anywhere from 40 to 80 percent of market value, is used primarily to cover operating expenses and the owner's debt service fees. If percentage rent is used, major tenants such as department stores could pay 1–2 percent of their gross sales in addition to base rent, while smaller retailers might pay 3–10 percent of gross sales in addition to base rent.

The duration of a downtown lease depends not only on market conditions but also on the nature of the retailer's business. Major department stores are known to sign leases for periods up to thirty years. Other large retailers lease for ten to fifteen years, and smaller merchants lease from seven to ten years. Many national chains (Kinney Shoes, for example) require lease terms of eleven or more years because that is the period over which they amortize their store fixtures. Strong market situations may predispose tenants to seek longer term leases. When these are granted, the lease usually includes provision for periodic increases in base rent. Percentage rent is a common requirement as well. Owners generally prefer shorter lease terms as a hedge against economic changes. Lenders, on the other hand, view longer lease terms as a protection for their financing of the retail project. Vacancy is a greater problem downtown than in the suburbs, however; and month-to-month tenancies are commonly used as a way of keeping space filled until a permanent tenant can be found. Because options to renew favor the tenant, the owner may require the retailer to meet certain sales performance criteria to qualify for such a renewal option. If there is a requirement to register or record long-term leases with a local jurisdiction, prospects have to be made aware of that fact, and it may be appropriate to note this in the lease itself. While leases for suburban retail space may require less scrutiny by the parties' attorneys, downtown leases typically require legal review in their entirety.

SUMMARY

Leasing retail space downtown requires a different approach than leasing space in suburban shopping centers. A city can encompass many shopping areas. Everything from a bustling central business district in a major city to the more sedate main street of a small town can be defined as "downtown," and each of these areas has a unique recipe for success.

While downtown retail spaces are as varied as the neighborhoods in which they are established, conventional enclosed shopping malls are being built more and more in the central business districts of cities that have a favorable economic climate. These malls are usually multilevelled and include a parking structure as part of the design. Like their suburban counterparts, they focus on fashion apparel and have at least one department store as an anchor tenant. Festival centers, catering to the tourist trade, are often developed in renovated historic structures. Restaurants and boutiques dominate these centers. Mixed-use developments, which can include hotels, private housing, offices, and recreational facilities in addition to retail space, are common in the downtown areas of large cities. Other types of retail spaces include traditional freestanding department stores; outdoor pedestrian malls; ground-floor, second-floor, and lower-level (basement) shops; and retail spaces in bus stations, train depots, and airports.

While no two cities are alike, most downtown retailers share problems that do not occur in the suburbs. Scarcity of space results in high construction and operating costs. Because rental rates in the city are sometimes twice those in a comparable site in the suburbs, prospective tenants must demonstrate proof of financial ability to meet these costs. Lack of adequate parking and perceived inconvenience to customers are other difficulties. Downtown retailers must also contend with negative images, buildings that were not designed for retail use, smaller spaces, and restricted store hours. Retailers must be able to work within and overcome these limitations in order to succeed.

Precise demographic information about downtown consumers is often difficult to obtain because city neighborhoods are generally in a state of flux. However, four categories of downtown consumers can be identified—city residents, residents of outlying areas who may or may not work in the city, downtown workers, and tourists and business travelers. The ratio of each of these four groups to the others changes with the type of city and the trade area. Downtown areas in big cities have the largest percentages of transient shoppers, while warehouse and industrial districts have large concentrations of laborers.

Tenant selection often depends on the characteristics of the nonretail facilities in the area—the kinds of businesses located nearby and the people who work for them. In order to place the best possible tenant in the available space, leasing agents must tailor their prospecting efforts to the nature of the city, the trade area being served, and the types of shoppers.

Appendixes

NOTE: Forms, documents, and other exhibits in this book are samples only. This publication is sold with the understanding that the publisher is not engaged in rendering legal, accounting, or any other professional advice. Because of varying state and local laws, competent advice should be secured before the use of any form, document, exhibit, or information herein.

The examples provided in appendix A represent the major contents of the specified forms. Exclusive and Nonexclusive Authorizations to Lease may also incorporate other specific terms, including provision for disposition of monies deposited by prospective tenants in the event a lease is not executed and for arbitration in the event of disagreement over payment of commissions. Guidance of legal counsel should always be sought when developing specific agreement forms.

A P P E N D I X   A.1

Exclusive Authorization to Lease

OWNER hereby grants to [company name] ("Broker") the exclusive right to negotiate a lease or leases with respect to the real property described below (the "Property") for a period commencing on _____, 19_____, and ending at midnight on _____, 19_____ (the "Listing Period"), unless this Authorization is extended in writing and signed by both Owner and Broker. The Property is located at _____ in the City of _____, County of _____, State of _____, and further described as _____

_____.

The price and terms of the lease(s) shall be as follows: _____

_____
_____
_____.

If during the Listing Period negotiations involving the leasing of the Property have commenced and are continuing, then the Listing Period shall be extended with respect to such transaction(s) and negotiations for a period through the termination of such negotiations or the consummation of such transaction.

In consideration of this Authorization and Broker's agreement diligently to pursue the procurement of a tenant or tenants for the Property, Owner agrees to pay Broker a commission or commissions as set forth in the attached SCHEDULE OF COMMISSIONS.

Owner shall pay such commission(s) to Broker if during the Listing Period: (a) the Property or any part thereof is leased to tenant(s) by or through Broker, Owner or any other person or entity; or (b) a tenant is procured by or through Broker, Owner or any other person or entity who is ready, willing and able to lease the Property or any part thereof on the terms above stated or other terms acceptable to the owner of the Property; or (c) any lease or contract for the lease of the Property or any part thereof is made directly or indirectly by the owner of the Property; or (d) this authorization is terminated or the Property is withdrawn from lease without the written consent of Broker or made unmarketable by Owner's voluntary act. Owner shall also pay said commission to Broker if within _____ _____ (   ) days after the expiration of the Listing Period (1) the Property, or any interest therein, is leased to any person or entity which during the term of the Listing Period made a written offer to lease the Property, or any interest therein, whether or not such transaction is consummated on the same or different terms and conditions contained in such offer; and (2) the Property or any interest therein is leased to any person or entity with whom Broker has negotiated or to whom Broker has submitted the Property in an effort to effect a transaction during the Listing Period and whose name appears on any list of such persons or entities (the "Registration List") which Broker shall have mailed to Owner at the address below stated within _____ (   ) days following such expiration. In the event title to the Property is transferred pursuant to foreclosure proceedings or by a deed in lieu of foreclosure during the Listing Period and within _____ (   ) days thereafter the Property or any portion thereof is leased to any person or entity which made a written offer to lease the Property, or any portion thereof, or which is named on the Registration List, Owner shall pay Broker said commission with respect to such transaction. The sale of the Property during the term of this Authorization or any extension hereof shall not be deemed to constitute a breach of this Authorization if the purchaser agrees in writing to be bound by this Authorization for the remainder of the Listing Period.

Owner agrees to cooperate with Broker in effecting a lease or leases of the Property and immediately to refer to Broker all inquiries of any person or entity interested in leasing premises in the Property. All negotiations are to be through Broker. Broker is authorized to accept a deposit and other funds from any prospective tenant. Broker is further authorized to advertise the Property and shall have the exclusive right to place a sign or signs on the Property if, in Broker's opinion, such would facilitate the leasing thereof.

It is understood that it is illegal for either Owner or Broker to refuse to present or lease real property to any person because of race, color, religion, national origin, sex, marital status, age or physical disability.

Owner hereby warrants and represents to Broker that (1) Owner is the owner of record of the Property or has the legal authority to execute this Authorization on behalf of such owner, (2) no person or entity has any right to lease the Property or any portion thereof by virtue of any agreement, option or right of first refusal, (3) there are no delinquencies or defaults under any deed of trust, mortgage or other encumbrance on the Property, (4) the Property is not subject to the jurisdiction of any court in any bankruptcy, insolvency conservatorship or probate proceeding, and (5) Broker has not made any promises or representations to or agreements with Owner not contained herein which in any manner affect Owner's and Broker's rights and obligations under this Authorization.

Owner agrees to defend, indemnify and hold Broker harmless from any and all claims, demands, liabilities and damages arising from any incorrect information supplied by Owner or any information which Owner fails to supply.

If there is a failure to make any payment to Broker at the time required herein, the delinquent sum(s) shall bear interest at the rate of _____percent (%) per year or the maximum nonusurious interest rate for loans permitted by law, whichever is lower.

Owner hereby authorizes Broker to represent and serve as agent for any prospective tenant or purchaser of the Property, and Owner hereby waives any conflict of interests which might arise as a result thereof.

The heirs, transferees, successors and assigns of the parties hereto are duly bound by the provisions hereof.

No amendments to or modifications of this Authorization nor the termination of this Authorization shall be valid or binding unless made in writing and signed by both Owner and Broker.

Owner hereby acknowledges that Broker is not qualified or authorized to give legal or tax advice; if Owner desires such advice Owner shall consult with an attorney or accountant.

Owner acknowledges receipt of a copy of this Authorization and the attached SCHEDULE OF COMMISSIONS which Owner has read and understands.

Other terms and conditions: _____

_____

_____

DATED: _____, 19_____   OWNER _____

ACCEPTED: [company name]   By _____

                               By _____

                               Address: _____

                               _____

By _____   Telephone: _____

Adapted from a form of Grubb & Ellis Company with permission.

A P P E N D I X A.2

Nonexclusive Authorization to Lease

OWNER hereby grants to [company name] ("Broker") the nonexclusive right to negotiate a lease or leases with respect to the real property described below (the "Property") for a period commencing on _____, 19_____, and ending at midnight on _____, 19_____ (the "Listing Period"), unless this Authorization is extended in writing and signed by both Owner and Broker. The Property is located at _____,

in the City of _____, County of _____, State of _____, and further described as _____

_____

_____.

The price and terms of the lease(s) shall be as follows: _____

_____

_____

_____.

If during the Listing Period negotiations involving the leasing of the Property have commenced and are continuing, then the Listing Period shall be extended with respect to such transaction(s) and negotiations for a period through the termination of such negotiations or the consummation of such transaction.

In consideration of this Authorization and Broker's agreement diligently to pursue the procurement of a tenant or tenants for the Property, Owner agrees to pay Broker a commission or commissions as set forth in the attached SCHEDULE OF COMMISSIONS.

Owner shall pay such commission(s) to Broker if during the Listing Period: (a) the Property or any part thereof is leased to tenant(s) by or through Broker; or (b) a tenant is procured by or through Broker who is ready, willing and able to lease the Property or any part thereof on the terms above stated or other terms acceptable to the owner of the Property; or (c) this Authorization is terminated or the Property is withdrawn from lease without the written consent of Broker or made unmarketable by Owner's voluntary act.

Owner shall also pay said commission to Broker if within _____ (   ) days after the expiration of the Listing Period (1) the Property, or any interest therein, is leased to any person or entity which during the term of the Listing Period made a written offer to lease the Property, or any interest therein by or through Broker, whether or not such transaction is consummated on the same or different terms and conditions contained in such offer; or (2) the Property or any interest therein is leased to any person or entity with whom Broker has negotiated or to whom Broker has submitted the Property in an effort to effect a transaction during the Listing Period and whose name appears on any list of such persons or entities (the "Registration List") which Broker shall have mailed to Owner at the address below stated within _____ (   ) days following such expiration. In the event title to the Property is transferred pursuant to foreclosure proceedings or by a deed in lieu of foreclosure during the Listing Period and within _____ (   ) days thereafter the Property or any portion thereof is leased to any person or entity which made a written offer to lease the Property, or any portion thereof, or which is named on the Registration List, Owner shall pay Broker said commission with respect to such transaction. The sale of the Property during the term of this Authorization or any extension hereof shall not be deemed to constitute a breach of this Authorization if the purchaser agrees in writing to be bound by this Authorization for the remainder of the Listing Period.

Owner agrees to cooperate with Broker in effecting a lease or leases of the Property. All negotiations are to be through Broker. Broker is authorized to accept a deposit and other funds from any prospective tenant. Broker is further authorized to advertise the Property and shall have the right to place a sign or signs on the Property if, in Broker's opinion, such would facilitate the leasing thereof.

It is understood that it is illegal for either Owner or Broker to refuse to present or lease real property to any person because of race, color, religion, national origin, sex, marital status, age or physical disability.

Owner hereby warrants and represents to Broker that (1) Owner is the owner of record of the Property or has the legal authority to execute this Authorization on behalf of such owner, (2) no person or entity has any right to lease the Property or any portion thereof by virtue of any agreement, option or right of first refusal, (3) there are no delinquencies or defaults under any deed of trust, mortgage or other encumbrance on the Property, (4) the Property is not subject to the jurisdiction of any court in any bankruptcy, insolvency conservatorship or probate proceeding, and (5) Broker has not made any promises or representations to or agreements with Owner not contained herein which in any manner affect Owner's and Broker's rights and obligations under this Authorization.

Owner agrees to defend, indemnify and hold Broker harmless from any and all claims, demands, liabilities and damages arising from any incorrect information supplied by Owner or any information which Owner fails to supply.

If there is a failure to make any payment to Broker at the time required herein, the delinquent sum(s) shall bear interest at the rate of _____ percent (%) per year or the maximum nonusurious interest rate for loans permitted by law, whichever is lower.

Owner hereby authorizes Broker to represent and serve as agent for any prospective tenant or purchaser of the Property, and Owner hereby waives any conflict of interests which might arise as a result thereof.

The heirs, transferees, successors and assigns of the parties hereto are duly bound by the provisions hereof.

No amendments to or modifications of this Authorization nor the termination of this Authorization shall be valid or binding unless made in writing and signed by both Owner and Broker.

Owner hereby acknowledges that Broker is not qualified or authorized to give legal or tax advice; if Owner desires such advice Owner shall consult with an attorney or accountant.

Owner acknowledges receipt of a copy of this Authorization and the attached SCHEDULE OF COMMISSIONS which Owner has read and understands.

Other terms and conditions:

_____

_____

_____

DATED: _____, 19_____   OWNER _____

ACCEPTED: [company name]   By _____

                                       By _____

                                       Address: _____

                                       _____

By _____   Telephone: _____

Adapted from a form of Grubb & Ellis Company with permission.

A P P E N D I X   A.3

Broker Cooperation Agreement

BROKER hereby agrees to conduct all negotiations for the purchase, sale, lease or other transfer of all or any interest in the below described property(s), whether for the account of BROKER or a third party, through [company name]. BROKER shall in no manner deal with the owner of the property(s) nor any agent of the owner other than [company name].

The property(s) to which the Agreement pertains is described as follows:

_____

_____

_____

_____

The undersigned hereby registers with [company name] the following prospective Buyers or Tenants for the above property(s).

_____

_____

_____

_____

In the event BROKER or any salesman or other broker working in cooperation with BROKER, desires to negotiate for the sale, lease or transfer of the property(s), all negotiations shall be conducted through [company name]. If such negotiations are successful and a transaction is consummated, _____ percent (%) of the total commission paid by the Seller or Owner shall be payable to [company name]. Except for those prospects registered above, [company name] may sell, lease, transfer or otherwise deal with the property without incurring any obligation to divide any commission or pay any portion thereof to BROKER.

For and in consideration of the execution of this Agreement and the supplying of valuable information concerning the property, BROKER agrees to be bound by this Agreement for a period of _____ (   ) months from the date hereof. BROKER agrees not to divulge any information concerning the above property(s) to anyone excepting prospects, salesmen engaged by BROKER and other brokers who agree to be bound by the terms hereof.

Receipt of a copy of this Agreement is hereby acknowledged.

DATED _____, 19_____

[company name]	BROKER _____
By _____	By _____
Address: _____	Address: _____
City _____State _____	City _____State _____
Telephone _____	Telephone _____

Adapted from a form of Grubb & Ellis Company with permission.

A P P E N D I X   A.4

Commission Agreement

For and in consideration of the efforts and services rendered by [company name] in connection with the lease of that certain property described as:

_____

_____

_____

_____

From _____

_____

_____ as Owner

To _____

_____

_____ as Tenant, the undersigned
agrees hereby to pay to [company name] the sum of $_____
in lawful money of the United States to be payable as follows: (a) when both parties have
signed an appropriate lease agreement, and all contingencies set forth in said lease
agreement have been satisfied or waived by the party for whose benefit such contingency has been included, or (b) if completion of lease is prevented by default of Owner,
upon Owner's default, or (c) if completion of lease is prevented by default of Tenant and
when Owner collects damages from Tenant, by suit or otherwise, then in an amount not to

exceed _____ percent (%) of the damages collected after first deducting
the expenses of collection, if any. [Company name] is hereby authorized to deduct the
foregoing sums from funds held in its trust account, if any, and the undersigned agrees
to pay any difference in cash in accordance herewith.

In the event an action is commenced to enforce the right of [company name] to payment,
the undersigned hereby agrees to pay to [company name] reasonable attorney's fees
and expenses, whether said action is prosecuted to judgment or not.

Receipt of a copy of this Agreement is hereby acknowledged.

DATED: _____, 19_____   OWNER _____

[company name]   By _____

By _____   By _____

Address _____   Address _____

City _____State _____   City _____State _____

Telephone _____   Telephone _____

Adapted from a form of Grubb & Ellis Company with permission.

A P P E N D I X   A.5

Schedule of Lease Commissions

The commission shall be calculated at the rate of ＿＿＿＿＿ percent (%) of the total rental or ＿＿＿＿＿ dollars ($) per square foot of gross leased space, whichever is the greater, payable subject to the following terms and conditions:

1. *Payment of Lease Commissions.* One-half commission shall be due and payable on execution of a lease by Owner and the Tenant, and one-half upon Tenant occupancy or commencement of lease payments.

2. *Term of More Than* ＿＿＿＿＿ (   ) *Years.* If a lease term be in excess of ＿＿＿＿＿ (   ) years, then the commission shall be calculated only upon the rental to be paid for the first ＿＿＿＿＿ (   ) years of the term of the lease.

3. *Month-to-Month Tenancy.* The commission rate in this instance shall be ＿＿＿＿＿ (%) of the first month's rent.

4. *Extension of Lease or Additional Space Taken.* Should the term of the lease be extended or the Tenant occupy additional space by virtue of provisions in the lease, or through subsequent modification of such provisions, then a leasing commission shall be paid at such time as said term is extended or additional space is occupied. Said leasing commission shall be computed in accordance with the provisions of this Schedule and by the rates applicable as if the initial term of the lease had included said extension period or the premises initially leased had included said additional space.

5. *Percentage Rent.* As to any leases which contain a percentage rent clause, the Owner shall pay a commission on the percentage rent at the same rate as applicable for the minimum guaranteed rent as above provided. This commission shall be due and payable within ＿＿＿＿＿ (   ) days after the Tenant's final payment and accounting of percentage rental for the preceding lease year. At the end of the ＿＿＿＿＿ full lease year there shall be a settlement as to any commission due on percentage rent for the remainder of the original term of the lease calculated upon the assumption that the percentage rent for each year of the remainder of the term will be the same as the percentage rent for the ＿＿＿＿＿ full lease year.

6. *Co-Brokerage.* In reference to the Schedule of Lease Commissions, [company name] will cooperate with all nonexclusive agents. In co-brokerage situations, nonexclusive agents will receive a full ＿＿＿＿＿ percent (%) cash-out commission or ＿＿＿＿＿ dollars ($) per square foot and [company name] will receive an additional one-half of that [i.e., ＿＿＿＿＿ percent (%) or $＿＿ per square foot.]

Adapted from a form of Henry S. Miller Management Corporation, a Grubb & Ellis Company, with permission.

APPENDIX B
Development Financing

EQUITY FINANCING

Most developers seeking to finance a large retail project will use a combination of debt and equity financing. Equity financing involves using cash available from other sources or raising capital through partnerships or other investment entities. This type of financing has the highest risk (because the investors might lose a large amount of cash) as well as the highest potential return on investment (because the "borrowers" do not pay interest on a "loan" as such, or they pay interest on a smaller loan amount). Equity capital usually must be raised before debt capital is committed, and the investor is "paid back" from the residual funds (cash flow or profit) after all the other expenses, including debt service, are paid.

High interest rates make financing a development expensive. In the past, comparatively low interest rates permitted 100 percent financing of a large retail property—all costs could be covered by a standard loan. When interest rates are high, however, it may be more sound economically to concentrate on raising capital up front to keep financing costs low. The type of equity financing employed is defined by how the interests of the investors are to be handled. The developer will have to structure the equity and debt financing to meet the needs of the project. Limited partnerships and joint ventures are the most common forms of equity investment. For urban retail projects, public involvement and government funding may be another alternative.

In a *limited partnership,* there is a mix of general partners, who assume liability, and limited partners, who are liable only to the extent of their investment. Limited partners are often involved in a single aspect of the project, one that requires specialized knowledge, such as accounting or legal affairs. Equity partners usually won't want to be exposed to cash demands such as improvements and expansion plans.

A *joint venture* may be a partnership between the landowner and the developer, or it may be among several entities who are partners in the development company. Typically, the owner contributes the land and the developer contributes his or her own expertise in addition to identifying and bringing to the project the expertise necessary to operate a retail property. A developer can also enter into a joint venture with a lending institution. In some shopping centers, especially in rehab projects where funds are limited, anchor tenants themselves sometimes provide part of the money.

Investing in real estate is a way of building estates—of accumulating and storing wealth. The relative stability of the United States' economy makes real estate investment attractive to foreign investors interested in the long-term goals of preserving capital. Foreign investment is particularly active when the U.S. dollar is weak because prices appear cheap when foreign currencies are converted to U.S. dollars. In general, equity investors are interested in the long-term concerns of the retail project and will take a more active role in the decisions involving leasing and tenant mix.

Equity financing usually reduces the loan amount needed and increases cash flow. However, debt financing is not unusual. Land acquisition, construction or interim loans, and permanent loans are the elements of shopping center development financing.

LAND ACQUISITION

Until the site is controlled by the developer, construction and long-term financing cannot begin. The first step is to acquire the right to build on the land. This may be done by purchasing the land outright or by leasing it from the owner. Developers sometimes choose a *ground lease* because it will preserve more capital at the outset. However, shopping centers built on a ground lease are often difficult to sell; because of this, developers prefer to purchase the land or enter a joint venture with the landowner.

Ground leases are preferably *subordinated,* which means that the owner offers the land as collateral for a portion of the entire mortgage commitment on the project. *Lenders usually insist on a subordinated ground lease.* Ground leases can also be *unsubordinated,* meaning that the land will not become collateral for the mortgage. However, financing for an unsubordinated lease is more difficult to obtain and the interest rate applied to it may be higher.

One factor to take into account when arranging a ground lease is its possible effect on future tenant-developer relationships. Most ground leases are for long terms—fifty years is common, and longer terms may be set. If the ground lease is terminated, there may be problems granting extended lease renewals to tenants. Also, tenants may ask for nondisturbance agreements in their leases.

CONSTRUCTION LOANS

Construction loans are usually short-term loans that are used during the building period to provide the immediate funds needed to start-up the store or center. They carry a higher interest rate than long-term or permanent loans because of the greater risk involved. Most developers apply for a permanent loan or mortgage once the property is operational; others rely solely on an extended construction loan and equity financing. Traditional construction loans are obtained from short-term lenders such as commercial banks and real estate investment trusts (REITs). Extended construction loans offer financing several years beyond the construction of the shopping center, allowing the developer to secure a permanent loan on more favorable terms because the center is already operational.

PERMANENT LOANS

Conventional mortgages are the most widely used form of permanent loans, although convertible mortgages are also viable. With an urban project, public or government financing may be an alternative. Whatever the chosen method, the developer, the long-term lender, and the short-term lender should cooperate from the start of the project. The following are sources of permanent financing for the developer:

- Commercial banks
- Savings and loan institutions and savings banks
- Life insurance companies and pension funds
- REITs and syndications
- Wall Street companies
- Finance and credit companies
- Government funds

Land sale-leaseback is another financing technique used for large shopping centers. In this arrangement, the shopping center land is sold to a financial backer, and the developer leases the land from the investor. In this type of arrangement, not only does the developer benefit from the reduction of the upfront investment, but the rent the developer pays is tax deductible, and the capital used for the actual construction of the center is depreciable.

PUBLIC AND PRIVATE COOPERATION
IN URBAN RETAIL DEVELOPMENT

One of the most effective ways of developing downtown retail projects is through establishment of a partnership between the private and public sectors, with financing provided by a combination of private investors and federal and state governments. Both parties benefit from urban development in a public-private partnership. The public sector often acts as a codeveloper, sharing the expenses, profits, and risks of building a new retail site or revitalizing an old downtown area. City governments are able to attract private investors by using public money. The city "profits" from the new retail activity as a result of the increased employment, an enhanced tax base, entry of more consumer dollars into the city, and overall rejuvenation of the urban area. Private developers usually welcome such cooperation because it means they can obtain financing at lower interest rates. The arrangement also offers other advantages such as lower land costs, tax relief, and easily attainable building permits.

Partnerships can be affected in several ways. Usually a private developer is hired by the city to manage the practical details of land acquisition, financing, and negotiating with local retailers. The city backs the developer by providing grants, loans, or tax breaks and by generating community support. Another possibility is to form a development team comprised of both public officials and private developers. (Sometimes large space users, such as department stores, will formulate their own development teams.) These teams work together to decide on design issues and promotion strategies. There are also private consulting firms that specialize in coordinating activities between the private and public sector and putting together financing packages.

Nonprofit investment and development groups are another alternative. These groups can be either public or private or a combination of the two. Private nonprofit groups may be formed by local businessmen, financial institutions, professional builders, and others interested in retail development. Structured as a corporation, they are protected from most of the risks that can be incurred by individual investors. Also, because they are not a branch of the local government, they are free from the bureaucracy and red tape that can hamper government-sponsored activities. They are also at liberty to acquire property, conduct private negotiations, and hire professionals without the restrictions and lengthy review processes that governmental agencies impose.

Public nonprofit groups are also structured as corporations. The difference between public and private corporations is that public groups have access to powers that are not available to private groups: They can sell tax-exempt revenue bonds, receive income from the sale of property, and levy taxes or fees for specific public improvements. Development may be expedited because land may be assembled through state delegation of the power of eminent domain to a public (local) jurisdiction. On the other hand, public corporations cannot make decisions as quickly as private organizations, and they may be limited by governmental restrictions on property development.

One way to gain the benefits that accrue to both private and public development groups is to form a quasi-public corporation. These are extremely useful joint ventures among private investors, lenders, members of community groups, urban development corporations, and city officials that can move quickly to coordinate retail projects. They are usually governed by a board of directors whose members are chosen from both the private and the public sector. Although these corporations may be under contract to the city for the purpose of facilitating a specific development, they are also free from the politics inherent in most other public organizations. The participation of community groups in these corporations stimulates public interest in the retail project, and the public sector can be of help in gaining tax abatements, assisting with land acquisition, and obtaining financial support in the form of loans and grants.

The role of the private developer working within a quasi-public corporation is to help achieve the city's goals for urban revitalization. This means that the developer must frequently compromise, conforming to the design the city wants for the project or including extra public facilities in return for tax breaks and lenient zoning regulations. For these reasons, the developer should be brought into the corporation at the early stages of the project, so that both public and private sectors will be clear about the roles they are expected to play. Developers' goals are usually short-term, and a city's goals are long-term; but these different viewpoints can be reconciled and used to achieve the same ends.

PUBLIC FINANCING

With certain types of retail projects, especially in urban areas, the investment costs will exceed the funding available to the developer from standard debt financing and equity investment. This creates a gap and the developer must look for other sources of financing. One alternative is to apply for grants and loans. These are distributed to the city by the federal and state governments, and the city must prove its eligibility for such aid from public funds. The city, in turn, will provide the funds to the private developer either as a loan or as an outright grant.

Several types of grants are available. One is the Urban Development Action Grant (UDAG). After receiving money from this source, the city loans it to developers at low interest rates, on the condition that it be used for projects that will improve the city—skyways, pedestrian walkways, parking garages, etc. Although UDAGs are popular and have been used successfully in many urban environments, they are difficult to acquire because there are not enough grants to go around. Community Development Block Grants (CDBGs) are part of a federally funded program to help combat inner-city neglect. They are often used to repair sewers and roads, to relocate buildings, and to rehabilitate older neighborhoods. The CDBG has an entitlement program—used primarily for metropolitan cities and urban counties—and a nonentitlement program, which can be used to improve neighborhood developments and community buildings in nonmetropolitan regions. Both grant programs are intended to help low-income and minority areas.

One of the major goals of public financing is to stimulate private investment, which provides the bulk of the economic support for a downtown project. Thus, timing is of the essence in most public funding programs. The city and the developer must put together a financing package which will attract equity investors early in the project. These investors will in turn attract lending institutions and other traditional sources of straight debt financing. Partnerships between individual investors, joint ventures with corporations, or syndicates of investors are all possibilities for investment. Other sources include REITs, banks, life insurance companies, savings and loan associations, and pension funds.

LENDER CONSIDERATIONS

Institutions that lend money to the developer impose many restrictions. Before financing a property, lenders will want to be assured that certain conditions have been met. These include tenant considerations, cost considerations, and market conditions.

Tenant Considerations

Most lenders require shopping centers to have conventional department store or supermarket anchors. However, other tenants with excellent credit ratings may also be acceptable. Lenders may require that a specified amount of the property's GLA be leased to retailers with high credit ratings. They may further stipulate that leases must run for a specified minimum number of years and that the minimum rents paid by tenants must total a specified amount to ensure that sufficient income is generated over a long enough period of time to cover the developers' debt-service costs. The initial leasing plan for the property would be developed with the objective of providing this type of information for lender review.

Lenders expect a new site to have a certain amount of its space leased before they will commit to long-term financing. Generally, leases should be signed for at least half of the space before the building is ready for occupancy. Otherwise higher interest rates will be applied to repayment of the loan if the developer falls short of the full (or minimum specified percent) lease-up requirement. This is why a construction loan or some other form of interim financing is necessary. Lenders usually require that the mortgage on the property take precedence over the tenant's lease rights to space in the property. If the developer defaults on the loan and the lender forecloses on the property, the lender will want full right of claim on the property.

As part of the loan application, owners can be required to submit tenant lease forms for lender approval before the leases are signed. Often lending institutions ask to be given the right to make nonmaterial changes in the language of the lease if they choose. The conditions laid down by the lender will have to be balanced with the rights and demands of the retail tenants. Legally, a lease agreement cannot be changed after it has been signed unless all the parties to it approve of the change.

The strength of the management and leasing program is also a factor. An experienced management company is an asset to a property because it will be more likely to remain competitive in the market.

Cost Considerations

Lenders may require that the estimated cost of the project fall within acceptable ranges for the current market. The net operating income (NOI) of the property should be expected to produce a fixed return in relation to current interest rates. The developers themselves should have a net worth and sufficient experience to warrant financing on a large scale; first-time developers may have to have a more experienced partner in order to obtain a loan. The amount of equity invested in the project is also important. Lenders require a cash or cash collateral contribution by the developer ranging from 5 to 25 percent of the total cost of the project. In a strong market, financing can sometimes be arranged without cash collateral, but in these cases, the lender must participate in cash flow or in increases in residual value.

Market Conditions

The lender will also take into account the strength of the other retail properties in the trade area and the economic situation in general. Market conditions influence the amount of equity available to the developer and the developer's financial prowess. In overbuilt markets, financing will not usually be approved until supply and demand even out. Lenders will also be concerned about the appropriateness of the site selection and whether demographic data support the choice of that location for a retail project.

APPENDIX C

Leasing Plan Examples

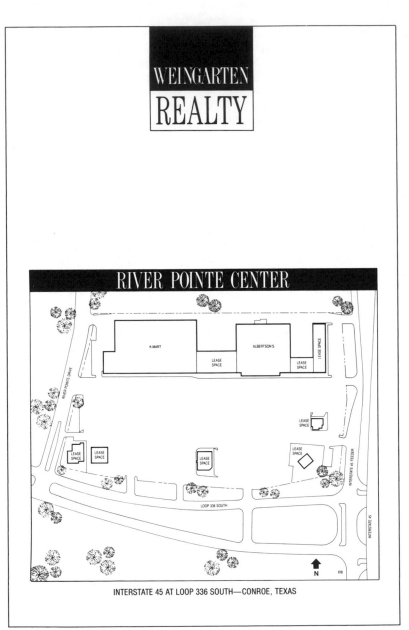

Face of marketing leasing plan for River Pointe Center. Reproduced courtesy of Weingarten Realty.

RIVER POINTE CENTER

Trade Area Population — 1988*
Conroe Urban Area
(including N.W. Montgomery Co.) 66,380
Woodlands & Oak Ridge North
(Southern Montgomery Co.) 43,174
Walker County 56,860
Total Trade Area 166,414

Median Family Income* $34,819

Retail Expenditure Potential in the Trade Area**
Retail Sales $845,257,518
Eating & Drinking 58,086,558
Drugs 24,970,680
General Merchandise 44,828,316
Apparel & Accessories 28,002,834
Furniture/Home Furnishings 28,419,012
Building Material/Hardware 132,463,512

Traffic Counts**

	Count	Date
IH-45 — north of Loop 336 North	53,000	1988
IH-45 — south of Loop 336 South	56,000	1988
U.S. 75 — north of Loop 336 South	10,800	1988
Loop 336 South — west of IH-45	21,000	1988****

Road Improvements
Loop 336 overpasses at Highway 105 to the East and FM 2854 to
the West – Under construction – Completion in 1990.

*Donnelley Marketing Information Services
**1987-88 Marketing Economics Guide (Montgomery County)
***Texas Highway Department
****Estimated by Texas Highway Department
Note:
Conroe and Northwest Montgomery County include census tracts #904; 905;
906.01; 906.02; 906.03; 907.01; 907.02; 907.03; 909; 910; 911.01; 911.02;
912.01 & 912.02.
Southern Montgomery County includes census tracts #902.01; 902.02; 902.03;
902.04; 902.05; 902.06 & 902.07.

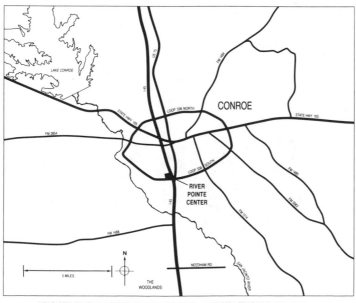

WEINGARTEN REALTY/2600 CITADEL PLAZA DRIVE/P.O. BOX 924133/HOUSTON, TEXAS 77292-4133/(713) 866-6000

Back of marketing leasing plan for River Pointe Center. Reproduced courtesy of Weingarten
Realty.

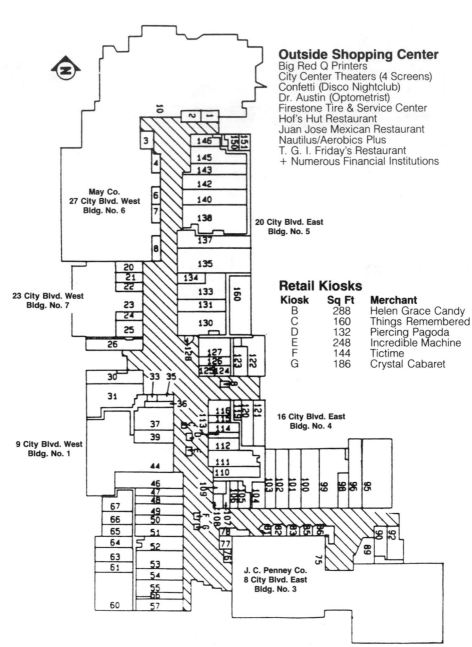

Outside Shopping Center
Big Red Q Printers
City Center Theaters (4 Screens)
Confetti (Disco Nightclub)
Dr. Austin (Optometrist)
Firestone Tire & Service Center
Hof's Hut Restaurant
Juan Jose Mexican Restaurant
Nautilus/Aerobics Plus
T. G. I. Friday's Restaurant
+ Numerous Financial Institutions

Retail Kiosks

Kiosk	Sq Ft	Merchant
B	288	Helen Grace Candy
C	160	Things Remembered
D	132	Piercing Pagoda
E	248	Incredible Machine
F	144	Tictime
G	186	Crystal Cabaret

May Co.
27 City Blvd. West
Bldg. No. 6

20 City Blvd. East
Bldg. No. 5

23 City Blvd. West
Bldg. No. 7

9 City Blvd. West
Bldg. No. 1

16 City Blvd. East
Bldg. No. 4

J. C. Penney Co.
8 City Blvd. East
Bldg. No. 3

Store layout portion of leasing plan for The City Shopping Center in Orange, California. Square footage and tenant identification information for retail buildings appears on the facing page. Reproduced courtesy of Tishman West Management Corporation.

Retail Building No. 1

Store	Sq Ft	Merchant
30	3349	Amy's Casuals
31	6987	Clubhouse Pizza
33	290	Modern Nail
35	560	Gentry Jewelers
36	1277	Cat's Meow
37	3956	The Limited
39	2150	Maling's Shoes
44	17457	R.E.I.
46	4483	Leed's
47	2000	Joel's
48	1900	Lynn's Stationers
49	2200	Lynn's Hallmark
50	2000	Software, Etc.
51	2233	Foxmoor Casuals
52	2604	Roy Step Shoes
53	3151	Wet Seal
54	2546	Swiss Colony
55	2567	Rooten's Luggage
56	1063	Obsession
57	2470	
60	6683	Smuggler's Inn
61	1531	US Postal Service (Boxes)
63	2400	Wade's Hair Design
64	1694	Jenny Craig
65	1826	Windsor Security/OPD/ Substation
66	1580	Benco Maintenance
67	2022	American Animal Hospital

Retail Building No. 3

Store	Sq Ft	Merchant
75	205586	J. C. Penney
76	457	Merle Norman Cosmetics
77	719	Motherhood Maternity
78	1066	Zales
81	568	Kit's Cameras
82	588	Ho-Ho Gifts
83	579	Deak International
85	579	Scorpion Jewelers
86	1108	Bobbi's
89	1736	Alexander's City Florist
90	1476	The Great American Short Story
92	1954	Shampoo by Judith Ann

Retail Building No. 4

Store	Sq Ft	Merchant
95	9100	Miller's Outpost
96	4620	Carl's Jr.
98	1280	Pro Image
99	5717	CVS
100	4403	House of Fabrics
101	3351	Footlocker
102	2975	Radio Shack
103	2975	Pat's Pets
104	1320	Stride Rite
105	866	Haroldson's Coffee World
106	963	Randy's Men's Wear
107	627	Orange Julius
108	740	Frost Art
109	1100	Bob's Ice Cream

Retail Building No. 4 (cont.)

Store	Sq Ft	Merchant
110	2400	Kid's Mart
111	3694	Thom McAn
112	1675	Cal-Hawaiian
113	938	Funny Business
114	1206	Aiko International
115	720	Tinder Box
116	1608	Hatfield's Jewelers
119	817	One Hour Photo Max
120	2336	Papa's Famous Popcorn
121	2278	China King Restaurant

Retail Building No. 5

Store	Sq Ft	Merchant
122	3228	True Grit Cafe
123	2072	
124	588	Papa's Famous Hot Dogs
125	735	Mrs. Field's Cookies
126	1121	C. J. Shoes (Florsheim)
127	2600	Celini
128	303	Unga Bunga Jungle Gifts
130	4757	B. Dalton Books
131	2727	ROCS
133	4355	Casual Corner
134	1200	Judith Ann Fashions
135	7541	Oshman's
137	4207	Jay Jacobs
138	7222	Lerner's
140	3909	Craft N Gifts
142	3909	Kinney Shoes
143	3048	Swan Hunter
145	2948	Kay-Bee Toys
146	1124	John Crandall Jewelers
150	1033	Merchant's Association
151	861	Community Hall
160	5700	

Retail Building No. 6

Store	Sq Ft	Merchant
1	863	US Post Office
2	831	Rock Party
3	790	Cafe Metro
4	750	Golden Square and Accessories
6	640	Wild Tops
7	697	Parklane
8	910	The Shoe Trend
10	160987	May Co.

Retail Building No. 7

Store	Sq Ft	Merchant
20	1298	General Nutrition Center
21	1062	Sunshine, The Natural Alternative
22	1180	Good Looks Beauty Supply
23	15460	United Artists Theater (6 Screens)
24	885	
25	1798	Ashly Jewelers
26	3257	Chuck Balboa's Label's

APPENDIX   D

Maintaining Prospecting Files

It is important to maintain accurate, current records of prospects contacted, their needs, properties shown, and the expiration dates of current leases. A good filing system will save valuable time when searching for information about a particular site, tenant, or prospect. Because so much of an agent's job involves following up a visit or a call, a system that allows the agent to make long-term schedules is absolutely necessary.

PROSPECT CARDS

After each contact with a prospect, the agent should record information about the potential tenant on a card or chart that permits tracking of a variety of information related to the prospect's current and future leasing potential. Space requirements and preferred locations are of particular importance. In fact, chain operations have these specifications for their stores down to a science. Also critical is the prospect's preferred rental range, any special needs regarding parking or other amenities, and information about leasing decisions (i.e., by whom and where they are made). Other information to record includes:

- Present store location
- Number of other stores
- Approximate date of opening new store
- Whether (when) credit reports and financial qualifications have been checked
- Date of the first contact
- Name of the person contacted
- Rate the agent quoted at the time, if any
- Comments about each contact

The agent can distinguish between an "active" record (if the prospect has not yet signed a lease and is still looking for space) and one that is "inactive." For an example of such a form, see figure 5.2 (page 110) in chapter 5, Prospecting.

TICKLER SYSTEM

To keep track of both long- and short-term transactions as well as plan monthly, weekly, and daily schedules, it is a good idea to maintain a "tickler" file of prospect contact data. Information from the prospect card can be incorporated into these files and updated from time to time. While the prospect card may be as large as a sheet of stationery (8½ × 11 inches) to allow for the amount and range of information to be recorded over time, a tickler file can be made on a smaller scale (3 × 5 inches).

The following items are needed to start the file:

* Twelve monthly dividers
* Five weekly dividers
* Seven daily dividers
* A supply of index cards
* A suitable file box

First arrange the twelve monthly dividers, starting with the current month. For example, if the month is July, the sequence would be July, August, September, etc., with June being the last month in the file. After the current month divider, insert the five weekly dividers, once again beginning with the most current week (the third week in July, for example). Then insert the seven daily dividers after the current week, with the current day first (Wednesday, Thursday, Friday, etc.).

On an index card, summarize information from the prospect card, including the prospect's name, address, and telephone number. Also note the date of the last contact and any significant comments regarding that meeting. In the top right hand corner, note future contact dates.

After a contact has been made, each card should be filed according to the date for the scheduled follow-up. Cards are sorted and refiled at the beginning of each week and at the beginning of each month, transferring cards from the monthly section to the weekly section and filing within the weekly section by days. The filing system will become more specific the closer it is to the current date.

As an example, suppose an agent visited a discount chain store owner in August of one year and learned that the prospect was thinking of expanding in the spring of the following year. The agent would note this information in the "comments" section on the tickler index card and file it under March (or earlier), making a notation to follow up with a phone call at that time next year. (When an appointment is so far in the future, the tickler system is an essential reminder for the agent to remember the scheduled date for the telephone call.) At the end of February, when the agent went through the "March" cards, a decision was made to call the discount store in the second week of March. The card was then filed under the appropriate weekly divider. In the second week of March, the agent transferred the index card to the daily divider section, under Tuesday. On Tuesday morning, the agent called the discount operator, learned that the prospect was definitely interested in moving into a shopping center that the agent was currently listing, and scheduled a second visit for the following week. The index card, marked with the results of the Tuesday phone call and the date of the follow-up visit, was then refiled under the third week of March.

While the foregoing example suggests a way to use the tickler file, it is important to "schedule" follow-up activities in a way that allows ample time for decision making by both parties. In particular, the lead time before move-in must accommodate not only the leasing decision but also the improvements to the tenant's space. The agent in the example might have done an even better job if follow-up had begun in December or January.

A tickler file is ideal for budgeting time or planning long-term objectives. By checking the cards each day, the agent can increase efficiency and stay on top of a busy schedule.

PENDING FILES

These files are intended primarily for transactions that are already underway and should be used in conjunction with tickler files for maximum efficiency. Standard-sized file folders can be used to hold contact names, parcel maps, descriptions of the property, and a chronological history of the transaction. It is a good idea to attach the business card of each prospect to the inside of the folder where it will be as accessible as possible. Pending files are maintained for easy reference if a client calls with questions.

It is particularly important to keep track of the dates and times of each meeting with a prospect and what was said during these meetings. If there is any disagreement between owner and tenant, the agent can sometimes resolve it by checking the pending file. A good idea might be to devise a form on which to easily record the chronology of meetings and transactions, keeping this form at the beginning of the folder as a reminder of what the file contains. Copies of all forms and letters sent to and received from the client should be arranged in chronological order, with the most recent one on top.

If a pending file shows that a deal is still a long way from closing, it should probably be moved to the tickler file. Conversely, if a tickler file shows that a prospect might be considering a transaction, the information about this prospect should be transferred to the pending file. Both filing systems should be reviewed each month to determine whether the status of any transactions has changed.

COMPUTER FILING

Information gathered during prospecting can also be stored in a computer. Computer filing systems permit organization of client information in a variety of ways, and programs can be written that will allow organization of the data on transactions on the basis of square footage, lease expiration date, tenants currently leasing space in a given shopping center, zip codes, etc. Combinations of different factors—for example, grouping clients whose leases will expire in three to five months and who occupy between 1,200 and 2,500 square feet—can also be arranged. The process of matching locations with prospects is simplified. By entering the prospect's space requirements, rental range, preferred location, and other details into the system, the agent can quickly produce a list of suitable retail sites.

Computers make prospecting easier as well. They can be used to arrange an agent's time schedule, replacing the tickler system. Updating information and adding new listings is also easier with a computer. Agents can "network" with computers from other brokerage agencies, exchanging information quickly and facilitating broker cooperation.

The computer system is an efficient, technologically up-to-date way of doing what the tickler and pending files have always done.

A P P E N D I X   E

Merchants' Association, Marketing Fund, and Quality Circle

Shopping center promotions are often planned long before the center is operating. When promoting a shopping center to the consumer marketplace, owners rely on the cooperation of all or as many as possible of the tenants to create an atmosphere of unity and cohesiveness. Merchants' associations and marketing funds are the most common methods of achieving these goals. A recent development, called the quality circle or "pilot circle," is also being tried in some large malls. Whichever vehicle is utilized, it is funded by fees collected from the tenants by the owner and transferred to a separate account.

It is sometimes difficult to organize tenants whose natural reaction is to resist paying extra fees for centerwide promotions, especially if they already spend substantial sums on their own advertising campaigns. On the other hand, ancillary tenants often welcome the opportunity to participate in promotional activities that they would otherwise not be able to afford. To assure each tenant's participation in the center's marketing efforts, the owner will often include a marketing clause in the lease that mandates attendance at merchants' association meetings or regular contributions to the marketing fund. The leasing agent may help negotiate these clauses.

THE MERCHANTS' ASSOCIATION

A merchants' association serves as an organized forum for promotion of a shopping center. It is a legal, usually not-for-profit, corporation that holds regular meetings at which tenant retailers attempt to solve mutual problems, discuss suggestions, and plan a program of promotional events for the entire center. Merchants' associations typically organize seasonal promotional events and centerwide decorations, plan special center promotions, publish news bulletins and merchant directories, and organize joint advertising programs. In enclosed malls, the merchants' association may also be responsible for enforcement of parking lot regulations and for setting store hours and night openings, which are usually the owner's prerogative in other types of shopping centers, and it may establish licensing fees for temporary tenants in kiosks. The latter provides additional revenue for center promotional activities and can reduce the burden on the permanent tenants. However, marketing and promotion are the most important responsibilities of the merchants' association.

Bylaws of the merchants' association stipulate the rules and regulations by which it operates. At their most basic, bylaws include the following:

- Election procedures and duties of officers
- Dates and order of business for monthly meetings
- Appointment of committees
- Establishment of a board of directors and standing committees (for example, finance, advertising, special events, publicity)

A president elected from among the tenants or the board of directors as a whole will work closely with the owner or property manager to plan a calendar of events and a budget for them. The property owner may (but usually does not) choose to actively run the association—direct the meetings, make decisions about advertising, and contact agencies and the media—or a marketing director may be hired to coordinate promotional efforts. The objective of the association is to have all the tenants work cooperatively to promote the center; the organization should *not* be directed exclusively by one person. However, the owner's representative will likely be the catalyst for the association.

The budget for the association depends on the type and size of the center and its planned promotional activities. Funds are contributed by both tenants and owner, and each tenant's contribution is negotiated separately and stated in its lease. Although other methods of calculation may be used, the amount of the individual tenant's share is usually based on the percent of the total GLA of the center that is represented by the tenant's individually leased space, or a percent of the tenant's gross annual sales, or both. Anchor tenants often contribute only a nominal amount, and a very strong anchor may contribute nothing at all. The rationale for this is the proportion of the anchor tenant's own budget that is spent for advertising which benefits the center indirectly because of the numbers of customers attracted to the major store in it. The owner or developer is responsible for 15–35 percent (20 percent on average) of the association's budget. Commonly this is calculated as 25 percent of the total collected from the tenants.

Ideally, the merchants' association will be in operation six months to a year before a new center is scheduled to open, and meetings are conducted formally, on a monthly basis. The owner may report on increases and decreases in the sales volume of the center as a whole. Few organized centers are operated without some form of mandatory tenant financial participation in the marketing program. Unless all tenants are consistently and equally active in the planning and funding of promotional activities, the marketing effort for the center as a whole will suffer.

There are significant disadvantages to merchants' associations, however. Often they are professionally incapable of managing an effective marketing program; the retailer members of the association may not be versed in contemporary marketing techniques or able to implement the best strategies for attracting customers to the center as a whole. Also, political infighting can arise during the meetings when some tenants think that others are dominating the meetings or are not contributing significantly; and leadership can change so often that it is difficult to maintain coherent long-term marketing plans. To circumvent these problems, an increasing number of owners have initiated marketing funds as an alternative way to generate the money needed for effective promotional campaigns.

THE MARKETING FUND

A marketing fund has replaced the merchants' association in a substantial number of centers. When a center has a marketing fund, tenants are required to contribute a specified amount of money to the marketing effort; association meetings and functions are eliminated in favor of total owner control over marketing and promotional programs, although there may be an advisory board established from among the tenants. In large malls, it is standard practice to hire a promotion director to administer the marketing fund. The director, being free from the administrative details involved in managing a merchants' association, can concentrate on the promotional program and on planning long-term marketing strategies.

Tenants pay their marketing fund fees along with their monthly rent, with anchor tenants often contributing only a small amount because they already spend 2–5 percent of their annual budgets on advertising. Typical marketing fees may be based on a percentage of a tenant's annual gross sales or of the percentage rent breakpoint, whichever is greater, or on a rate basis related to the tenant's GLA (dollars per square foot). The owner provides up to 25 percent of the total fund, and this contribution may take the form of salaries for marketing staff, employee benefits, insurance, office space, etc. All financial records of the fund should be open for tenants' examination; likewise, each tenant may be required to show proof of its advertising.

Marketing funds are often more cost effective than merchants' associations. Decisions are made more quickly because advertising agencies and the media deal with one marketing director instead of retailer representatives. In addition to paying a regular fee, the lease may also require the tenant to advertise in center-sponsored media such as in-mall directories, catalogs, and newsletters. The lease may also require individual tenant advertising to mention the center.

THE QUALITY CIRCLE

An innovation in mall marketing is a compromise between the merchants' association and the marketing fund. Quality circles or "pilot circles" are being tested as a way of allowing tenants to participate in the center's overall plan without having to direct the marketing effort. Several types of quality circle programs have met with success.

The mall marketing director begins the program in January with a general meeting of all the merchants in the shopping center. The director of marketing, who serves as the coordinator of all the quality circles, supplies each merchant with an information packet covering the marketing objectives, past marketing campaigns, and scheduled promotions for the coming year. Each merchant is asked to sign up for a "pilot circle" that will be responsible for supervising at least two marketing "flights" or promotional campaigns. These groups will be comprised of eight to ten merchants who will meet to discuss plans. Each marketing flight, with the exception of Christmas, has two months' lead time. The pilot circles meet regularly with the marketing director to present their specific plans. The pilot circles are responsible for generating ideas about the type of advertising and public relations to incorporate into the flight; the marketing director and staff are responsible for contacting the media and controlling the budget. This quality circle technique lets each merchant share in the marketing effort while retaining centralized management of the campaign to assure continuity of theme and overall control of expenditures.

Another quality circle technique allows the tenants less independence. Management divides the tenants into groups of ten and assigns them to particular flights. Again, a general meeting in January is attended by representatives of each quality circle to learn the center's marketing plans for the coming year. Each group then meets separately to develop a promotion that will tie in with the marketing director's plans. The groups meet on a monthly basis; once every three months all the groups get together to discuss their progress.

Although quality circles are just beginning to be established in the shopping center business, their popularity is likely to increase, particularly in festival centers where the independent tenants need a very specialized marketing campaign. A standardized marketing fund would not permit enough input by these tenants, and a merchants' association might not function efficiently with such a large number of varied participants.

A P P E N D I X   F

Description of Standard Landlord-Tenant Work

[The following is a general description of the work that can be done to prepare a retail space for occupancy; it is included in this book as an example and a guideline only. Because specifications for individual sites vary with location, applicable zoning codes, and the age of the property, each retail site should develop its own landlord-tenant work standards for incorporation into its leases.]

Description	Landlord's Work	Tenant's Work
1. Structure	Steel and pre-cast concrete supported on concrete spread footings.	Any structural alterations required for the support of any special equipment or roof openings may only be done with prior approval of landlord.
2. Floors	Concrete slab on grade.	
3. Exterior walls	Pre-cast concrete as per drawings.	
4. Storefronts	Landlord will provide as shown on drawings.	Tenant will not alter storefronts without landlord's prior approval, which may be unreasonably withheld.
5. Trash	Shielded trash areas are provided as indicated on general site plan.	Trash containers located only in designated locations which must be utilized by tenant as set forth in the lease.
6. Roofing	A fifteen (15) year bondable type roof.	No penetration of roof will be allowed without obtaining prior written approval from landlord.
7. Carpentry	Any exterior wood, as shown on drawings.	All interior wood surfaces and finishes including, but not limited to, doors, frames, paneling, built-in cabinets, vanities, ceilings, and trim.
8. Exterior	Where shown in drawings, exterior doors are aluminum storefront type, or landlord may provide tenant with one 3'0" x 7'0" hollow metal door in metal frame, painted.	Any additional exterior doors required for servicing or special conditions with prior written approval of landlord.
9. Interior doors	None provided.	All interior doors required will be 3'0" x 7'0" solid core wood or hollow metal doors set in wood or hollow metal frames.

Description	Landlord's Work	Tenant's Work
10. Hardware	All doors supplied by landlord to have standard duty quality or better hardware in accordance with applicable codes.	All doors supplied by tenant to have standard duty quality or better hardware in accordance with applicable codes. Finish is to be coordinated with landlord's.
11. Demising partitions	Partitions only required by code as "area separation walls" as shown and detailed on drawings, and those required to delineate the exterior dimensions of the leased premises. Wall to be fire-taped only.	All partitions provided between tenancies to be constructed of metal studs 24" on center and 5/8" fire-rated board on tenant side only, taped and ready for finishing as shown on drawings.
12. Interior partitions	None provided.	All required partitions to be constructed of metal studs, 24" on center with ½" gypsum board on each side.
13. Ceilings	2×4 fissured tile suspended acoustical ceiling (fire-rated).	
14. Floor finishes	None provided.	Carpet, or other approved hard surface flooring will be utilized throughout in all rental areas. Sealed concrete in service areas may be allowed.
15. Painting/staining	All exterior wood or metal surfaces as shown on drawings.	All interior painting or staining to completely finish all retail areas. Walls may be left unpainted in service areas.
16. Wall finishes	None provided.	Any applied finishes including vinyl wall surfacing, wood paneling, grass cloth, ceramic tile, or plastic laminated panels will become a part of the premises and have a flame spread rating in accordance with all codes and ordinances.
17. Special equipment	None provided.	Any special equipment to be installed only after obtaining written approval from landlord.

Description	Landlord's Work	Tenant's Work
18. Plumbing	Landlord will provide one 4" sewer stub to each space.	Tenant, if granted permission by landlord, may be permitted to put in the necessary plumbing at its expense for toilets, etc.
	Landlord will provide one water stub to each space.	Tenant will be required to obtain water meter for any special use other than tenant toilets.
19. HVAC	Landlord will provide fully functional three (3) ton HVAC roof-top unit with diffuser at front and rear of space, necessary ductwork to diffusers, control and power wiring and gas piping.	Tenant will provide exhaust fans, humidification, and any other special requirements of its tenancy.
		Tenant will be required to provide and pay for all A/C required in its premises in excess of the amount provided by landlord. Tenant will be required to supplement the installed system so it conforms to the landlord's design conditions. The determination as to whether tenant's system complies with landlord's design conditions will be made solely by landlord's architect/engineer.
20. Electrical	Landlord to provide electrical stub into tenant space for tenant signage.	Tenant will provide its own wiring to equipment and motors, outlet boxes, switches, transformers, and special electrical equipment, in strict conformance with all codes. Tenant will be responsible for any changes to landlord-furnished service (above or below 200 amps) including appropriate conduit from landlord's distribution board into space. Determination as to whether tenant's system complies with landlord's criteria or design conditions will be made solely by landlord's architect or engineer.
	Landlord will provide one (1) 100 AMP electrical panel.	
	Landlord will provide one (1) 2x4 light troffer per 250 sq. ft. of tenant's space with wiring (functional).	

Description	Landlord's Work	Tenant's Work
21. Telephone	Landlord will provide empty telephone conduit of adequate size to ceiling space of retail area.	Tenant will provide all conduit, final wiring, and instruments required within the tenant space.
22. Signs		All signs will be provided by tenant and be in strict conformance with the shopping center design criteria.
23. Fees		Tenant agrees to pay all hookup, tap or utility fees, and installation costs for water, electrical, and gas extensions necessary to service the leased premises.

APPENDIX   G

Lease Negotiation Checklist

Date Prepared _____   Prepared By _____

Action 1.   6.
Items: 2.   7.
        3.   8.
        4.   9.
        5.   10.

Owner _____
Tenant _____
Name and _____
Address of Site _____
Space Identification _____   Square Feet _____
Beginning _____   Ending _____
Term _____ years
Type of Lease _____ (net or gross)
Options: Expansion _____
         Renewal _____
         Other _____
A. Rent
    1. Fixed Minimum Rent   _____
    2. Escalation   _____
    3. Percentage Rent:
        a. Rate   _____
        b. Payable   _____
        c. Reports due   _____
        d. Recapture:
            (1) Taxes   _____
            (2) Insurance   _____
            (3) Construction costs   _____
            (4) Promotional Fees   _____
    4. Rent Commencement:
        a. Date Certain _____
        b. _____ days after signing lease
        c. _____ days after receipt of building permit
        d. Upon receipt of owner contribution _____
        e. Upon opening for business _____
B. Other Direct Costs
    1. HVAC
        a. Mall   _____
        b. Restaurant   _____
    2. Utility Charges   _____
    3. Insurance:
        a. Liability   _____
        b. Casualty   _____ (for shopping center)
        c. Waiver of Subrogation   _____
    4. Common Area Expense Proration _____
    5. Tax:
        a. Separately assessed   _____
        b. Not separately assessed   _____
    6. Owner's Contribution for Tenant's Work:
        a. _____ upon completion; _____
        b. $_____ _____% of percentage rent

C. Marketing Considerations
   1. Parking   _____
   2. Signs:
      a. Storefront   _____
      b. Outside Building   _____
      c. Pylon   _____
      d. Other   _____
   3. Restrictions on Food Service Applicable   _____
   4. Site Layout
      a. Ingress and Egress   _____
      b. Visibility   _____
      c. Change in Layout of Property   _____
      d. Parking   _____
   5. Retail Restrictions   _____
   6. Garbage Removal   _____
   7. Hours of Operation   _____
   8. Merchants' Association Dues   _____
   9. Permitted Uses and Trade Names   _____

D. Secondary Considerations
   1. Audit of Books by Owner:
      a. Certified statement by CPA   _____
      b. Office of Tenant   _____
   2. Utilities   _____
   3. Security   _____
   4. Equipment Financing   _____
   5. Alterations   _____
   6. Maintenance   _____

E. Architectural, Engineering, and Construction Considerations
   1. Days for Completion of Tenant's Work   _____
   2. Plans Submission Requirements:
      a. Original Submission by Tenant   _____
      b. Review and Return by Owner   _____
      c. Resubmission by Tenant   _____
   3. Commencement of Work
      a. _____ days from signing lease
      b. _____ days from approval of plans
      c. _____ weeks after tenant's receipt of permits
   4. Utilities to Premises (specifications):
      a. Sewer (_____ inch pipe)
      b. Water (_____ inch pipe; _____ psi)
      c. Gas (_____ M BTU/hour)
      d. Electrical Wiring (_____ volts, _____ phase _____ amps)
   5. Parking Lot Lighting _____
   6. Submissions required for owner contribution _____

F. Legal Considerations
   1. Legal Description:
      a. Premises   _____
      b. Surrounding Property   _____
      c. Easements   _____
   2. Indemnification   _____
   3. Defaults
      a. By Tenant
         (1) Rent   _____
         (2) Other   _____
         (3) Waiver if commence to cure   _____
      b. Owner to use best efforts
         to relet if tenant in default   _____
      c. By Owner   _____
   4. Condemnation   _____
   5. Destruction of Premises   _____
   6. Reimbursement on Termination
      for Condemnation and Destruction   _____
   7. Nondisturbance Agreement   _____
   8. Assignment and Subletting   _____

APPENDIX H

Steps in Leasing a New Shopping Center

The agent working to lease space in a new shopping center will work with the owner to develop a leasing plan that states the types of tenants and merchandise, and the applicable rental rates, for the spaces that are available for lease. Following the leasing plan, the agent will contact prospective tenants and attempt to interest them in opening another store in the new center or in relocating there. Those prospects indicating an interest will be evaluated to determine how they fit best into the proposed tenant mix (location, store size, etc.) and qualified as to their financial responsibility. This, along with a determination of the level of retailing expertise, is especially important when the prospects are local retailers. The prospect will have been shown one or more specific spaces in the center (if it is nearing completion of construction) or the plans for them (if construction has not progressed sufficiently). After all these preliminaries are completed (see chapter 5), the agent begins the following step-wise process to acquire a signed lease and establish the retailer in the new center.

1. Proposal to Lease

Agent drafts a *proposal to lease* for individual spaces in the center as serious prospective tenants for them are identified. The proposal is submitted for approval by the developer or owner and the developer's (or owner's) attorney. Review and approval by the property manager and possibly the lending institution that is financing the project may be necessary or appropriate. The proposal is submitted to the prospect after approval by the above parties. This allows for preliminary negotiation of lease terms between the prospect and agent before the actual lease is drafted. The tenant's shell space and improvement allowance, if any, should be clarified at this time.

Sometimes called a *letter of intent,* the proposal to lease is usually nonbinding and generally outlines the business terms of the proposed lease, including: (1) the parties, (2) the project or property (center), (3) identification and area of the particular space (premises), (4) duration of the lease (including dates for commencement of occupancy and commencement of rent), (5) the use of the space, (6) minimum or base rental rate, (7) percentage rent (and breakpoint), (8) pro rata charges and their basis, (9) allocation of maintenance costs, and (10) marketing fund participation.

2. First Draft of Lease

Agent (or the landlord's attorney) prepares a draft copy of the lease and exhibits based on the terms set forth in the letter of intent. If a letter of intent is not used, the first draft lease may be prepared from the agent's records of points and terms already discussed with the prospect.

2. First Draft of Lease (continued)	Minimally the exhibits will include a site plan showing the proposed leased space within the center, a legal description of the center, an explanation of how expenses charged to the tenant will be prorated, a work-letter covering improvements to the space, and the rules and regulations of the center. Other exhibits may cover signage requirements or limitations.
	The minimum number of typewritten copies needed should account for distribution to individuals or departments as required for internal approval according to the development company's standards. Landlord's attorney should review the typed drafts if he or she did not prepare them.
3. Lease Log	Agent (or a leasing secretary) should maintain a log detailing every lease prepared and its movement within the organization and among the various outside contacts involved. (It is desirable to keep a record of the dates and substance of *all* meetings and correspondence with the prospect, beginning with the first contact.)
4. Negotiation	Attorneys, property manager, and other landlord representation may or may not participate in this process. The agent's role is to guide the negotiations in a direction that is acceptable to ownership while at the same time keeping in mind the importance of the tenant's perspective. Agent must be well-versed in what is or is not acceptable to ownership.
	Points to be discussed include: financial responsibility (including possible guarantors, especially for a local retailer or a new business); options; tenant improvement allowances, if any; percentage rents; concessions and rent reductions; merchants' association dues; tenant's share of operating expenses, insurance, property tax, and common area maintenance; use clauses and other restrictive covenants; subletting and assignment clauses; and hours of operation. The range of points to be negotiated will vary with the size (importance) and retailing experience of the prospect.
5. Revised Draft of Lease	Changes are made to the draft lease based on the results of specific negotiations, and, if necessary, a revised lease is prepared. (Sometimes minor changes to the lease can be handwritten and initialed by the signers without necessitating preparation of a new lease; sometimes only individual pages are retyped.) At least two original leases are prepared for signatures (one each for landlord and tenant). The number of additional originals depends on whether the attorneys involved and the landlord's lending institution require them.

6. Prospect Signs Lease

In most cases (with the exception of anchors or other major tenants), the prospect is usually required to sign the lease before the landlord. A guarantor's signature or a partner's signature may also be necessary. Prospects may wish to have their attorneys examine and approve the lease before they sign it. (The agent should encourage the prospect to have the lease reviewed by legal counsel.) The agent should be sure to advise the prospect that the landlord retains the right not to sign.

7. Lease Approval and Transmittal

Upon receipt of the lease documents signed by the prospect, agent should double-check the documents for accuracy and signatures. Agent prepares a *lease summation report* highlighting key terms and unique aspects of the lease. All attachments should be accounted for—including site plans, a credit report, at least two copies of the agent's commission statement, and a copy of the security deposit check. The lease is then transmitted to the developer (owner) for signature.

8. Landlord Signs Lease

After the lease has been checked for accuracy and completeness by the landlord and the agent—also by an attorney (if desired) and the property manager (if necessary or appropriate)—the landlord signs the lease (all originals).

9. Setting Up Files

Upon receipt of the signed lease, a leasing division (or legal) file is set up. Only copies of the signed lease should be kept in the official file. However, agent's file should be retained in case of a later dispute about the lease and the correspondence and discussion that resulted in any unique provision(s).

10. Distribution of Lease Copies

The property manager should be given a copy of the documents so that arrangements for move-in (including ordering of signs) can be made. Copies of the lease should be sent to lenders, if required. Copies of the signed lease or the lease summation report or both should be distributed within the development company as appropriate so that the landlord's part of the construction on the tenant's space can begin, commissions can be paid, etc.

Agent should transmit a signed copy (original) of the final lease to the tenant. It may be hand-delivered or sent by certified or registered mail, return receipt requested, to assure delivery. A lease is not fully executed until delivered. The tenant is responsible to provide copies for its attorneys and other internal distribution.

11. Landlord Construction

If landlord is to provide the space in other than standard shell condition, various aspects of construction in the tenant's space may require consideration in advance, including estimates of cost for the work to be done, etc., details of which should have been set forth in the *workletter* exhibit.

12. Space Acceptance

When construction is completed, appropriate in-house personnel should inspect and approve the work. The tenant should also approve the work. When the space is accepted, tenant should sign a *final acceptance* form and an *estoppel certificate,* and copies of these should go to the leasing manager and others as necessary (including the lender).

13. Tenant Construction and Installation of Fixtures

For complex installations, development, authorization, and approval by landlord of working drawings may be required. When a tenant improvement allowance is involved, cost estimates may be made for preliminary, revised, *and* final plans. Normally landlord's tenant construction coordinator or property manager works with and reviews tenant's contractors to assure compliance with the workletter and minimize disruption to others.

14. Rent Effective Letter

Before tenant opens for business, property manager sends a letter welcoming the tenant to the center and verifying the rent commencement date of the lease and move-in date. Copies of this letter go to the leasing manager and the accounting department.

15. Lease Follow-Up

After the tenant has moved in (which may be a considerable time after the lease has been signed) agent should follow up with regular visits to the site to encourage referrals.

Glossary

AAA rating   The highest credit rating given to businesses by Dun & Bradstreet; useful when determining a prospect's financial status.

Addendum   In retail leasing, a supplement to a standard lease, usually attached to it.

Agent   An individual authorized to act on behalf of another person or entity called the principal. (See also *leasing agent*.)

Anchor tenant   A major shopping center tenant that will draw the majority of customers.

Ancillary tenant   A shopping center tenant that occupies a smaller space and a location that is secondary in relation to the anchor tenant.

Assignment   The transfer of title, right, and interest in certain real property. The document used to convey a leasehold is called an "assignment of lease" rather than a "deed." (Compare *sublease*.)

Base rent   Minimum monthly rent payments, as set forth in a retail lease, excluding pass-throughs, percentage rents, and other additional charges. (See also *minimum rent*.)

Base year   The year in a lease term used as a standard in a rent escalation clause. Operating costs in the next year are compared with costs in the base year, and tenant's rent is adjusted either up or down.

Block group   A subdivision of the census tract covering an urban population of 10,000 or more. (See also *enumeration district*.)

"Boilerplate" lease   The owner's lease form containing clauses that are usually standard for all tenant-owner relationships.

Breakpoint   In retail leases, the point at which the tenant's percentage rent is equal to the base rent and beyond which the tenant will begin to pay overages; also called natural breakpoint. Sometimes tenant and owner negotiate an artificial breakpoint which allows the tenant to begin paying percentage rent either before or after the natural breakpoint is reached.

Broker   An agent with a real estate license who acts as a representative for an owner or tenant, within specific limits of authority.

Broker cooperation agreement   A document signed by broker, owner, and brokerage firm, stating that broker is working for a particular owner on a particular property; it registers the names of prospective tenants, and outlines terms of broker's commission. It may also constitute an agreement between an original and an outside broker.

Brokerage firm   An agency that has brokers working for it who bring in business by canvassing the territory for prospective tenants or for listings on properties.

Build-to-suit   An arrangement between a shopping center developer and a large tenant (supermarket, department store, fast food franchise, bank, etc.) whereby the developer agrees to construct the tenant's building according to the tenant's specific instructions. The tenant will then lease that building and the site from the developer.

Buy-out   A form of concession whereby an owner or developer arranges to pay for the rest of a tenant's lease term so that the tenant will relocate to the owner's shopping center or move out of a space that the owner wants to use for another purpose.

Canvassing   Contacting prospective tenants by telephone or in person in order to interest them in leasing retail space. (See also *cold calling*.)

Capitalization rate   A rate used to calculate an estimate of a property's value based on that property's income.

Cash flow   The amount of spendable income from a real estate investment; cash available after all payments have been made for operating expenses and mortgage principal and interest.

Census block   The smallest subdivision used by the U.S. Bureau of the Census to compile population data, usually by streets or roads in urban areas.

Census tract   A subdivision of the census data for a standard metropolitan statistical area (SMSA) which refers to an area that has a population not exceeding 4,000.

Central business district (CBD)   The central shopping or business area in an urban environment; also called downtown.

Chain store   One of a group of retail stores operating under the same ownership that carries similar goods. National, regional, and local chains are defined in terms of the geographic areas they serve and the numbers of stores they operate.

Closing After final negotiations, the signing of a lease.

"Cluster" anchors A group of smaller stores that sell similar or complementary merchandise and operate in the place of the traditional anchor tenant in certain "specialty" centers.

Cold calling Calling on prospects with whom the agent has had no previous contact in order to interest them in leasing retail space.

Commission The fee, usually a percentage, that the agent receives after a leasing transaction; usually guaranteed through a legal document called a commission agreement. (See also *schedule of commissions*.)

Common area maintenance (CAM) charges clause In a retail lease, this clause stipulates how much the tenant will pay for maintaining the common area— that area within a shopping center or mall which tenants use in common; i.e., courtyards, escalators, sidewalks, skyways, parking areas, etc.

Community Development Block Grant (CDBG) A federally funded program to rehabilitate inner-city and older neighborhoods; the CDBG entitlement program is used primarily in metropolitan areas; the nonentitlement program is applied mostly in smaller communities.

Community shopping center A shopping center commonly anchored by a junior department store, discount store, or variety store and having a GLA of 150,000–400,000 square feet.

Comparison goods Merchandise that consumers will usually shop for at several stores before buying.

Comparison grid A form used to compare the base rents, additional charges, location, amenities, structure, age, and sales potential of both similar and dissimilar shopping centers.

Concession A benefit granted by the owner to encourage the leasing of new space or to retain a tenant; usually related specifically to the rental rate or improvement allowance.

Construction loan Money borrowed to build improvements on vacant land; a form of interim financing.

Construction rider (See *workletter*.)

Consumer Price Index (CPI) A way of measuring consumer purchasing power by comparing current costs of goods and services to those of a selected base year.

Continuous occupancy clause A lease clause that requires the tenant to occupy the space continuously throughout the lease term.

Continuous operation clause A retail lease clause that requires tenants to keep their stores fully stocked at inventory levels equal to (1) when they first opened for business, (2) their stores in other locations, or (3) stores offering similar merchandise in the area. There may also be requirements regarding store hours, staffing, and business name.

Convenience center   A small shopping center anchored by a quick-stop food store and occupied by other service-oriented tenants.

Convenience goods   Milk, soft drinks, chewing gum, candy, personal items, and similar goods that consumers will buy at stores closest to where they live or work, without making a special trip to purchase them.

Cooperating broker   An agent who brings a suitable prospect for a particular location to the broker who represents the owner of the site, or vice versa, thereby qualifying for a portion of the commission fee; also called an outside broker.

Debt service   Regular payments made on a loan.

Declining percentage rent   A negotiated percentage rent structure such that the tenant pays a smaller percentage of gross sales after a specified sales volume is reached.

Default   Failure to make either a mortgage or lease payment; nonperformance of the terms of a loan or lease.

Delinquent   The state of being past due. In real estate, delinquency is commonly used in reference to rent or other payments.

Demand   In marketing terms, the willingness and ability to purchase a commodity or service. (Compare *supply*.)

Demographic profile   The social and economic statistics of a specific population, including population density, age, education, occupation, and income.

Depreciation   In real estate, the decrease in value of a property due to age and wear and tear; in accounting, the process of converting a fixed asset into an expense.

Depth   In retail properties, the distance between the front window of a store and its back wall; in retailing, the variety of goods stocked for sale.

Developer   The individual or entity that invests in building a retail property and is responsible for construction, marketing, and leasing; may also be the owner of the land. The developer's investment may consist solely of time and expertise.

"Dignified" use clause   The provision in a retail lease that the merchant will not use the property in a way that will damage the image or reputation of the center as a whole.

Downtown retail space   Refers to a mall, freestanding store, or space in a mixed-use development in an urban environment, primarily the central business district, but not limited to it.

Effective rent   The amount of rent a tenant actually pays when extra improvement allowances and other concessions are taken into account; contrasts with the quoted base rent that is stated in the lease.

Effective space   The amount of retail space in a given trade area that is capable of drawing consumers.

Enumeration district   A subdivision of a census tract in a rural area with a population of 10,000 or more. (See also *block group*.)

Equity   An owner's interest or value in a retail property over and above any mortgage or claim on it by others based on money invested.

Equity financing   Capitalization of a retail project through partnerships or other investment entities that acquire an interest in the project.

Escalation clause   In a retail lease, a provision requiring the tenant to pay more rent based on increased operating costs, changes in a given economic index, or an agreed-upon schedule stated in the lease.

Estoppel certificate   A document by which the tenant states the terms of the rent agreement and the full amount of rent to be paid for the entire term of the lease; commonly requested as part of a transfer of ownership or refinancing.

Exclusive authorization to lease   A document stating that the agent will receive a commission for any prospect that signs a lease within a certain time period, regardless of who actually negotiated the transaction.

Exclusive use clause   A clause preventing the owner from leasing space to other retailers that sell merchandise similar to that specified in the tenant's lease.

Exhibit   A lease attachment elaborating on points in the standard lease.

Festival center   A type of specialty center, usually located in an historical section of a city, which creates a unique shopping environment using imaginative architecture and nearby natural resources. Draws mostly from the tourist trade; merchandising concentrated in restaurants and souvenir-type goods; may be anchorless.

Fixed expense   A regular expense that does not vary according to sales volume.

Fixed rate option   The tenant's guaranteed right to renew at the end of a lease term at a previously determined rental rate.

Floor area   (See *gross leasable area (GLA)*.)

Food court   An area in a shopping center, usually in an enclosed mall, where different kinds of food are available from individual vendors selling from separate stalls.

Franchise   An exclusive right to sell a product or perform a service; in retailing, an individual will purchase this right from a chain store or other type of parent corporation and operate the store according to the rules and regulations of the franchisor.

Freestanding retail space   A store that is not an integral part of a shopping center, enclosed mall, or mixed-use development; also called pad space. Many downtown department stores are freestanding. (See also *outlot*.)

Frontage   The section of a store that faces the street or the pedestrian walkway in a mall; also refers to window display area and entrance.

GAFO   A way of categorizing merchandise; stands for General merchandise, Apparel, Furniture, and Other.

Gross leasable area (GLA)   The size of a tenant's space, usually expressed in square feet. The total square feet of floor space in all store areas of a shopping center (excluding common area space); also called floor area.

Gross lease   A lease that allows the tenant to pay a fixed rent while the owner pays all operating expenses for the property. (See also *net lease*.)

Gross profit   The retailer's sales income minus the cost of the goods sold; sometimes the cost of returns is also subtracted from the total.

Gross sales   The total sales that the retailer makes during a financial period, usually a calendar year.

Ground lease   A lease that gives the tenant the right to use and occupy the land under a property. Under a subordinated ground lease, the owner offers the land as collateral for the mortgage commitment on the property. If the ground lease is unsubordinated, the land will not become collateral for the mortgage.

Guaranteed rent   (See *minimum rent* and *base rent*.)

Guaranty   A lease clause or addendum that promises the owner that, in case of tenant default, the tenant's rent will be paid and all other obligations performed. The individual or organization making such a pledge is called a guarantor.

Hypermarket   A very large individual store, sometimes occupying in excess of 150,000 square feet of GLA, that offers groceries, apparel, appliances, furniture, and other types of merchandise at discount prices.

Independent retailer   A local, nonchain store owned by a single individual or family.

Index escalation clause   A provision in a retail lease whereby the rental rate is adjusted according to a specified cost-of-living index.

Industrial shopping center   A type of specialty center based around stores and services having to do with plumbing fixtures, hardware items, or the care of automobiles.

Inflation   An increase in the prices of goods and services as a reflection of increased spending in relation to the supply of goods.

In-house agents   Leasing representatives who work for a particular developer, owner, or retailer; they are paid a salary and normally do not receive commissions as part of their compensation.

Initial markup   In pricing merchandise, the first markup of a new item after purchasing it wholesale.

Interim loan   Short-term, generally higher interest financing for new or existing projects. (See also *permanent loan*.)

Joint venture   A partnership, usually between landowner and developer but may be among several entities who are partners in the development company.

Keystone markup   A standard apparel markup that sets a selling price for merchandise at double its cost. (See also *markup*.)

Kiosk   A booth or stall set up in a shopping center, sometimes on a temporary basis, to sell goods such as tobacco, newspapers, magazines, seasonal merchandise, candy, keys, and other small impulse-purchase items.

Landlord   The owner of the leased premises. (See also *lessor*.)

Lease   A contract between owner and tenant that transfers to the tenant the right to use a piece of property for a specified length of time under specific conditions.

Leasing agent   The individual in a real estate brokerage firm (or management organization or development company) who is directly responsible for renting space in assigned properties. In some states, leasing agents must have a real estate broker's license.

Leasing plan   For a given retail site, the statement of rental rates and suitable tenants for specific spaces, usually presented to the owner or developer in the early stages of prospecting.

Lessee   The tenant in a lease agreement.

Lessor   The landlord in a lease agreement; the property owner.

Leverage   The use of borrowed funds to increase one's purchasing power.

Maintained markup   The average markup of an item sustained over a period of time, allowing for future markdowns and other reductions in selling price. (See also *markup*.)

Margin   Refers to the amount of profit a retailer makes from a certain item; it is always expressed as a percentage of the sales price. (Compare *markup*.)

Markdown   A retail price reduction taken for a hard-to-sell item.

Market   The interactions between consumers and retailers.

Marketing   Promoting a store or retail center through advertising and public relations.

Marketing fund   An account controlled by the landlord that is specifically for funding shopping center promotions and advertising and to which all merchants in the center must contribute based on a predetermined amount stated in their leases. (Compare *merchants' association*.)

Market penetration   Percentage of a specific type of retail market that a retailer has captured.

Market price   The amount actually paid for a property.

Market rent   The rent a retail site could command under prevailing market conditions.

Market research   The gathering of information about a trade area and a particular retail site pertaining to population, economy, local industries, per capita expenditures, the competing retail sites, and sales potential.

Market segmentation   The process of reducing the number of available tenant prospects by classifying retailers into categories on the basis of type of goods sold, form of ownership, size of store, and other criteria.

Market share   That portion of consumer dollars spent on a particular merchandise category which a given retailer can capture.

Market value   The estimated selling price a retail site would command on the open market.

Markup   The difference between the selling price of an item and its cost; also called mark-on. (Compare *margin*)

Megamall   An enormous enclosed mall three or four times the size of an ordinary regional shopping center and including retail space, hotels, restaurants, entertainment facilities, and amusement park-type amenities.

Merchandising   The buying, promoting, and selling of goods.

Merchants' association   An organization formed in shopping centers and controlled by the tenants to plan promotions and advertisements for the good of the center as a whole; usually all tenants are required to participate and both tenants and landlord pay dues. (Compare *marketing fund*.)

Minimum rent   The rent which will always be due each month in a tenant's lease term, regardless of sales volume and exclusive of any additional charges. Often used in conjunction with a percentage rent arrangement; sometimes called fixed-minimum rent. (See also *base rent*.)

Mixed-use development (MXD)   A type of real estate project, often found in central business districts, that develops a single property for several different purposes, including hotel, office, residential, retail, and entertainment.

Negotiation   The process of bargaining by tenant and owner to reach a mutually profitable agreement on rental rates, term of the lease, options, and other points.

Neighborhood center   A shopping center typically anchored by a supermarket or drugstore and having a GLA of 50,000–150,000 square feet.

Net lease   A lease specifying that tenant will pay a share of the owner's operating expenses, real estate taxes, and insurance premiums, usually in return for a lower base rent. The terms net-net and net-net-net (or triple net) are also used, depending on the extent of the costs that are passed through to the tenant.

Net operating income (NOI)   The money available to an owner or developer after deducting a property's operating expenses from its effective gross income. Debt service is deducted from NOI to determine cash flow.

Net sales   A retailer's sales income after exchanges, refunds, and allowances have been deducted from the total.

Nonexclusive authorization to lease   A document stating that the leasing agent will only receive a commission if he or she actually executes a lease with a prospect within a certain time frame.

Notice clause   In a retail lease, the clause that establishes the proper method and time frame each party must use to inform the other of matters that require notification as provided in the lease.

Occupancy cost   The retail tenant's cost for the leased space; includes base and percentage rent plus pass-through prorations such as insurance, real estate taxes, utilities, common area maintenance, management and marketing fees, etc.

Occupancy level   The relation of space already rented to the total amount of leasable space (GLA) in a center, expressed as a percentage. (See also *vacancy rate*.)

Off-price center   A type of specialty shopping center comprised of tenants offering name-brand merchandise at large discounts (20–60%) off normal retail prices, usually apparel items that are factory overruns, seconds, and overstock items from conventional department stores. (Compare *outlet center*.)

Operating expenses   The expenditures for real estate taxes, salaries, insurance, maintenance, utilities, and similar items paid in connection with the operation of a retail site or center and which are properly charged against income.

Operating statement   The record of a retailer's or developer's income and expenses over the course of a year; details expenditures and the percentage of income that can be expressed as profit.

Option   In a retail lease, a statement of the tenant's right to obtain a specific condition within a specified time; often incorporated as an addendum. Typical options are renewal, expansion, and cancellation.

Outlet center   A type of specialty center comprised of at least 50 percent factory outlet stores offering name-brand goods at discounted or wholesale prices; usually the manufacturer will operate the store, eliminating the retail markup. (Compare *off-price center*.)

Outlot   In a shopping center, a site which is not attached to the main center, sometimes located in the parking lot; freestanding space; also called out parcel or pad space. Tenants include fast food restaurants, gas stations, and drive-up banking services.

Overage   (See *percentage rent*.)

Overhead   The cost of doing business (i.e., wages, salaries, rent, common area fees, insurance, taxes, utilities, etc.) that cannot be charged to a particular part of the operation; in retailing, usually all expenses exclusive of the cost of goods sold or inventory.

Owner   The individual or entity with the legal right of possession of a property; can also be the developer. (See also *landlord*.)

Parking area ratio   The relationship between the size of the parking area and the size of the retail building.

Parking index   The number of parking spaces per 1,000 square feet of GLA.

Partnership   A form of ownership that binds the participants in shared responsibility for its debts. In a general partnership, all partners are equally and fully liable for its debts; in a limited partnership, there are one or more general partners who actively manage the business plus one or more passive partners whose liability is limited to the amount of their investment.

Pass-through escalation clause   In a retail lease, the article that passes increases in operating expenses to the tenant.

Pedestrian flow   The direction and patterns in which people move through a shopping center; can be influenced by architecture and design.

Pedestrian mall   In downtown shopping areas, a blocked-off set of streets containing stores where people can shop without interference from automobile traffic.

Per capita expenditure   A way of measuring how much each individual spends in a particular retail category over the course of a year.

Percentage rent   Rent a tenant pays that is based on a percentage of gross sales or net income; often set against a guaranteed minimum rent and therefore considered overage.

Permanent loan   A long-term loan used to finance the purchase of an existing project or to replace the construction loan for a new development; a mortgage.

Preleasing   The leasing of a large retail project before and during construction to ensure a high occupancy level when completed; often necessary to obtain financing.

Pro forma   A financial statement developed by the owner and projecting costs for a retail site based on assumptions about construction, financing, leasing rates, and operating costs; also projects gross income and net operating income of a property.

Promotional aid   A handout, giveaway, or gift item marked with the name of the leasing agency or the developer and given to retailers to interest them in leasing at a retail site.

Property manager   The person who supervises the operation of a property, making sure it is properly leased, well maintained, competitive with other sites, and otherwise managed according to the owner's objectives.

Pro rata share   The leasable area (GLA) of the tenant's site divided by the GLA of the premises, the resulting fraction being used to compute the tenant's share of operating expenses, HVAC charges, common area maintenance (CAM) fees, taxes, insurance, etc.

Prospect   A potential tenant for a retail site.

Prospecting   The search for potential tenants by referrals, canvassing, and cooperation with other brokers.

Quality circles A marketing program for shopping centers whereby retail tenants are divided into groups, also called pilot circles, with each group responsible for planning and supervising at least two promotional programs or marketing "flights" in a year's total program. The quality circle is a compromise between the *merchants' association* and the *marketing fund*, which see. (All of these programs are described in detail in appendix E.)

Radius clause Article in a retail lease that prevents a retailer from opening and operating another business, whether competitive or not, within a certain radius from the shopping center.

Regional analysis An examination of the general economic and demographic conditions and physical aspects of an area surrounding a shopping center and the trends that affect it.

Regional center A shopping center with one or more full-line department stores and a GLA of 400,000–1,000,000 square feet.

Rent schedule A listing of the rental rates for each space in a shopping center.

Residual analysis A method of calculating the portion of the sales potential in a market that is available for a new store to capture.

Sales potential The total number of consumer dollars available to retailers for the entire trade area.

Schedule of Commissions A document that outlines the terms of the commission agreement stating how and when the fee is to be paid. (See also *commission*.)

Security deposit A payment by tenant to ownership before occupancy as a guarantee that lease conditions will be met.

Shell space The condition of a tenant's space before occupancy and before any tenant improvements. For retail space, definition may vary with regional location and type of shopping center.

Site plan A drawing of the retail site as it will look when it is completed, including individual tenant spaces, common areas, elevators, escalators, food courts, service areas, parking, and access routes.

Site presentation packet A marketing tool presented to a serious prospect, usually during the site visit, including a site plan, demographic data, and other market- or site-related information.

Specialty center A shopping center characterized by the use of a dominant theme or image and concentrating on a particular type of merchandise. Often these centers have no conventional anchor tenant.

Standard form lease A basic lease form into which specific clauses or provisions may be written.

Standard metropolitan statistical area (SMSA)   A division of U.S. census data designating a central city and contiguous jurisdictions with a population exceeding 50,000.

Stock turnover   The rate at which inventory is sold in a retail store, normally expressed in turns per year; also called stock turn.

Store split   A method of reducing a store's GLA and re-leasing the newly created space to another retailer(s) as a means to increase sales potential and improve tenant mix.

Strip center   A type of shopping center designed in a single, unenclosed strip facing the street.

Sublease   A lease given by one tenant to another to create a subtenancy, usually only for the duration of the original tenant's lease term. Original tenant remains liable to owner in case of default by subtenant. (Compare *assignment.*)

Subordination   The condition whereby a tenant's lease is transferred to the mortgagee in the event of a foreclosure on the owner's mortgage.

Super regional center   A shopping center anchored by at least three full-line department stores and having more than 1,000,000 square feet of GLA.

Supply   In marketing terms, the quantity or amount of goods or services available. (Compare *demand.*)

Take back clause   A lease article giving the owner the right to take back subleased space in order to rent it to a new tenant.

Target market   The specific group of consumers whom the retailer wishes to attract.

Temporary tenant   A tenant that rents for a short period of time, often seasonal or month-to-month. These tenants sometimes occupy kiosks or carts.

Tenant   The individual or entity that pays rent in order to exclusively occupy a retail site for a specific length of time. (See also *lessee.*)

Tenant improvement allowance   Funds allowed by the owner for the tenant to use to improve the shell space before move in; exact amount, if any, is negotiable.

Tenant mix   The combination of retailers and service vendors leasing space in a shopping center.

Term   The duration of a tenant's lease.

Trade area   The geographic area from which a shopping center will obtain most of its customers; size depends on the type of center, location of competition, and other factors.

Trade area zones   A way of subdividing the trade area on the basis of distance, travel time, and other factors; usually classified as primary, secondary, and tertiary.

Traffic count   The number of automobiles passing an intersection or point along a street within a given time period; used by market researchers to determine if a site will support a shopping center.

Turnkey operation   A concession whereby the owner agrees to provide a completely finished store space for a retail tenant.

Urbanized area   A densely populated urban area and its surrounding suburbs.

Urban Development Action Grant (UDAG)   A federal or state government grant given to a city which, in turn, lends the funds to developers at low interest rates to finance urban improvements.

Use clause   A lease provision that restricts a retail tenant's use of the rented space by indicating what can and cannot be sold.

Vacancy rate   The ratio of vacant space to total rentable area (GLA), expressed as a percentage. (See also *occupancy level*.)

Valuation   The method of determining the current or probable market value of a new or existing retail property; useful for developers, brokers, investors, and lending institutions.

Waiver of subrogation   A lease clause whereby tenant and owner both agree not to file insurance claims against each other for any damages to the property.

Workletter   An addendum to the tenant improvement clause of a retail lease that lists in detail all the work to be done for the tenant by the owner; sometimes called a construction rider.

Zoning   A public regulation to control the character and intensity of land use.

Bibliography of Resources

The publications and other sources listed in these pages are offered as a guide to the array of material that is available to the leasing agent through direct subscription or at libraries. Additional book titles can be identified through library card files and in *Books in Print* published by R. R. Bowker. This bibliography of sources and publications is not intended to be complete.

PUBLICATIONS

The following list of publications is not intended to be all encompassing. The various books and articles address specific topics related to retail space leasing as well as to retailing itself. The trade magazines and newsletters devote part or all of their contents to topics on retailing and retail space leasing and management. In addition to those listed here, there are numerous other magazines and newsletters that are directed toward specific aspects of retailing and types of merchandise, many published by associations devoted to the market specialties. These can be identified in *Periodicals in Print* published by R. R. Bowker or by inquiring at the local library.

Books and Monographs

Basile, Ralph J., et al.: *Downtown Development Handbook* (Washington, D.C.: ULI—the Urban Land Institute, 1980).

Black, J. Thomas, et al.: *Downtown Retail Development: Conditions for Success and Project Profiles* (Washington, D.C.: ULI—the Urban Land Institute, 1983).

Bohon, Davis T.: *Complete Guide to Profitable Real Estate Leasing* (Englewood Cliffs, N.J.: Prentice-Hall, Inc., 1969).

Brue, Nordahl L.: *Retailer's Guide to Understanding Leases* (New York: National Retail Merchants Association, 1980).

Brue, Nordahl L.: *Retailers' Guide to Shopping Center Leasing* (New York: National Retail Merchants Association, 1980).

Casazza, John A., and Spink, Frank H., Jr.: *Shopping Center Development Handbook: Second Edition* (Washington, D.C.: ULI—the Urban Land Institute, 1985).

Davies, R. L., and Rogers, D. S. (eds.): *Store Location and Store Assessment Research* (Chichester, U.K.: John Wiley & Sons, 1984).

Development Trends 1987 (Washington, D.C.: ULI—the Urban Land Institute, 1987).

The Dimensions of Parking, Second Edition (Washington, D.C.: ULI—the Urban Land Institute, 1983).

Downs, James C., Jr.: *Principles of Real Estate Management (12th ed.)* (Chicago: Institute of Real Estate Management, 1980).

Factory Outlet World, Third Edition, 1985 (Suffern, N.Y.: DPN Enterprises, Inc., 1985).

Flynn, Robert J. (ed.): *Carpenter's Shopping Center Management: Principles & Practices (3d ed.)* (New York: International Council of Shopping Centers, 1984).

Friedman, Jack. P.: *The 1987 Real Estate Almanac* (Boston: Federal Research Press, 1987).

Halper, Emanuel B.: *Shopping Center and Store Leases* (New York: Law Journal Seminars—Press, Inc., 1988).

Hines, M.A.: *Shopping Center Development and Investment* (New York: John Wiley & Sons, 1983).

Increasing Retailer Productivity: A Guide for Shopping Center Professionals (New York: International Council of Shopping Centers, 1988).

Issues in Downtown Retail Development: An Overview of Recent Experience (New York: International Council of Shopping Centers, 1984).

Lawrence, Edward, and Elkin, Norman: *Downtown Retail Markets: An Analysis of Downtown Retail Sales in Metropolitan Areas Over One Million Population* (Chicago: The Downtown Research Corporation, May, 1986). [Prepared for Urban Investment and Development Co.]

Levin, Michael S.: *Measuring the Fiscal Impact of a Shopping Center on Its Community* (New York: International Council of Shopping Centers, 1975).

Licensed Departments: Rates, Policies, and Expenses in Department and Specialty Stores (New York: National Retail Merchants Association, 1977).

Lighting Energy Management in Retailing (2nd ed.) (Washington, D.C.: National Lighting Bureau, 1985).

Managing the Shopping Center (Chicago: Institute of Real Estate Management, 1983).

Morgenstein, Melvin, and Strongin, Harriet: *Modern Retailing: Management Principles and Practices (2d ed.)* (New York: John Wiley & Sons, 1987).

Parker, Frank J., and Schoenfeld, Norman P.: *Modern Real Estate: Principles & Practices* (Lexington, Massachusetts: D.C. Heath & Company, 1979).

Parking Requirements for Shopping Centers: Summary Recommendations and Research Study Report (Washington, D.C.: ULI—the Urban Land Institute, 1982).

Roca, Ruben A. (ed.): *Market Research for Shopping Centers* (New York: International Council of Shopping Centers, 1985).

Senn, Mark A.: *Commercial Real Estate Leases: Preparation and Negotiation* (New York: John Wiley & Sons, 1985).

Shopping Center Operating Cost Analysis Report (New York: International Council of Shopping Centers, 1987).

Sternlieb, George, and Hughes, James W. (eds.): *Shopping Centers: USA* (Rutgers, N.J.: The State University of New Jersey: Center for Urban Policy Research, 1981).

Standard Method for Measuring Floor Area in Office Buildings (Washington, D.C.: Building Owners and Managers Association International, 1980). [Shows standard for measuring usable area.]

Standard Manual of Accounting for Shopping Center Operations (Washington, D.C.: ULI—the Urban Land Institute, 1971).

Successful Leasing and Selling of Retail Property (2d ed.) (Chicago: Real Estate Education Company, 1983).

Troy, Leo: *Almanac of Business and Industrial Financial Ratios, 1988 Edition* (Englewood Cliffs, N.J.: Prentice-Hall, Inc., 1988).

Articles

Alexander, Alan A.: Are percentage rents meaningful for analyzing retail sales? *Journal of Property Management* 50(1):22–23, January–February 1985.

————: At what price concessions? *Journal of Real Estate Development* 4(4):71–73, Spring 1989.

————: Developing leasing plans for shopping centers, *Journal of Real Estate Development* 1(1):58–68, Summer 1985.

————: Evaluating the first-time retail tenant, *Journal of Property Management* 47(5):38–39, September–October 1982.

————: The leasing contract, *Journal of Property Management* 50(3):6–8, May–June 1985.

————: Negotiating large rental increases: Solve lease renewal problems before they begin, *Real Estate Business* 3(3):18–19, Summer 1984.

————: Shopping center strategies, *Journal of Real Estate Development* 2(2): 94–96, Fall 1986.

————, and Muhlebach, Richard: Negotiating the shopping center lease with a national tenant, *Journal of Real Estate Development* 2(1):79–85, Summer 1986.

Arnheim, Stuart A.: Escalation clauses—Do they adequately protect your cash flow? *AMO Quarterly*, Spring 1977, pp 16–17.

Bearson, Robert: Break-even calculation an essential tool for leasing space, *Shopping Center World* 13(8):14–16, August 1984.

————: Using professional guidelines makes good retailers even better, *Shopping Center World* 12(5):64–72, May 1983.

Friedman, Jack P.: Lease provisions for developing a single-tenant retail store, *Journal of Real Estate Development* 4(4):51–55, Spring 1989.

Gorman, Bridget: Trends in retail development, *Journal of Property Management* 54(4):26–31, July–August 1989.

Greer, R. L.: The shops around the corner, *Real Estate Today* 11(7):33–37, August 1978.

Halper, Emanuel B.: Alteration clauses in shopping center leases, *Real Estate Review* 7(1):78–85, Spring 1977.

————: The FTC and shopping center leases, *Real Estate Review* 11(4):49–56, Winter 1981.

————: Insurance clauses in shopping center leases, *Real Estate Review* 7(3):72–78, Fall 1977.

————: Repair clauses in store leases, *Real Estate Review* 8(1):65–73, Spring 1978.

————: The self-occupancy ground lease—Parts I and II, *Real Estate Review* 18(3): 32–42, Fall 1988; 18(4):40–48, Winter 1989.

————: Use clauses in apparel store leases, *Real Estate Review* 6(3):58–64, Fall 1976.

————: What is a net net net lease? *Real Estate Review* 4(4):9–14, Winter 1974.

How to negotiate shopping center lease restrictions, *Mortgage and Real Estate Executives Report*, March 1, 1979, pp 5–6.

Karras, Stath: Soft market strategies: A leasing plan for workout properties—Parts I–III, *Real Estate Review* 18(1):64–68, Spring 1988; 18(2):86–88, Summer 1988; 18(3):92–96, Fall 1988.

Klapper, Jules Z.: The CPI in rental adjustments: Dirty work or useful tool? *Shopping Center World* 10(1):127, 130, January 1981.

————: Downtown deals call for new look at minimum plus percentage lease, *Shopping Center World* 9(8):24–26, August 1980.

Landon, Richard: More than a renovation: The reconfiguration of a shopping center, *Journal of Property Management* 54(4):48–50, July–August 1989.

Lasker, Arthur E.: Shopping center leases are not nonnegotiable, *Real Estate Review* 6(1):116–122, Spring 1976.

Leasing: The trend is toward more and more sophistication, *Shopping Center World* 7(4):88–92,150,152, May 1978.

Manning, Joseph P., and Haynie, Susan P.: How to read your customers' minds, *American Demographics* 11(7):40–41, July 1989.

Muhlebach, Richard: Make shopping center leasing your strong suit, *Real Estate Today* 19(8):48–50, November–December 1986.

————: Updating the shopping center lease, *Journal of Property Management* 51(3):23–28, May–June 1986.

————: Working with financially troubled retail tenants, *Journal of Property Management* 48(1):12–13, January–February 1983.

————, and Alexander, Alan: The shopping center: How is it different? *Journal of Property Management* 54(4):58–60, July–August 1989.

————, and Ryan, Frank E.: The retail tenant in the office building, *Journal of Property Management* 47(2):18–19, March–April 1982.

Murray, W. Michael: Auditing percentage rents has little to do with accounting, *Shopping Center World* 9(5):216, 220–225, May 1980.

New approaches to shopping center leasing, *Mortgage and Real Estate Executives Report*, March 1, 1979, pp 2–4.

Opsata, Margaret: The art of negotiating a shopping center lease, *Shopping Center World* 10(8):20–22, August 1981.

————: Re-leasing: the secret of successful older centers, *Shopping Center World* 8(5):102–106, 210, May 1979.

Pelosi, Ray: How to lease to mom and pops, *Shopping Center World* 9(6):24–28, June 1980.

Phelps, John W., and Muhlebach, Richard: Proper tenant mix: It's more than the merchandise, *National Mall Monitor* 11(5):56–57, July–August 1981.

Rent adjustment clauses and the consumer price indices, *Real Estate Law Report*, April 1978, pp 2–3.

Rosenberg, Iris S.: Hypermarkets now! *Stores* 70(3):54–61, March 1988.

Schlesinger, James A.: Center redevelopment: How to hit the ground running, *Journal of Real Estate Development* 4(3):28–32, Winter 1989.

Schonberger, Susan R.: Specialty stores—Especially now, *Monitor* 18(5):44–48, July–August 1988.

Some important items shopping center leases should cover, *Real Estate Investment Ideas*, December 1978 (2nd issue), pp 7–8.

Stambaugh, David R.: The evolution of the shopping center lease, *Real Estate Today* 11(7):20–23, August 1978.

————: The regional mall from the ground up, *Real Estate Today* 11(7):24–28, August 1978.

Sullivan, John H.: Mysteries of the operating expense recovery formula, *Real Estate Review* 18(3):50–53, Fall 1988.

Waldron, William D.: Balanced shopping center lease helps both lessee and lessor, *Mortgage Banker*, May 1976, pp 42–44.

Periodicals

The Appraisal Journal (Chicago: American Institute of Real Estate Appraisers, quarterly).

Buildings: The Facilities Construction & Management Magazine (Cedar Rapids, Iowa: Stamats Communications, Inc., monthly).

Chain Store Age Executive (with Shopping Center Age) (New York: Lebhar-Friedman, Inc., monthly).
    A newsmagazine for retail management.

Commercial Property News, formerly *Real Estate Times* (New York: Gralla Publications, twice monthly).

Journal of Property Management (Chicago: Institute of Real Estate Management, bimonthly).

The Journal of Real Estate Development (Boston: Federal Research Press, quarterly).

Metro Chicago Real Estate (Chicago: Law Bulletin Publishing Company, twice monthly).

Monitor, formerly *National Mall Monitor* (Clearwater, Fla.: National Mall Monitor, bimonthly).
    Articles about development, tenant mix, retailing, and marketing ideas.

National Real Estate Investor (Atlanta, Ga.: Communication Channels, Inc., monthly).

Real Estate Outlook (Boston: Warren, Gorham & Lamont, Inc., quarterly).

Real Estate Review (Boston: Warren, Gorham & Lamont, Inc., quarterly).

Real Estate Today (Chicago: National Association of Realtors, monthly).

Shopping Centers Today (New York: International Council of Shopping Centers, monthly).
> Covers a variety of topics related to retailing.

Shopping Center World (Atlanta, Georgia: Communication Channels, Inc., monthly).
> Aimed toward regional shopping centers covering topics such as floor planning and merchandising; publishes a chain store survey annually.

Urban Land (Washington, D.C.: ULI—the Urban Land Institute, monthly).

Newsletters

AndrewsReport (Indianapolis: Report Communications, monthly).
> A newsletter for owners, developers, managers, and marketers of small shopping centers.

Car Care Mall News (Wayne, N.J.: Automotive Week Publishing Company, weekly).

CarlsonReport (Indianapolis: Report Communications, monthly).
> A newsletter for shopping center management professionals.

Commercial Lease Law Insider (New York: Brownstone Publishers, Inc., monthly).
> A newsletter for owners, managers, attorneys, and other real estate professionals.

Commercial Leasing Law & Strategy (New York: Leader Publications, monthly).

Crittenden Retail Space News (Novato, Calif.: Crittenden News Service, Inc., weekly).
> A newsletter that reports on retailer's moves.

Crittenden Restaurant Real Estate News (Novato, Calif.: Crittenden News Service, Inc., weekly).

Dealmakers' Weekly (Kendall Park, N.J.: DPN Enterprises, Inc., weekly).

Inside Retailing (New York: Lebhar-Friedman, Inc., biweekly).

JonesReport (Indianapolis: Report Communications, monthly).
> A newsletter for shopping center marketing professionals.

Landlord Tenant Law Bulletin (Boston: Quinlan Publishing Co., Inc., monthly).

Mortgage & Real Estate Executives Report, The (Boston: Warren, Gorham & Lamont, Inc., twice monthly).

Real Estate Financing Update (Boston: Warren, Gorham & Lamont, Inc., monthly).

Real Estate Insight (New York: Laventhol & Horwath, monthly).

Real Estate Leasing Report (Boston: Federal Research Press, monthly).

The Real Estate Newsletter (New York: Laventhol & Horwath, monthly).

The Retail Leasing Reporter (Kendall Park, N.J.: DPN Enterprises, Inc., monthly).
Offers helpful information about current transactions and leasing deals.

Who's Looking for Retail Space (Bethesda, Md.: Euler Enterprises, Inc., weekly).

OTHER RESOURCES

Market Research

In doing market research, the leasing agent will require a variety of types of information. The United States government generates data on varied aspects of U.S. population and U.S. commerce and industry. State data centers distribute demographic information for communities and townships within their borders as well as statewide. Regional or local planning commissions collect demographic data at census tract levels. Utility companies, business bureaus, and chambers of commerce are sources for local information. Local newspapers often collect data on shopping habits of their readers in the course of subscriber surveys. Various associations and other organizations related to retailing and to shopping centers and their management publish directories listing retailers, markets, and shopping center developers, usually on an annual basis. Often the local Board of Realtors has library copies of these and other real estate publications. What follows covers a wide range of potentially useful sources, including a number of commercial services.

The U.S. Department of Commerce, *Bureau of the Census,* generates consumer demographic information on an ongoing basis, and a number of its services, in addition to the decennial census of the population, are useful in market research. *The Census Catalog and Guide* is published every decade. The *Census of Retail Trade,* published every five years in years ending in two and seven, yields data for cities and counties defined as standard metropolitan statistical areas (SMSAs) and listed by major retail categories. *Current Business Reports* compiles data on monthly retail trade sales and inventories. *American Housing Survey* includes income, housing quality and costs, neighborhood quality, and other data of interest to retailing. The *CPI Detailed Report,* issued monthly, reports changes in the Consumer Product Index. The *Bureau of Labor Statistics* conducts and publishes a *Survey of Consumer Expenditures* that describes U.S. households by their retail spending patterns. Information is organized by merchandise categories. Census data are also compiled and published annually in the *Statistical Abstract of the United States,* available from the *Government Printing Office* in Washington, D.C.

Other sources for demographic data include:

- American Demographics Press in Ithaca, New York, offers various publications and marketing and market research tools, including the monthly magazines *American Demographics* and *The Numbers News.*
- CACI in Fairfax, Virginia, offers demographic and income forecasts, census profiles, residential neighborhood profiles, and sales potential data.

- CDP Marketing Information Corporation in Hauppauge, New York, provides targeted market research.
- Claritas in Alexandria, Virginia, provides targeted market research.
- Donnelly Marketing Information Services in Stamford, Connecticut, provide individual household level analysis.
- Intelligent Charting, Inc., of Perth Amboy, New Jersey, prepares custom demographic maps.
- *Metro Insights* published annually by DRI/McGraw-Hill in Lexington, Massachusetts, provides up-to-date demographic data on selected SMSAs.
- National Decision Systems in Encinitas, California, prepares custom marketing maps.
- *Rand McNally Commercial Atlas & Marketing Guide* is published annually by Rand McNally & Company in Skokie, Illinois.
- The REIS Reports, Inc., issued from New York City, are retail market analyses for major metropolitan areas.
- Survey Sampling, Inc., of Fairfield, Connecticut, conducts consumer and business sampling for market research.
- United States Institute of Marketing—Management and Marketing Consultants publishes and distributes business reference books and reports on advertising.
- Urban Decision Systems, Inc., of Los Angeles, California, offers demographic, business, consumer spending potential, lifestyle, and shopping center data.

Numerous directories and other listings of retailers and leasing information are published periodically. Most are annuals although some may be issued twice a year or on another schedule. Often they are published as a special issue of an established trade magazine.

- *Chain Store Guide—Directory of Leading Chain Stores in the United States* is published annually by Business Guides, Inc., in New York City.
- *Crittenden Retail Space News* and *Crittenden Restaurant Real Estate News,* weekly newsletters published by Crittenden News Service, Inc., in Novato, California, follow the activities of various retailers and restaurant operators and list individual contacts.
- *Directory of Major Malls,* published annually by MJJTM Publications Corporation in Spring Valley, New York, lists existing and planned shopping centers, developers, retailers, and markets.
- *Directory of Retail Space Site Selectors,* published by Euler Enterprises, Inc., in Bethesda, Maryland, is distributed to subscribers to the weekly newsletter, *Who's Looking for Retail Space.*
- *Fairchild Fact File—Department Store Sales,* published annually by Fairchild Publications in New York city, reports sales estimates for department store chains and numbers of store units.
- *Fairchild's Financial Manual of Retail Stores* is published annually by Fairchild Publications in New York City.
- Food Court Survey is conducted annually and published at mid-year in *CarlsonReport.*
- *The Franchise Annual Directory* is published annually by Info Press, Inc., in Lewiston, New York.

- *Leasing Opportunities* is published annually by the International Council of Shopping Centers in New York City.
- *Main Streets Across the World* is published twice a year by Healey & Baker, Inc., in London, U.K., and distributed in the U.S. from their New York office.
- *Means Square Foot Costs,* published annually by R. S. Means Company, Inc., in Kingston, Massachusetts, provides construction costs for various types of buildings and components.
- *Retail Tenant Directory* is published annually by *Monitor* magazine.
- *Shopping Center Directory,* published by the National Research Bureau in Burlington, Iowa, provides diversified information on established shopping centers.
- *WomenScope—Surveys of Women* is published monthly by Marketing to Women in Oneonta, New York.

Lease Forms

Chapter 7 of *Leasing Retail Space* has described in detail the various important clauses in a retail space lease, but no example of a lease form is included. The following are sources of examples.

Senn, Mark A.: *Commercial Real Estate Leases: Forms* (New York: Wiley Law Publications, John Wiley & Sons, 1986).

Shopping Center Study Lease: 1987 Edition (New York: International Council of Shopping Centers, 1987).

Sample Shopping Center Lease Form (Washington, D.C.: National Association of Home Builders).

Professional Organizations

Several professional organizations provide opportunities for leasing agents and other real estate professionals to exchange ideas. The *Institute of Real Estate Management,* headquartered in Chicago, Illinois, is an association of property management professionals whose expertise encompasses leasing and management of all types of real properties, including shopping centers and other forms of retail space. In the 1990s, they will begin publication of an income and expense analysis report on shopping centers. The *International Council of Shopping Centers,* headquartered in New York City, holds national and regional meetings to discuss current topics in shopping center leasing, management, and development. ICSC publishes *Leasing Opportunities,* an annual directory of shopping centers with space to lease and retailers seeking space. The ICSC *Research Quarterly* reports statistical information on shopping centers—gross leasable areas (GLA), retail sales, vacancies, etc.—as it is changing. *ULI—the Urban Land Institute,* based in Washington, D.C., is an association of developers, architects, and others interested in land use, especially for commercial development including retail projects. ULI publishes *Dollars & Cents of Shopping Centers,* a report of operating expenses and income of super regional, regional, community, and neighborhood centers that is compiled and issued every three years. ULI also publishes *Dollars & Cents of Off-Price Shopping Centers*, *Dollars & Cents of Fashion Malls*, and *Dollars & Cents of Superstore Centers* as special reports. *National Retail Merchants Association, Inc.*, in New York City, is another possible source for information related to retailing.

Seminars and Courses

Seminars and courses related to shopping center development, management, and leasing, are offered periodically by the *Institute of Real Estate Management,* the *International Council of Shopping Centers,* the *Institute for International Research* also based in New York City, and *ULI—the Urban Land Institute.* The professional organizations distribute catalogs and conduct direct-mail promotion of their various offerings. Privately offered seminars on shopping center leasing and management with a focus on retailing are offered by ABM—Advisors to Business Management in Long Beach, California. There is also a four-year degree in mall management available through the Youngstown State University, Warren P. Williamson Jr. School of Business Administration.

NOTE: Many of the publications cited in this bibliography are sources for specific data on shopping center income and operating expenses, minimum and percentage rents, retailer space requirements, and sales volumes. Information on rental income and operating expenses for different types of shopping centers can also be found in a variety of other published sources. In seeking out such information, the reader is cautioned to be aware of publication dates as well as when original surveys were conducted. The passage of time renders these data less reliable for current planning although they may be useful for comparison. Also, some reports include figures for anchor tenants as well as ancillary tenants and rental and fee rates established in older long-term leases, thus stating apparently *lower* figures for a center as a whole. Published data cannot substitute for personal experience.

Index

Urban Land Institute (ULI), 105, 196,
208, 231, 234, 302–303
parking standards, 133–134
Use clause, 154–155, 194, 291. *See
also* Continuous operation clause
Utilities, 159–160

V
Vacancy, 42, 156–157
Vandalism, 129
Ventilation (HVAC), 65
Visibility, as site attribute, 38

W
Waiver of subrogation, 162
Working women, shopping habits, 36
Workletter, 169, 173, 291

Z
Zoning
parking lot size, 134
retail sites, 29